Treatment of
Chronic Medical Conditions

Treatment of

Chronic Medical Conditions

Cognitive–Behavioral Therapy Strategies and Integrative Treatment Protocols

Len Sperry, MD, PhD

American Psychological Association
Washington, DC

Published by
American Psychological Association
750 First Street, NE
Washington, DC 20002
www.apa.org

To order
APA Order Department
P.O. Box 92984
Washington, DC 20090-2984
Tel: (800) 374-2721; Direct: (202) 336-5510
Fax: (202) 336-5502; TDD/TTY: (202) 336-6123
Online: www.apa.org/books/
E-mail: order@apa.org

In the U.K., Europe, Africa, and the Middle East, copies may be ordered from
American Psychological Association
3 Henrietta Street
Covent Garden, London
WC2E 8LU England

Typeset in Goudy by Stephen McDougal, Mechanicsville, MD

Printer: United Book Press, Baltimore, MD
Cover Designer: Naylor Design, Washington, DC
Technical/Production Editor: Harriet Kaplan

The opinions and statements published are the responsibility of the authors, and such opinions and statements do not necessarily represent the policies of the American Psychological Association.

Library of Congress Cataloging-in-Publication Data

Sperry, Len.
    Treatment of chronic medical conditions : cognitive-behavioral therapy strategies and integrative treatment protocols / Len Sperry. — 1st ed.
        p. ; cm.
    Includes bibliographical references and index.
    ISBN-13: 978-1-4338-0389-5
    ISBN-10: 1-4338-0389-5
    1. Chronically ill—Mental health. 2. Cognitive therapy. I. American Psychological Association. II. Title.
    [DNLM: 1. Chronic Disease—psychology. 2. Chronic Disease—therapy. 3. Cognitive Therapy—methods. 4. Combined Modality Therapy. WT 500 S751t 2009]
    RC108.S662 2009
    616'.044—dc22   2008010831

British Library Cataloguing-in-Publication Data
A CIP record is available from the British Library.

Printed in the United States of America
First Edition

CONTENTS

ACKNOWLEDGMENTS

Over the past 3 years, it has been my good fortune to serve as a consultant to a unique experiment in primary care psychology at New Mexico State University, Las Cruces, and the Southern New Mexico Family Medicine Residency Program. The experiment aims to train graduate psychology students and others for professional practice in primary care settings. What is unique about this federally funded training program is that it emphasizes border health care for those living in U.S.–Mexican border communities. I would like to especially acknowledge the support and encouragement of my colleagues Eve Adams, Kay Ennis, Charles Huber, and Luis Vazquez of the doctoral counseling psychology program faculty at New Mexico State University as well as Robert Mayfield, Kathleen Hales, and Bert Garrett of the faculty and medical staff at the Southern New Mexico Family Medicine Residency Program at Memorial Medical Center in Las Cruces. During the past 3 years, I have worked with several doctoral psychology and social work students at New Mexico State University and family medicine residents at the Southern New Mexico Family Medicine Residency Program in this remarkable program. In seminars, meetings, and consultations, much of the material in this book and in its companion volume, *Psychological Treatment of Chronic Illness: The Biopsychosocial Therapy Approach*, was field tested. These faculty, students, and family medicine residents have truly enriched my life, and I want to publicly recognize their contributions to this unique health care experiment. Thanks also to Barbara Abernathy, a graduate assistant, who was involved in some of the early literature reviews. Finally, I want to acknowledge the invaluable assistance and expertise of the editorial staff in the American Psychological Association Books Department, particularly Susan Reynolds, acquisitions editor; Margaret Sullivan, development editor; and Harriet Kaplan, production editor.

Treatment of
Chronic Medical
Conditions

INTRODUCTION

As the population ages, clinicians are increasingly finding that the patients they treat for psychological disorders have chronic medical conditions as well. According to the National Centers for Chronic Illness Prevention and Health Promotion (2007), chronic medical conditions—such as heart disease, cancer, and diabetes—are the leading causes of death and disability in the United States. They account for 70% of all deaths in the United States, which is 1.7 million each year. They also cause major limitations in daily living for almost 1 out of 10 Americans, or about 25 million individuals. Most telling, prevalence rates of chronic medical conditions are more than 3 times higher than the rate of all mental disorders. What does this mean for professional practice? It means that because of these extraordinarily high prevalence rates, clinicians will encounter individuals with chronic medical conditions in their practice, even if these clients primarily present with psychological issues.

Working with patients who are chronically ill can be challenging for the mental health clinician. Establishing and maintaining effective therapeutic relationships with these patients, performing comprehensive assessments, and developing and implementing treatment plans requires the same knowledge, competencies, and skills needed in traditional psychotherapy plus additional ones: an understanding of patients' illness representations and treat-

3

ment expectations, the skills to elicit and negotiate these representations and expectations, a targeted focus on illness-related therapeutic tasks, and a knowledge of the kinds of interventions most likely to be effective in clinical practice in the context of chronic medical illness. Moreover, the clinician must have an understanding of the patient's specific chronic disease and must be able to integrate what is known about the patient and the disease to plan and implement effective treatment interventions.

Although there are some similarities between the assessment and treatment of psychotherapy clients and of chronic illness patients, there are some differences. In my previous book, *Psychological Treatment of Chronic Illness: The Biopsychosocial Therapy Approach* (Sperry, 2006b), I described what the clinician needs to know in order to perform a comprehensive biopsychosocial assessment and devise an appropriate treatment plan. In this context, I presented an approach for identifying and assessing over a dozen key markers of illness dynamics and their determinants that affect treatment decisions for chronic medical conditions in general. The biopsychosocial model emphasizes the reciprocal interaction between biological, psychological, and social variables and the patient's experience of and response to his or her illness.

This book shares the biopsychosocial model of my previous book, but it incorporates an integrative approach to systematically treat 10 of the more common chronic medical conditions the clinician is likely to encounter in general psychotherapy or primary care settings. As a companion to the previous volume, this book helps the clinician develop, plan, and implement assessment and treatment strategies for these various chronic medical conditions.

Currently, a number of books are available that deal with the biopsychological assessment and treatment of a single chronic medical condition, such as diabetes, hypertension, chronic pain, and cancer. These books address the needs of *specialists*, that is, researchers and health psychologists who work in subspecialty medical units and clinics or in subspecialty surgical units and clinics in academic medical centers or other settings. In contrast, the current book addresses several common medical conditions that psychologists and psychotherapists will commonly encounter in a general psychotherapy practice or in a primary care clinic setting. Accordingly, the primary audiences for this book are *generalists*, that is, psychotherapists, primary care psychologists, and others who provide psychologically oriented treatment for people with a broad range of chronic medical conditions. Similarly, graduate students in clinical, counseling, and rehabilitation psychology and psychotherapists in training in other mental health disciplines (e.g., counseling, clinical social work, couples and family therapy, pastoral counseling) who need a broad knowledge of chronic medical conditions and their treatment should find the book useful as well. Some readers may already work with patients with chronic illnesses, and this book will help them become even more effective in their clinical work.

Best practices and evidenced-based guidelines are beginning to become available for the medical treatment of common chronic diseases. Unfortunately, such practices and guidelines for the psychological treatment of these chronic conditions have yet to appear, and it may be several years before a full set is available. In the meantime, *Treatment of Chronic Medical Conditions: Cognitive–Behavioral Therapy Strategies and Integrative Treatment Protocols* is the most current and comprehensive compendium of integrative treatment protocols and cognitive–behavioral strategies for the most common chronic medical conditions.

Cognitive–behavioral therapy (CBT) is the most often used and, generally speaking, the most effective psychotherapeutic intervention for chronic medical conditions. This book emphasizes various cognitive–behavioral strategies for working effectively with such clinical challenges as noncompliance, illness denial, symptom exacerbation, and spiritual and life meaning issues as well as with specific medical conditions. These strategies are discussed and illustrated with case material and extended transcriptions.

The book also emphasizes integrative treatment protocols or action plans rather than just medical or psychological treatments. Because effective treatment of chronic medical conditions requires both medical and psychological interventions, the integrative protocols described and illustrated here combine medical, psychoeducational, and psychotherapeutic strategies. Such strategies are based on more than 100 randomized clinical trials and various meta-analyses and provide the clinician with an unparalleled source of treatment options. Protocols for arthritis, asthma, cancer, chronic pain, diabetes, epilepsy, hypertension, irritable bowel syndrome, and systemic lupus erythematosus are described and illustrated with case material.

The book is arranged in three sections. Part I sets the stage for working with chronic medical conditions. Chapter 1 emphasizes the importance of establishing an effective therapeutic relationship with such patients and the necessity of identifying and incorporating *illness representations* (the patients' beliefs about their illness, treatment, and clinical outcomes) into a case conceptualization and treatment plan. Chapter 2 discusses the necessity of assessing other factors similar to illness representations and the value of planning treatment interventions that are tailored to patient need, personality, and context. This chapter follows the format of the assessment and intervention components of the integrative protocols.

Part II consists of four chapters that focus on four common clinical challenges in working with chronic medical patients: illness denial, noncompliance, symptom exacerbation, and spiritual and life meaning issues. Cognitive–behavioral strategies targeted to these challenges are described and illustrated 'with case material and session transcriptions.

Part III consists of 10 chapters and provides extensive clinical background information and assessment and intervention protocols for 10 common chronic medical conditions: arthritis, asthma, cancer, cardiac disease, chronic pain, diabetes, epilepsy, hypertension, irritable bowel syndrome, and systemic lupus erythematosus. Each is described in terms of medical information of the disease: its pathology, epidemiology, types, severity, cause, gender and culture, psychiatric comorbidities, and its prognosis. The heart of chapters is the clinical application section, which includes a protocol for biopsychosocial assessment, including patient profile and illness profile; a protocol for intervention planning; a protocol for intervention implementation, with detailed information, including research support, on the use of psychoeducational interventions, CBT, other types of psychotherapy, medical treatment and medication, and combined treatment; and a protocol for intervention monitoring. A brief case study illustrates the application of each protocol. For many of the chronic medical conditions, certain treatment interventions are common. For example, for all 10 of the chronic diseases, psychoeducational therapy and CBT are often used and have proven records of results. Empirically supported interventions for some diseases, but not all of the medical conditions, include, for example, hypnotherapy, social support groups, or mindfulness-based approaches.

The protocols are integrative, systematic, and comprehensive in that they combine knowledge of the specific medical conditions, empirically supported assessment and treatment interventions, and a detailed patient and illness profile. These protocols enable the clinician to develop the assessment and treatment approach that is most likely to succeed for a particular patient. Once the reader has achieved some level of mastery using one of the protocols for a particular chronic illness, he or she will find that applying another protocol for a different chronic illness will come naturally. In addition, the protocols are written in such a way that as research continues to be reported on assessment methods or treatment interventions for the illness, the clinician can update the protocols to reflect these new findings.

As the clinical practice of psychology as a health care specialty continues to evolve, psychologists will become even more indispensable in the treatment of chronic medical conditions. My hope is that the knowledge and protocols provided in this book will enhance clinicians' conceptual understanding of chronic illness and their clinical effectiveness in treating patients with these conditions.

I

TREATMENT OF CHRONIC MEDICAL CONDITIONS

Working effectively with patients with various chronic medical conditions requires a broad knowledge base and competence that is similar in some respects, but quite different in others, from that needed for working effectively with psychotherapy clients. Part I sets the stage for working with such patients by providing an overview of the process of treating medical conditions. Chapter 1 emphasizes the necessity of establishing an effective therapeutic relationship with such patients and the importance of identifying and incorporating illness representations (i.e., the patients' beliefs about their illness, treatment, and clinical outcomes) into a case conceptualization and treatment plan. Chapter 2 describes a strategy for assessing patient and disease variables and the value of planning treatment interventions that are tailored to patient need, personality, and context. The reader will note that this chapter follows the format of the assessment and intervention components of the integrative protocols in Chapters 7 to 16. As such, it connects Part I with Part III.

1

THERAPEUTIC RELATIONSHIP, CASE CONCEPTUALIZATION, AND ILLNESS REPRESENTATION

Despite all the spectacular advances and breakthroughs of technological health care, the health and well-being of individual patients does not seem to have increased appreciably. In fact, it could be argued that health and well-being have actually declined in proportion to reliance on technological advances. Such observations inevitably lead to nostalgia about the "high-touch, low-tech" health care of the past. In this context, "high-touch" refers to the health care professional's ability to provide "good bedside manner," or a positive treatment relationship. What is needed today is not so much a return to the past as a shift to what might be called "high-touch, high-tech" health care. So it should not be too surprising that contemporary health care professionals are "rediscovering" the importance and value of establishing an effective working relationship or good bedside manner with patients. A basic assumption of this chapter and this book is that an effective therapeutic relationship is essential if patients are to collaborate with clinicians and the treatment process and thereby improve their well-being and quality of life.

Accordingly, working with chronically ill patients can be both challenging and rewarding. It is challenging in that establishing and maintaining effective therapeutic relationships with chronically ill patients requires the same competencies and skills needed with traditional psychotherapy patients plus extra attention to their illness representations, treatment expectations, and readiness and capacity for change (Prochaska, DiClementi, & Norcross, 1992). It is rewarding in that patients who experience a positive, caring relationship with a health care professional, whether it be termed "good bedside manner" or "positive therapeutic alliance," seem to respond with good treatment compliance as well as improved treatment outcomes. This chapter addresses the therapeutic relationships in medical and psychological treatment with chronically ill patients. It begins with a description of the components of effective therapeutic relationships and emphasizes and illustrates the importance of achieving a "meeting of the minds" between clinician and patient with regard to case conceptualizations. The next section describes illness representations and how to elicit and modify them, when indicated. Emphasized are explanatory models and treatment expectations. Finally, a case example illustrates these points, including that therapeutic relationship, case conceptualization, and illness representation are mutually interactive.

THERAPEUTIC RELATIONSHIPS

The *therapeutic relationship*, also referred to as *therapeutic alliance*, is the context in which the process of psychological treatment is experienced and enacted. Although there are notable differences in the way the therapeutic relationship is described among the various therapeutic approaches, most acknowledge the importance of the relationship in affecting the process and outcome of treatment. Across these various approaches, a high correlation has been found between the therapeutic relationship and treatment outcome. On the basis of his analysis of psychotherapy research, Strupp (1995) concluded that the therapeutic relationship is "the sine qua non in all forms of psychotherapy" (p. 70). Research, including a number of meta-analyses, suggests that the quality of the therapeutic relationship has a strong positive impact on treatment outcome (Lambert & Barley, 2002; Martin, Garske, & Davis, 2000; Orlinsky, Grawe, & Parks, 1994; Wampold, 2001). More specifically, it has been estimated that at least 30% of the variance in psychotherapy outcome is due to "relationship factors" (Lambert, 1992), and others have suggested it may be closer to 80% (Wampold, 2001). In short, patients who are engaged in and collaborate in the treatment process appear to benefit significantly from the experience. Similarly, there is evidence that a poor therapeutic relationship predicts poor compliance and early, unilateral termination (Shick-Tyron & Kane, 1993, 1995).

An effective therapeutic relationship involves a meeting of hearts and minds between clinician and patient. Research operationalizes this in terms of three factors of a therapeutic alliance: bond, goals, and methods (Bordin, 1994). *Bond* refers to a meeting of hearts, and *mutual agreement on goals and methods* refers to a meeting of the minds.

Important to the formation of a strong therapeutic bond is what Carl Rogers called the "core conditions" of effective counseling and psychotherapy: empathy, respect, and genuineness (Rogers, 1951). It appears that when patients feel understood, safe, and hopeful, they are more likely to take the risk of disclosing painful affects and intimate details of their lives as well as risk thinking, feeling, and acting in more adaptive and healthier ways. However, these core conditions must actually be felt by the patient, and these core conditions will be experienced differently by patients depending on their individual psychodynamics and social and cultural dynamics. Duncan, Solovey, and Rusk (1992) contended that the most helpful alliances are likely to develop when the clinician establishes a therapeutic relationship that matches the patient's—rather than clinician's—definitions of empathy, respect, and genuineness. Besides the therapeutic bond, clinicians need to attend to mutually agreed upon therapeutic goals and methods. This entails a recognition of the patient's explanatory model and expectations for treatment goals and methods and the way treatment will be provided. Such expectations are influenced by cultural factors and norms. Among some cultures, it is customary for family members to accompany the designated patient to appointments. Because there may be an unspoken expectation that family members be included in the treatment process, effective clinicians will inquire about such expectations. Similarly, there may be silent expectations about the type of intervention that will be used. Some patients prefer action-oriented approaches over strictly talk-oriented approaches.

Sometimes, the silent expectation is that healing requires some measure of touch or contact. I vividly recall a psychological consultation to evaluate "agitation and noncompliance" in a hospitalized elderly woman of Iranian descent. In short, she refused to take her prescribed medication and became belligerent whenever the nursing staff approached her with it. As I was talking with the patient, a cardiologist who had also been called to consult on the case entered the room and asked if he could interrupt. I agreed, and he spoke with her briefly and immediately ordered a topical form of the medication that had been prescribed by her internist. The consulting physician, with great care, applied the nitroglycerin ointment over her heart region. Immediately, the woman relaxed and smiled. Afterward, I spoke with the physician at the nurses' station as he was writing a progress note. He indicated that patients from the Middle East tend to believe that healing only comes by touch and that the only medications that "really work" for them are those that are applied topically, that is, rubbed on the skin. It seemed clear that not having her silent expectations honored by the nurses and other health care professionals accounted for her agitation, lack of cooperation, and treatment noncompliance.[1]

Accordingly, the effective clinician will elicit and be sensitive to the patient's expectations for treatment, including expectations about objectives, outcomes, methods, and clinician and patient roles and responsibilities. Unrealistically high or low patient expectations need to be noted and discussed. The patient needs to be queried about what they expect from treatment—symptom relief, improvement in functioning, personality change, and so on—as well as about expected modalities (i.e., individual therapy; medication; couple, group, or family session) and treatment methods (i.e., psychodynamic interpretation, behavioral interventions, etc.).

CASE CONCEPTUALIZATIONS: CLINICIAN'S VERSUS PATIENT'S

Effective clinicians quickly develop a formulation or case conceptualization of the patient's illness, including its causes, impact, and treatability. These case conceptualizations give form and meaning to clinical information and provide a bridge to planning interventions and effecting change. Typically, this explanation is based on psychological and scientific theory. Clinicians, and particularly trainees, are often surprised to learn that patients also have their own formulation or conceptualization, that is, their own explanation for the cause, impact, and treatability of their medical or psychological condition.

Effective clinicians are skilled at eliciting, developing or formulating, and negotiating case conceptualizations. What do I mean by "eliciting case conceptualizations"? Although patients may not consciously be aware of their conceptualizations, these conceptualizations are nevertheless powerfully operative in the treatment process. Effective clinicians not only recognize the presence of these conceptualizations but elicit them, formulate them, and then negotiate a common conceptualization with their patients. In a very real sense, the process of developing a conceptualization should be considered a "reformulation of the client's existing explanation" (Good & Beitman, 2006, p. 105).

What are these patient conceptualizations like? They closely resemble the structure of the clinician's case conceptualization. First, the patient's description of his or her presenting problem or concern, including symptomatic distress and self-rating of impairment in the various areas of life functioning, is analogous to the clinician's clinical formulation, as is the patient's

---

[1]It should be noted that although the physician's "laying on of hands" was ethically appropriate in this example, the ethics codes governing the practice of psychologists and other mental health professionals view touching patients and clients as a boundary violation.

explanatory model of his or her condition or presenting problem. The patient's expectations for treatment are analogous to the clinician's treatment formulation.

Where the patient's and clinician's case conceptualizations usually differ is in content. Whereas the clinician develops a case conceptualization based on a critical understanding of the scientific basis—that is, biological, psychological, and sociocultural—of human behavior, the patient's explanation is more likely to be based on a highly personal, idiosyncratic, and uncritical understanding or theory of human behavior. Social psychologists refer to this phenomenon as *naive personality theory*.

Why is it important to recognize the patient's own case conceptualization? Because the more it differs from the clinician's conceptualization, the less likely treatment is to be effective and the more likely noncompliance or nonadherence will be present. This can show itself in many ways: Patients may come late or not show up for sessions; they may fail to do homework or take medication as prescribed; or they may prematurely terminate from therapy, that is, drop out. For example, imagine that the patient's nonelicited explanatory model for panic symptoms and difficulty doing grocery shopping and other outside household responsibilities is that it is caused by "a chemical imbalance in my brain." Imagine also that this patient's nonelicited treatment expectation is for a prescription for Ativan "because it really worked for a neighbor" but not for "talk therapy." Then, imagine that his clinician—who is considered a specialist in the behavior therapy of anxiety disorders and is adamantly against the use of tranquilizers like Ativan—comes up with a diagnostic formulation of panic with agoraphobia, a clinical formulation of symptoms being caused by avoidance behavior, and specifies a treatment formulation of exposure therapy—that is, the patient will be trained to gradual exposure to feared stimuli such as large stores and other open spaces. What is likely to happen? Probably that the patient will directly or indirectly reject the plan for exposure therapy: directly by refusing to participate in the exposure protocol or by premature termination, or indirectly by half-heartedly being involved in the early exposure attempts. Now, if this clinician elicited the patient's case conceptualization, the clinician could then provide the patient with reasons why Ativan and other medications in that class are only short-term treatments and have high addictive potential and why exposure therapy is preferable. It may be that after further discussion, both agree that a safer and more effective medication like Prozac—which has Food and Drug Administration approval for use with panic and agoraphobia—will be used along with the behavioral approach.

The effective clinician's task, then, is to elicit the patient's case conceptualization. This means eliciting the presenting problems; symptoms; areas of impaired functioning; treatment expectations; and, particularly, the patient's explanatory model. An *explanatory model* is the patient's personal explanation for what is causing their problems, symptoms, and impaired functioning. In other words, an explanatory model is akin to the clinician's professional and scientific explanation for the patient's problems, symptoms, and impaired functioning.

Effective clinicians are able to reconcile differences between what are often two disparate explanations or conceptualizations. Reconciliation involves negotiation. This negotiation process begins with the clinician acknowledging the patient's explanation and its similarities to and differences from the clinician's conceptualization. The ensuing discussion allows the clinician to educate the patient about his or her illness and clarify misconceptions about it and the treatment process. Furthermore, discussion of the patient's or patient system's expectations for the treatment process and outcomes facilitates negotiating a mutually agreeable direction for treatment and a therapeutic relationship based on cooperation. Then, the specifics of treatment selection can be discussed.

SHIFTING FROM AN EXCLUSIVELY BIOLOGICAL EXPLANATION TO A BIOPSYCHOSOCIAL EXPLANATION

A common scenario is for a patient to receive a diagnosis that they cannot accept. They are convinced they have a bona fide medical diagnosis such as epilepsy and are told they have a somatoform disorder instead. For example, after an exhaustive medical evaluation, a young adult is diagnosed with nonepileptic seizures. The clinician finds when eliciting her illness perceptions that the patient is convinced she has epilepsy and that the cause of her symptoms is neurological. Arguing with such a patient in such a situation is counterproductive. Instead, the clinician explains and discusses illness dynamics while validating the patient's concern and normalizing her experience (Watson, 2007). The goal is to frame the patient's symptoms as stress related and then focus on efforts to manage specific stressors in place of seeking conventional epilepsy treatment. In the following, a psychological consultant (CL) talks with the patient (PT) and begins the process of reframing a physical cause to a more biopsychosocial one.

> CL: *Psychological* means that emotional factors rather than neurological ones are the cause. It doesn't means that you're making these symptoms up or faking them or doing them on purpose. In fact, these symptoms are not under your conscious control. Also, it doesn't mean that you are mentally ill. Actually, most people with this problem are strong, intelligent individuals, but they're not particularly good at recognizing when something is bothering them. So stresses build up and symptoms develop. What do you think of what I've said?

PT: Well, I've been to other doctors, and they've also said that I don't really have epilepsy. They say it's all in my head. Isn't that what you're basically saying, too?

CL: No, I'm absolutely not saying that it's all in your head. I'm saying that it is both in your body *and* in your head. That's because your body and mind are very closely connected. So when something is bothering you physically, like a bad cold or the flu, it also has an effect on your mind and mood. It works the other way, too. When something is affecting you emotionally, it also affects your body. So, when a close relative dies, the body feels heavy and listless. And when you're really upset with somebody, you might lose your appetite or get restless. What happens in the body affects the mind and vice versa. To say it's all in your head dismisses the physical connection as if it isn't important or real. It's really not accurate to say that. What you're experiencing is not unreal or trivial or easy to deal with. Stress affects both mind *and* body. Does that make sense to you?

PT: It's starting to. I guess it means that I've got to get rid of the stress in my life.

CL: Reducing the source of specific stresses might really help. But the goal isn't to get rid of or eliminate stress in your life, since that really isn't possible. Rather, the goal is to find better ways of managing your stress so these symptoms don't result. So, it's basically a matter of controlling and managing your stress.

PT: You know, I guess I do have some specific stresses. My symptoms seem to start up when I'm really feeling in a bind about my job and home responsibilities.

SHIFTING FROM AN EXCLUSIVELY PSYCHOLOGICAL EXPLANATION TO A BIOPSYCHOSOCIAL EXPLANATION

Somewhat less commonplace is when a patient's explanation of causality is mistakenly attributed as psychological when the most likely explanation is biological. For example, a patient with a long history of treatment for hypertension reports a new symptom: impotence.

CL: So what do you make of this new symptom? Where does it come from?

PT: Oh, I'm not really sure. I thought you'd tell me.

CL: I know you're not a doctor. But I wonder if you might have some thoughts about its cause.

PT: Well, I'm a little embarrassed to say it, but I think it's because of the impure thoughts I've been having about the new receptionist at my job. You know I'm married and all.

CL: Uhm-hm.

PT: And [*pause*] I think God is punishing me for having those thoughts. You know, my guilt and all.

CL: It's not easy for you to talk about this.

PT: No, it's not.

CL: [*looking at patient's medical chart*] I'm noticing that you were recently started—just 2 weeks ago—on a second medication for your blood pressure: Inderal. It's a really good medication, but it has a troubling side effect for some men. It's impotence.

PT: So you're saying it's only a medication problem?

CL: No, I'm not. I'm saying medication is likely having some effect, but I'm also thinking that relationships and guilt feeling can be playing a part, too. So, it might well be some combination of biological, psychological, and social factors that are all involved.

PT: Well, what do you suggest doing about it?

CL: Here's my thought. Let's look to see if the new medication dose can be lowered or discontinued. And, at the same time, let's start talking about your concerns about your feelings about your marriage and the new receptionist and related matters. How does that sound?

PT: Yeah, that sounds good.

Here, the patient initially attributes his impotence to a primarily psychological or psychosocial cause. In the process of explaining, reframing, and refocusing, the clinician first educates the patient about medication side effects and then suggests a broader explanation and a treatment plan based on it. The shift is from a psychosocial to a biopsychosocial explanation and treatment plan, and the patient's willingness to accept the treatment focus represents his tacit acceptance of a broader causal explanation. It is noteworthy that the clinician did not insist that the patient accept a biopsychosocial explanation. Initially, that is, before the medication could be ruled out as causing the side effect, it was probably more important to the patient that the clinician was willing to therapeutically process the patient's conflicting feelings, including guilt about being married and having sexual thoughts about another woman while the medication is changed.

ILLNESS REPRESENTATIONS

As noted earlier, illness is not the same as disease. Whereas *disease* is the objective manifestation of a medical condition, *illness* is the subjective experience of a disease or medical condition. A key aspect of that subjective experience is one's illness perceptions. Clinical experience and research (Leventhal, Diefenbach, & Leventhal, 1992; Leventhal, Leventhal, & Cameron, 2000) have revealed that individuals cluster their ideas about an illness around five coherent themes. Together, these five themes reflect a individual's perceptions and beliefs about his or her illness. These themes provide individuals a framework to make sense of their symptoms, assess their health status, predict treatment compliance, and take corrective action and cope with their medical condition.

The five illness representation themes are as follows:

1. *identity*, which involves the diagnostic label and the symptoms viewed to be part of their disease or condition;
2. *cause*, or personal ideas about causality—also called *explanatory models*—whether it is a simple, single cause or a more complex, multiple causality;
3. *timeline*, or how long the individual expects the illness will last (the three time categories are *acute*, *chronic*, and *periodic*);
4. *consequences*, or the expected impact or effects and outcome of the illness; and
5. *cure/control*, or how one anticipates recovery from, and control of, one's illness. (Leventhal et al., 1992)

Why should clinicians be interested in illness representations? The answer is because such perceptions are related to treatment compliance as well as treatment outcomes. First of all, educating and negotiating a more accurate and mutually agreeable illness perception has been suggested as critical for developing and maintaining an effective therapeutic relationship (Sperry, Carlson, & Kjos, 2003). Recall that besides achieving a bond of trust and caring, an effective therapeutic alliance requires an alignment of beliefs and goals as well as methods of treatment between both patient and clinician (Bordin, 1994). An effective therapeutic alliance therefore increases patients' receptivity to treatment. Increasingly, research is demonstrating that such a therapeutic relationship is most predictive of effective treatment outcomes (Lambert & Barley, 2002). The obvious implication is that assessing and modifying, when necessary, patients' illness perceptions is essential for effective counseling.

So how do illness representations develop? It seems that an individual's perceptions of illness develop over time from diverse sources, ranging from firsthand experiences with a family member who suffered from a particular medical condition to information gleaned from written material or the media as well as from relatives and friends. These perceptions tend to remain dormant until activated by a person's own illness or that of someone close to him or her. Illness perceptions are essentially private theories or models. Thus, it should not be too surprising that individuals can be reluctant to discuss

TABLE 1.1
Questions for Eliciting Illness Perceptions

Question	Illness perception theme
How much do you experience symptoms from your illness?	Identity
What do you think has caused your illness?	Cause
How long do you think your illness will continue?	Timeline
How much does your illness affect your life?	Consequences
How much do you think your treatment can help your illness?	Cure/control
How much control do you feel you have over your illness?	

their beliefs about their illness with health care providers for fear of being viewed as ignorant or misinformed. Assessment of illness perceptions is accomplished through direct questioning or by paper-and-pencil inventories.

Interview

Awareness of a patient's illness representations is clinically useful in tailoring and implementing counseling interventions. The first step involves assessment. Clinicians—whether physicians or counselors—can assess an individual's illness perceptions by eliciting answers to the questions in Table 1.1.

Inventories

Illness perceptions were initially elicited through direct questioning, but over time a paper-and-pencil instrument was developed. Currently, three validated instruments are available. The first inventory was developed by Weinman, Petrie, Moss-Morris, and Horne (1996), the Illness Perception Questionnaire (IPQ). This inventory consists of 38 items, covering all five of the illness perception themes derived from Leventhal et al.'s (1992) self-regulation model and research. Subsequently, a revised version of the IPQ was developed to address minor psychometric concerns with two subscales and to add subscales dealing with emotional representation, illness coherence, and cyclical timeline. It consists of 80 items and is called the Revised Illness Perception Questionnaire (IPQ-R; Moss-Morris et al., 2002). To meet the need for a shorter version of the IPQ-R that could rapidly assess illness perceptions in clinical settings as well as monitor treatment progress, the Brief Illness Perception Questionnaire was developed and validated by Broadbent, Petrie, Main, and Weinman (2006). It consists of 9 items and can be completed in 3 minutes or less. All three instruments are available in English as well as in several other languages, including Spanish. They are available at the IPQ Web site (http://www.uib.no/ipq).

ILLNESS REPRESENTATIONS AND SELF-EFFICACY

Self-efficacy is concerned with patients' beliefs in their capabilities to exercise control over their own functioning and over events that affect their lives (Bandura, 1986). Beliefs in personal efficacy affect life choices, level of motivation, quality of functioning, resilience to adversity, vulnerability to stress and depression, compliance with treatment regimens, and health status. Along with illness representations, self-efficacy is a key construct in clinical health psychology. Recently, it has been suggested that the two constructs are intimately related.

Lau-Walker (2006) studied the relationship of illness representation components in predicting measures of self-efficacy in patients with coronary heart disease. In a longitudinal study, she assessed general self-efficacy, diet self-efficacy, and exercise self-efficacy twice, once while patients were hospitalized and then 9 months following discharge. She found that the relationship between illness representation components and specific self-efficacy changed over time. Specifically, consequence and timeline were significantly related to self-efficacy measures initially; however, identity or symptom and control/cure were the variables that were significantly related to self-efficacy measures 9 months later. After statistically controlling individuals' baseline self-efficacy measures, demographics, and illness characteristic effects, symptom and control/cure were found to make significant contributions to exercise and diet self-efficacy, respectively, 9 months later. In short, a significant relationship existed between illness representation and self-efficacy. The clinical implications of this relationship for interventions planning and implementation are just beginning to be studied.

ILLNESS REPRESENTATIONS AND CASE CONCEPTUALIZATION

Clinicians would do well to consider a patient's illness representations in the case conceptualization process. Particularly important are a patient's representations about causality, consequences, and cure/control. The following case example demonstrates how a clinician elicits illness representations and surmises that the patient's illness representations are probably operative and drive her demand for a specific treatment. Accordingly, the clinician first elicits relevant illness representations and then works collaboratively with the patient to examine and renegotiate or revise those operative representations. Sometimes, the therapeutic process of eliciting, examining, and revising a patient's illness representations is sufficient to resolve the impasse that led to the referral.

Case Example

Jill is a 27-year-old married woman with a 19-year history of asthma. After graduating from college and working 2 years as a nurse, she married

Jack, a sales executive. Jill had hoped to be admitted to a competitive graduate program and knew she needed a high Graduate Record Examination score to have any chance of being admitted. She complained of recently experiencing an "anxiety attack," which then triggered an asthma attack, while studying for the exam. Until recently, her asthma had been relatively well controlled by medication and an inhaler. She had asked Steven Jenkins, her physician, for an antianxiety medication to curb her anxiety, but because of the high likelihood of negative interaction between that drug class and her asthma medications, he was reluctant to add such a medication. Instead, Jenkins suggested a referral for counseling. Jill was hesitant to take the referral, indicating that she did not think she had mental problems. Her thought was the medication would provide the short-term relief she needed to pass the test. She seemed to think she could put up with any medication side effects for a couple of weeks.

Not sure how to proceed, the physician excused himself and talked briefly with Jerry Winters, a clinical health psychologist with expertise in dealing with illness issues. Winters consulted at the clinic on three afternoons a week and typically saw patients with issues like Jill's for all 15 of the clinic physicians. Winters agreed to join Jenkins and Jill and talk with her briefly. Jenkins introduced Winters to Jill and said that he had asked the psychologist to evaluate her anxiety symptoms and treatment options. She agreed. When Jenkins left the exam room, Winters proceeded to calm her down and then inquired about her anxiety attacks and their triggers. Ruling out panic attacks, he learned more about Jill's fear of getting a low score on the exam and her difficulty in studying for it. It seemed that her difficulty concentrating appeared to be due largely to distractions because she and Jack lived in an apartment with "paper-thin walls, and noise travels." Jack's music listening in another part of the apartment appeared to be a prime source of distraction for her. The transcription picks up at this point.

CL: How much would you say your asthma affects your life?

PT: Until lately, not very much. I'm so thankful that Dr. Jenkins has been pretty good at controlling it with changing my medications as the allergy season comes and goes. But lately, I've become almost a basket case with all this anxiety and worry.

CL: So, using a 10-point scale, where 1 is very little and 10 is very high, how much control would you estimate you have had over your asthma before this anxiety started? And, how much control would you say you have now?

PT: I'd say about an 8 or 9 before, and about 3 or so now.

CL: Thanks, that's helpful. So, what do you think has caused your asthma?

PT: Well, it seems to run in the family. Heredity. My mother and sister have it. I've had it since I was 8, and I was told that allergies to tree pollen and mold just make it worse.

CL: Do you see a connection between your stress, which you experience as anxiety, and allergy symptoms?

PT: Definitely.

CL: How do you understand that connection?

PT: Well, I guess that stress aggravates it. The more stress and worry I have, the worse my asthma gets and the harder to control it. That's why I asked for a new medication for it.

CL: So, psychological stress activates your asthma just as environmental stress like pollen and mold do. Psychological factors can affect your asthma in addition to environmental and hereditary factors. Is that what you're saying?

Here, Winters is attempting to expand Jill's perception of causality to include both biological and psychological factors. A positive response to his question suggests that she is more receptive to a multiple cause explanation, that is, a biological and psychological formulation, compared with a single causative one, that is, a biological formulation.

PT: Yes. [*pause*] I suppose I am.

CL: So, generally speaking, biological treatments like your asthma medication and inhalers are the usual treatment for biologically caused aspects of a medical condition like asthma. And, while medications can be a treatment for more psychologically caused aspects of it, psychological treatments like stress management and counseling are the usual treatments for it, particularly when medications are contraindicated, such as when there is potential for causing serious side effects. Does that make sense?

PT: [*pause*] It does. But I'm not keen on therapy stuff. That's why I'm willing to try the medications even though there may be side effect problems.

CL: Dr. Jenkins mentioned to me that the antianxiety medication you were hoping he would prescribe has been shown to cause short-term memory loss and concentration difficulty in a number of those who take it. Particularly in the first few weeks of use. Are you saying that you're willing to take the chance of failing your exam by taking a medication which could reduce your anxiety at the price of negatively affecting your test preparation because of memory and concentration difficulties?

PT: Well, if you put it that way . . . no. I guess that isn't what I want.

CL: I hear your concern about going into therapy. You seem to be viewing yourself more as someone with a medical problem who wants a biological treatment than as someone with a psychological problem wanting a psychological treatment. Would that be accurate?

PT: Yes, it is.

CL: Well, then, I think I can be of some help to you. Right now. Today. [*pause*] You see, it is possible to apply some very brief focused stress management and counseling techniques in this medical setting today that could make a big difference. Since medication seems out of the question at the present time, I'm willing to work with you now for the next 15 to 20 minutes or so to deal with your stress, worry, and anxiety so that they don't trigger more asthma symptoms or disrupt your concentration while you're studying. There may be a need for a follow-up session. But if there is, it would be short. Are you willing to give it a try?

PT: I am. I've got to do something.

Case Commentary

Jill came to the medical clinic with one objective: to get relief from anxiety that was aggravating her asthma. On the basis of her perception of the biological cause of her asthma, she believed she needed a biological treatment, that is, an antianxiety medication. Thus, Jenkins's talk of referral for psychological counseling was alien to her illness perception of causality, and it is not surprising that she did not immediately embrace this plan. Fortunately, Jenkins was able to call in an on-site consultant. As Winters increased her awareness of an additional causative factor, the psychological cause, Jill was much more receptive to a more psychologically based intervention. In short, as Winters helped Jill expand her illness perception of causality, her receptivity to counseling was significantly increased. It turned out that her work with Winters, which lasted about 20 minutes, was sufficient to effect a plan for preparing and passing the exam with minimal anxiety. In short, this very brief intervention resulted in a positive therapeutic outcome and spared her the untoward side effects of the medication she was initially seeking.

CONCLUDING NOTE

This chapter has described the importance of effective therapeutic relationships in medical and psychological treatment with chronically ill patients. Such relationships require a meeting of both "hearts and minds" between patient and clinicians. It was noted that the purpose of developing an effective therapeutic relationship is for the patient to collaborate with clinicians in the treatment process. A key indicator of collaboration is for patients to commit themselves to self-management of their medical condition. *Self-management* is the capacity of a patient to take appropriate responsibility for dealing with all aspects of their chronic illness, including symptoms, treatment, physical and social consequences, and lifestyle changes. With effective self-management, patients—working in tandem with health care providers—can monitor their own condition and make whatever cognitive, behavioral, and emotional changes are needed to maintain a satisfactory quality of life (Barlow, Wright, Sheasby, Turner, & Hainsworth, 2002).

This chapter has emphasized how this can be accomplished by eliciting illness representations, especially explanatory models and treatment expectations, and by forging a mutually agreed upon case conceptualization. Eliciting and assessing other patient data and planning interventions tailored to patient need is the next step. Chapter 2 focuses on these topics.

2

ASSESSMENT AND INTERVENTIONS

During the process of forming a collaborative therapeutic relationship with the patient, the clinician is also assessing the patient and his or her illness experience. Such an assessment forms the basis for case conceptualization, intervention planning, and intervention implementation as well as monitoring the treatment process and outcomes. This chapter begins with a discussion of a comprehensive assessment of the biopsychosocial factors that predispose and describe the patient's response to his or her illness. Then it describes the components for planning interventions tailored to the patient's unique needs, expectations, and circumstances. Next, it describes the components for implementing and monitoring these interventions. As an overview, this discussion is necessarily broad and general because it is an introduction to chapters in Part III, which apply and illustrate these assessment and intervention components for 10 common chronic medical conditions. Exhibit 2.1 lists the various assessment and intervention components of an integrative protocol that can inform and guide the treatment process.

BIOPSYCHOSOCIAL ASSESSMENT

Although there are some similarities between the assessment of psychotherapy clients and chronic illness patients, there are some differences. This section focuses on these differences. In an earlier volume (Sperry, 2006b),

EXHIBIT 2.1
Assessment and Intervention Components of the Integrative Protocol

BIOPSYCHOSOCIAL ASSESSMENT

Patient profile

- Illness representations and treatment expectations
- Capacity, readiness, and previous change efforts
- Personality, roles and relationships, and culture

Illness Profile

- Comorbidities and risks
- Type and severity
- Illness phase
- Biomarkers and behavioral markers

INTERVENTION PLANNING

- Patient profile factors
- Illness profile factors
- Treatment targets

INTERVENTION IMPLEMENTATION

- Psychoeductional
- Cognitive–behavioral therapy
- Psychotherapy
- Medical treatment and medication
- Combined treatment

INTERVENTION MONITORING

- Track biomarkers
- Track behavioral markers

I advocated an approach to assessment that identifies 13 key markers of illness dynamics and determinants. These include illness representation, disease progression and functional impact (Sharpe & Curran, 2006), health behaviors and exposure history, early parental bond and adverse childhood experiences, personal schemas and family narratives, personality style, family competence and style, religious and spiritual beliefs, capacities and resources, readiness, treatment relationships with previous providers, alignment between clinician–patient explanations and treatment goals, and phase of illness. In the present volume, these are formulated somewhat differently as components that specify a patient profile and an illness profile. Each of these components is briefly introduced here.

Illness Representations and Treatment Expectations

Illness Representations

Illness representations are introduced in chapter 1 of this volume. Briefly, a patient's perceptions of the identity, cause, timeline, consequences, and cure and control of her medical condition represent the five dimensions of their illness representation. Research on illness representations supports clinical observations that discrepancies between patients' and clinician's views can negatively impact treatment. One study found that when there were large discrepancies between such views, the result was worsened health status for the patient and a subsequent increase in healthcare utilization (Heijmans et al., 2001). Another study found that those who believed they would experience negative medical consequences of their illness reported that they became very depressed compared with those who believed there would be only minimal medical consequences from their rheumatoid arthritis (Schiaffino, Shawaryn, & Blum, 1998).

Treatment Expectations

What a patient expects of the treatment process and outcomes and what role and responsibilities he or she expects the clinician to assume is what constitutes one part of treatment expectations. The other part is the clinician's expectation of the patient's role and responsibilities in collaborating with the treatment process. Patients can have high, low, or ambivalent expectations for change, and these expectations may be realistic or unrealistic. Generally speaking, patients with moderate to high realistic expectations of change do experience more change than patients with unrealistic or minimal expectations or who assume little responsibility for change (Sotsky et al., 1991).

Capacity, Readiness, and Previous Change Efforts

Capacity

The likelihood that patients will succeed with their self-management efforts is in large part a function of their capacity for change, readiness for change, and previous success with change efforts. Treatment capacity reflects the degree to which patients are capable of controlling or modulating their affects, cognitions, and impulses. Perhaps the most important capacity for a patient is *self-management*, that is, taking appropriate responsibility for dealing with all aspects of their chronic illness. An underlying premise of self-management is that *self-efficacy* (i.e., the patient's belief in his or her own ability to accomplish a specific behavior or achieve a reduction in symptoms) leads to improved clinical outcomes. The clinician supports the patient's self-management efforts by collaborating with a patient in various ways, such as building confidence and making choices, which leads to improved self-management and better clinical outcomes.

Readiness

Readiness for treatment refers to the patient's desire for and capacity to make therapeutic changes. Five stages of readiness to engage in change efforts have been articulated (Prochaska, Norcross, & DiClemente, 1994). They are (a) *precontemplation*—denial of need for treatment; (b) *contemplation*—

acceptance of need for treatment; (c) *decision*—agreeing to take responsibility and collaborate with treatment effort; (d) *action*—taking responsibility and collaborating in change effort; and (e) *maintenance*—continuing effort and avoiding relapse. Knowledge of treatment and readiness for change are critical in anticipating treatment outcomes because patients who have accepted the need for treatment, decided to cooperate with treatment, and made efforts to change and maintain change are more likely to have positive treatment outcomes than patients who have not. Recently, it was reported that level of readiness for change predicted treatment outcome in eating disorder patients and should be considered in the assessment profile of patients (McHugh, 2007). Furthermore, it has also been reported that readiness for change is reflected in patients' illness representations (Stockford, Turner, & Cooper, 2007). The implication is that in eliciting illness representations, the clinician is indirectly eliciting readiness for change.

Previous Change Efforts

Success in self-management effort is also a function of previous change efforts. Thus, a patient who was able to stop smoking and remain abstinent 5 years ago or who regularly and consistently has arranged his schedule and walked for 20 minutes a day for the past year is more likely to regularly monitor daily blood glucose levels or be compliant with antihypertensive medication than someone who has not had such success with previous change efforts.

Personality, Roles and Relationships, and Culture

Personality

Among the factors impacting a patient's chronic illness experience, personality is a significant one. *Personality style* refers to an individual's consistent and enduring pattern of thinking, feeling, behaving, and relating (Sperry, 2003). A personality disorder is present when a personality style becomes sufficiently inflexible and maladaptive to cause significant impairment in occupational or social functioning or result in great subjective distress. Not surprisingly, personality-disordered patients with chronic illness are a challenge to health care personnel with regard to keeping appointments, compliance with treatment recommendations, and relating to particular health care personnel. Assessment of personality style or disorder provides the clinician with information about the health–personality dynamics of patients with chronic illness. Treatment implications of the six most common personality styles or disorders noted in diabetic patients are highlighted in Table 2.1. See Harper (2004) and Sperry (2006a, 2006b) for more information on chronic illness and other personality disorders.

Roles and Relationships

All individuals are defined by the roles they assume, for example, wife, mother, teacher, friend, life-long learner. Associated with each role are clusters of norms and behavioral expectations that are shared with significant others, and knowing what to do in a particular role makes the social environment more predictable and provides a sense of fulfillment and satisfaction. The more valued the role, the more fulfillment and satisfaction it provides as long as the role can be enacted. However, the inability to successfully execute role prescriptions can be devastating. For example, divorce may be construed as failure in the roles of wife and mother, whereas being fired from a teaching position would constitute failure in the role of teacher. The end result is that these undesirable stressors may deprive individuals of a sense of meaning, and the vacuum created by the loss of meaning may promote inactivity and noncompliance and inhibit otherwise effective coping behaviors. In short, roles that are valued highly are a major source of meaning in life, and stressors arising in these roles can undermine this sense of meaning (Krause, 1998). The same may hold for a chronic medical condition. Furthermore, it cannot be assumed that because a patient was married or was working that her relationship with her husband or child or returning to her teaching job is important to her and thus should be a treatment focus. For this reason, the clinician must identify the patient's valued roles and how life meaning and satisfaction is being undermined by the chronic medical condition. It may no longer be possible to fully enact one or more of these valued roles, but partial enactment may be possible, or another lesser valued role can be emphasized. Psychotherapeutic inquiry can promote a sense of meaning in the face of adversity and help the patient better cope with stressful events that threaten these valued roles.

Culture

Cultural factors, including ethnicity, gender, age, and religious and spiritual beliefs, can significantly influence a patient's perception of his or her chronic illness (R. Cox, 2003; Danielson, Hamel-Bissell, & Winstead-Frey, 1993; Fennell, 2003). It is not surprising that these beliefs can also affect the patient's decisions about treatment and compliance. Patients can refuse to take medication because of their beliefs about what their medications or their illness signify. Similarly, religious and spiritual beliefs can be significant factors that influence commitment to and response to treatment. For example, patients may be reluctant to take medication because they believe that their illness is a punishment from God and that they do not deserve to be relieved of their suffering. Sometimes older patients hold two disparate beliefs. The first is that life is meant to be a struggle and painful at times and that enduring such suffering is redemptive, that is, makes them worthy of a heavenly reward. The second belief is that authority figures like physicians should be honored and respected (i.e., you do not question or dispute their judgment). The resolution of holding such discrepant beliefs is evident when they are given a prescription by their physician: They will graciously accept the prescription but have no intention of filling it or taking it.

TABLE 2.1
Personality Style and Issues, Risks, and Strategies With Diabetes Patients

Personality style	Key issues	High risks	Key strategies
Avoidant	1. Shy, anticipate rejection of clinicians, and are anxiety prone, which leads to glucose fluctuations that are not (primarily) diet related. 2. Often misunderstood by clinicians, who attribute glucose control problems to patient's nonadherence or misbehavior, leading to interpersonal tension and clinician recrimination, the patient's feeling rejected, quitting IM, and fear that seeking care will be ultimately rejecting. 3. "Test" clinician or provider, anticipating curt or critical response.	1. Stressful situations significantly alter glucose metabolism. 2. Use of "testing" (e.g., changing or canceling appointments at a moment's notice and other provocative behaviors) early in the course of treatment.	Once rejected, they remain fearful about seeking alternative care, which they anticipate as ultimately rejecting. Therefore, manifest patience and a patient-centered orientation, and discuss and monitor all stressful factors that contribute to problematic glucose regulation.
Borderline	Tend to be rejection sensitive; consistently inconsistent; and given to overmodulated cognitions, behaviors, and affects. To the extent they lack a cohesive sense of self and the capacity to self-modulate, they will experience difficulty monitoring and regulating glucose levels. Even in higher functioning patients who intellectually accept the responsibility to be accountable for glucose control, emotionally keeping the promise can be extraordinarily difficult, particularly when tempted by certain nonallowed foods or substances.	1. Moods and cognitive instability affect endocrine surges, making glucose control a major challenge; such instability is complicated by impulsive dietary indiscretion and substance abuse as well as nicotine and caffeine use, which constricts small blood vessels. Emotional and interpersonal conflicts often result in neglect of insulin regulation. 2. Even if initially successful in implementing a diet and glucose-monitoring plan, maintaining it	1. Establish and maintain clear boundaries about expectations of the treatment process and the clinician–patient relationship. 2. Because the implementation phase of their IM is typically problematic rather than the planning phase—unless they are smokers or obese—anticipate this and muster the necessary resources. 3. Because instability is usually triggered by interpersonal issues, consistently monitor the relational aspect of their lives.

without relapse or departing from the schedule tends to be their downfall.

3. Self-neglect during a relational conflict can precipitate a DM crisis, often occurring because of transient psychotic decompensation or deliberately stopping insulin, bingeing on food, or drinking excessively. Their sugar levels can become unstable, and this can result in a crisis to elicit guilt or remorse from the therapist.

4. If their relationships are typically tumultuous and fragile, psychotherapy should be regarded as an essential component of IM.

Dependent

Instead of acting independently, they seek a nurturing authority figure (the clinician) to provide security, take care of, and make decisions for them, leading to significant IM problems.

Unrealistic demands and expectations, little sense of closeness to clinician and/or prospect of a long-term treatment relationship, and lack of perceived incentive to engage in disciplined behavior is a recipe for illness denial and IM failure with regard to lack of glucose self-monitoring and regulation.

1. Conceptualize IM as a conjoint undertaking that reinforces their need to feel part of the IM process.

2. Reframe problems as opportunities for conjoint problem solving instead of failures.

3. Emphasize the role of self-discipline as essential to IM, and make demands and expectations manageable and achievable so that success is relatively assured throughout stages of treatment.

4. Provide opportunities to report success and effective glucose control, especially in early stages of IM.

5. Schedule ongoing, fixed appointments, and enthusiastically recognize and reinforce their IM efforts, leading to increased self-efficacy (the reverse of standard

(continues)

TABLE 2.1 (Continued)

Personality style	Key issues	High risks	Key strategies
			medical care, where absence of symptoms or health problems results in a reduction of appointments with a nurturing authority figure).
			6. Regularly elicit whatever apprehensions and concerns arise from becoming more self-disciplined and responsible.
Histrionic	High need for attention; given their fragmented, undisciplined style, they require much longer and more varied training to achieve sufficient proficiency in IM.	1. Regulating blood sugar levels, calculating calories, and evaluating food choices when dining out. 2. Because of strong need for attention, they can use hypoglycemia or hyperglycemia as weapons to demand attention and caretaking by precipitating a DM crisis, especially when a valued relationship is threatened.	1. Help them process difficult interpersonal situations and find less medically risky solutions than DM crises. 2. Given their gregarious nature, introduce a social dimension in their IM training (e.g., skill training and dining-out groups).
Narcissistic	Tend to be self-aggrandizing, self-indulgent, and preoccupied with lofty fantasies of their own self-importance; thus, they are not well suited to the humbling task of self-discipline required of IM. They are also overly sensitive to criticism, and narcissistic injury in response to recommendations, such as smoking	1. When narcissistically injured, they may "fire" the offending clinician, somatize, sue, or bolt from treatment. 2. The more burdensome the routines required to control diabetes, the less likely they will be to make and keep such commitments.	1. Establish and maintain sufficient rapport so they keep appointments, and use "mirroring" rather than corrective feedback in the early phase of treatment. 2. Emphasize simple, straightforward, and easy-to-use here-and-now directives for glucose monitoring and regulation

Personality style		

(in contrast with standard patient counseling directives, which emphasize the importance of long-range adherence and future risk of complications).

3. Cavalier and dismissive behavior should be expected from patients who may perceive and treat their condition as the medical team's responsibility.

4. Consider engaging a spouse or significant other who is responsible for meal preparation; this can be invaluable in establishing and maintaining limits to their self-indulgent excesses.

1. Avoid being too harsh in evaluating their deviations from treatment regimens because their struggle to conform can be counterproductive. Harshness leads to preoccupation with punishment, increased rigidity, discouragement, and noncompliance.

2. Communicate acceptance and support while conveying confidence that they are doing enough to manage their illness despite occasional lapses.

cessation or the like, can infuriate and test the resolve of clinicians who may be tempted to "fire" such patients.

3. They engage in provocative behavior and condescending responses.

Noncompliance and other problems are more likely to emerge in early IM rather than later.

Very high self-demands for perfection and doing things right make them best suited of all personality styles for IM because diabetes requires lifelong self-monitoring, discipline, self-denial, and self-regulation.

Obsessive–compulsive

Note. IM = illness management; DM = diabetes management.

Comorbidities and Risks

A common barrier to successful self-management is that chronic conditions often occur as comorbidities. Patients with chronic medical conditions who are asked to identify barriers to self-management often complain that the symptoms or treatment of a comorbid medical or psychiatric condition further aggravates or complicates the self-management efforts (Lorig, 2003). Generally speaking, prevalence rates of anxiety, depressive disorders, and other psychiatric disorders are 2 to 4 times higher among those with chronic medical conditions than in the general population. There are also various factors that increase a patient's risk for treatment failure. These may include onset of symptoms at an early age, symptom severity, low socioeconomic status, family history, and so on. In light of these comorbidities and risk factors, clinicians must consider how to combine and sequence interventions to optimize treatment.

Type and Severity

Type

Disease type can be essential in effectively planning treatment. For example, neurogenic hypertension differs significantly from essential hypertension and appears to be primarily mediated by psychological factors, particularly repressed emotions. Repressed emotion, genetic predisposition, and overweight have been shown to be additive risk factors for neurogenic hypertension, and it appears that trauma and severe stress may trigger this form of hypertension (Mann & James, 1998). Rather than conventional medication treatment, psychotherapy focused on repressed emotions may be indicated along with an alternate medication.

Severity

Severity of symptoms is another useful indicator in planning treatment. Typically, patients with moderate and severe conditions, for example, levels of chronic pain, may require more intensive and combined treatments than patients with milder conditions. Also, when the condition and symptoms are severe, such as in the terminal stage of cancer, some cognitive–behavioral therapy (CBT) techniques may be inappropriate, for example, reframing (White, 2001).

Illness Phase and Course

Phase

Various phases of adaptation occur in chronic illnesses. The four-phase model describes the events of chronic illness and the response to it that typically occurs at each phase (Fennell, 2003). This model is briefly described here. Phase 1 involves *crisis*, and the basic task for patient and clinician is to deal with the immediate symptoms, pain, or traumas associated with this new experience of illness. Phase 2 is called *stabilization*, and the basic task is to stabilize and restructure life patterns and perceptions. Phase 3 is referred to as *resolution*. Its basic task is to develop a new self and to seek a personally meaningful philosophy of life and a concomitant spirituality. Phase 4 is called *integration* and involves the basic task of finding appropriate employment if able to work, to reintegrate or form supportive networks of friends and family, and to integrate one's illness within a spiritual or philosophical framework. It has been noted that "without sustained guidance from a clinician most patients find themselves either perpetually in crisis (Phase 1) or in an endless loop between the first two phases" (Fennell, 2003, p. 8). Needless to say, identifying illness phase is essential in effectively planning treatment.

Course

The course or trajectory of a chronic disease can defy easy characterization. Some disease processes take a progressive debilitating course, whereas others follow a course that is mild and relatively stable with only occasional periods of exacerbation. Nevertheless, it is possible to consider the course of a disease state as mild and stable, moderate with a waxing and waning course, or progressively deteriorating and debilitating. Because illness is the subjective experience of a disease state, the impact of a progressively debilitating disease may be minimal for some individuals, whereas a mild and stable condition may significantly and negatively impact another individual. The clinician needs to be able to accurately note course, progression, and impact.

Specific Biomarkers and Behavioral Markers

There are biomarkers for nearly all chronic diseases, ranging from lab tests to biopsies. Unlike physicians, who rely on these biomarkers for diagnosis and treatment, other clinicians may find only a couple of these to be useful. These include, for example, blood pressure readings in hypertension and hemoglobin A_{1c} (designated as HbA_{1c}) blood tests to measure long-term glucose control in diabetes. On the other hand, there are a myriad of behavioral markers used for specific illnesses that clinicians will find extremely useful in planning and monitoring treatment. These include patient self-rating scales, clinician rating scales, patient diaries and logs, and so on.

INTERVENTION PLANNING

Patient Profile Factors

A patient profile provides a useful map of the attributes of the patient experiencing a particular chronic medical condition. Some key attributes useful to clinicians in planning treatment are illness representations, treatment expectations, capacity, readiness, previous change efforts, personality style, valued roles and relationships, and cultural factors. Because of its salience in intervention planning, illness representation is highlighted here.

Illness Representation

When the patient's elicited illness representation has the potential to hinder treatment, the clinician does well to consider the impact of personality style on the patient's perceptions of their illness and treatment before attempting to modify them. For example, the illness representations of histrionic patients are likely to be emotionally charged, dramatic, and attention getting. If a clinician simply attempts to provide accurate, objective information about the disease process, the histrionic patient may easily distort it. Instead, the more concrete the illness representation information that can be linked to the patient's specific experience and need to be pleasing to the clinician, the more likely treatment compliance will be. In other words, although other patients might find that objective information increases their sense of control over the illness, this may not be of much importance to the histrionic patient, who is more likely to be focused on pleasing and attention seeking. "Rather what will be important will be how the information and behavioral expectations are linked to the patient's sense of relationship to the physician, which will determine its importance" (Harper, 2004, p. 121).

Illness Profile Factors

Where the patient profile maps key attributes of the patient experiencing a particular chronic medical condition, the illness profile provides the clinician a map that reflects the unique features of a specific chronic disease experienced by the patient. Factors that constitute this profile that can be useful in intervention planning include the type and severity of the disease or illness, unique risks and comorbidities, and the phase and course.

Treatment Targets

Unlike psychotherapy clients for whom typical treatment targets include reducing symptoms and impairment, personality change, integration, and self-actualization, treatment targets for medical patients are somewhat different. These include modifying treatment-interfering illness representations, increasing treatment compliance, reversing illness denial, reducing symptom amplification, and dealing with life meaning and spirituality issues, to name some of the more common ones.

INTERVENTION IMPLEMENTATION

Psychoeducational Interventions

Although psychoeducation and patient education appear to be similar, they actually differ significantly. The goal of patient education is to increase a patient's knowledge of their disease and its treatment in anticipation that such knowledge will lead to behavior change that improves clinical outcomes.

On the other hand, the primary goal of psychoeducation is to increase the patient's sense of self-efficacy and commitment to self-management in anticipation that the patient will engage in specific behaviors that will lead to improved clinical outcomes. The clinician's primary role in patient education is simply to provide accurate and objective information, whereas in psychoeducation, the clinician's primary role is to support the patient's self-management efforts. This includes processes that develop patient problem-solving skills, improve self-efficacy, and translate treatment information into real-life situations that matter to patients (Coleman & Newton, 2005). Increasing evidence indicates that clinician support of patient self-management efforts reduces hospitalizations, emergency room use, and overall health care costs (Lorig et al., 2001).

There are many types of psychoeducational interventions, ranging from problem-solving skills training to mindfulness meditation, as well as lifestyle change interventions such as smoking cessation, weight management, and exercise. The clinician's challenge is to tailor such interventions to patient need, personality and coping style, and circumstances.

Cognitive–Behavioral Therapy

CBT is considered the psychotherapeutic treatment of choice for most chronic medical conditions (White, 2001). Whether used alone or in combination with other psychological or medical treatments, numerous randomized controlled trials (RCTs) provide evidence of CBT's effectiveness in increased psychological well-being and, in several instances, physical well-being as well. For example, CBT was provided to patients with rheumatoid arthritis. It resulted in reduced fatigue, depression, and helplessness and enhanced use of active coping strategies (Evers, Kraaimaat, van Riel, & de Jong, 2002). In another study, CBT was used to modify illness representations. Among patients with systemic lupus erythematosus, a self-selected controlled trial of an intervention program containing a module to explain and attempt to improve illness representations led to enhanced patient perceptions that treatment could control their lupus. It also reduced their perceptions of the emotional impact of their lupus and their overall stress (Goodman, Morrissey, Graham, & Bossingham, 2005a). Similarly, in patients who had recently experienced an acute myocardial infarction and perceived their illness in terms of a chronic time line, serious consequences, and lack of control, these illness representations were modifiable in an RCT-designed study in which CBT was shown to improve symptoms of angina sufficiently so patients could return to work (Petrie, Cameron, Ellis, Buick, & Weinman, 2002).

CBT is particularly suited for changing maladaptive health behaviors and cognitions. These include modifying treatment-interfering illness representations, increasing illness acceptance, and dealing with compliance problems. They also include changing negative thinking, increasing self-efficacy and self-esteem and reducing substance use, avoidance of activity, overdependence on others, interpersonal conflicts, and support issues. Interventions include cognitive restructuring, positive reattribution, breathing and relaxation, social problem solving, coping skills training, and communication skills training.

One particularly potent CBT strategy useful with patients with medical conditions is the cognitive behavioral analysis system of psychotherapy (CBASP). CBASP was developed for the treatment of chronic depression (McCullough, 2000, 2005). Several large multisite studies comparing use of CBASP and medication in the treatment of chronic depression have been published in the recent past. Results from the acute phase of the study indicated that the antidepressant nefazodone alone and CBASP appeared to be equally effective, with response rates of 52% for CBASP and 55% for nefazodone. However, response rates for the combination group, which received both CBASP and the antidepressant, were significantly better at 85% (Keller et al., 2000). With regard to CBASP for longer term or maintenance treatment, findings support the use of CBASP as a maintenance treatment for chronic forms of major depressive disorder (Klein et al., 2004). Other large-scale trials are underway comparing CBASP with interpersonal therapy and supportive–expressive psychotherapy.

Recently, CBASP has been extended to various other Axis I and Axis II conditions as well as relational problems (Driscoll, Cukrowicz, Reardon, & Joiner, 2004). CBASP has recently been adapted for use with medical illness in individuals and couples (Sperry, 2005). Unique to this approach is an inquiry about behaviors and interpretations or beliefs that result in unwanted outcomes or consequences compared with alternative behaviors and beliefs that can result in desired outcomes or consequences.

Noteworthy is that this approach is easily accepted by clients with medical conditions. There are a number of reasons for this. First, the approach is direct and focuses on the here and now. Second, clients like it because it is neither mysterious nor too removed from their experience. Rather, in a systematic and detailed fashion, it analyzes only the material—the thoughts or interpretations and behaviors for a particular situation—that the client is willing to share. Third, it not only increases the client's understanding but promotes specific behavior changes that the client—rather than therapist—proposes and plans. Fourth, in addition to analyzing their own thoughts and behaviors, clients have the experience of analyzing the effects or consequences of these thoughts and behaviors in terms of whether they help or hurt in achieving the client's desired outcome. This tangibly motivates and promotes behavior change. Finally, patients, especially higher functioning ones, have indicated that they have used the approach in solving problems and making decisions on their own without any prompting or suggestion from their therapist. This speaks to the perceived value that clients attribute to the approach. Not surprisingly, clients with medical conditions who would not likely seek out and engage in therapy find this approach accessible, nonthreatening, and effective.

CBASP provides a "cognitive map" for therapeutic processing of a situation. The adapted form (Sperry, 2005) consists of nine steps in the form of clinician-initiated queries. These steps and queries are as follows:

Step 1: Can you describe what happened? Elicit situation narrative with beginning, middle, and end.

Step 2: What was your interpretation of your thoughts about the situation?

Step 3: What were your behaviors? What did you say, what did you do? What were your feelings?

Step 4: What did you want to happen? What did you desire or expect would happen?

Step 5: What actually happened?

Step 6: Did your behaviors and thoughts promote your health and well-being or detract from it?

Step 7: Can we analyze this together to see what happened and what might be different?

Step 8: Taking each specific thought and behavior: did this thought or behavior help or hurt you in terms of getting you what you wanted?

Step 9: What alternative thought or behavior might have better helped you get what you wanted? Specifically, how would this new thought or behavior get you what you wanted?

Other Psychotherapeutic Interventions

Other psychotherapeutic approaches besides CBT have been used with chronic medical conditions. Beginning with efforts to treat the so-called psychosomatic illnesses, various psychotherapeutic approaches, individual and group, have been used to increase psychological well-being and, in a few instances, physical well-being as well. Dynamic psychotherapies have long been used in the treatment of chronic medical patients. Needless to say, there are relatively few RCTs that address the effectiveness of dynamic therapies and other approaches.

Medical Treatment and Medication

Medical treatment includes modalities such as medications, surgery, diet modification, physical therapy, and exercise. Rehabilitation techniques may also be used to prevent dysfunction and decrease the severity or duration of disability. For the most part, though, medications are the primary modality, which means that medication noncompliance may lead to referral for psychological interventions.

Combined Treatment

In all chronic medical conditions, combined and integrated treatment eventually becomes the treatment of choice for most patients with moderate and severe symptoms and impairment. Treatment with such patients may begin with a single modality, such as medication, but because of minimal response, untoward side effects, or noncompliance, introducing a psychological intervention is considered. In typical combined treatment, a medical treatment, usually a medication, is combined with one or more psychological interventions. Occasionally, combined treatment involves two or more psychological interventions and no medical intervention. Perhaps the most common form of combined treatment is medication, psychoeducation, and CBT.

INTERVENTION MONITORING

Track Biomarkers

Clinicians may find that monitoring biomarkers such as blood pressure readings and HbA1c levels can be useful in monitoring a patient's compliance and progress toward treatment goals. These biomarkers usually are recorded in a patient's medical chart. If a clinician is providing service in a location where access to these data is not available, it may be advantageous to arrange to be forwarded such data. In either instance, patient consent should be secured.

Track Behavioral Markers

A number of behavioral markers for specific illnesses might be useful to clinicians in monitoring a patient's compliance and progress toward treatment goals. These include patient self-report (e.g., scaling, diaries, and logs of symptoms and functionality). There are also many rating scales that clinician can use to rate symptoms, functionality, and other markers of session-to-session progress with regard to illness phase, compliance, illness acceptance, relational functioning, and personal integration.

CONCLUDING NOTE

This chapter has discussed the components of assessment, intervention planning, intervention implementation, and intervention monitoring. It has provided a general overview of an approach to clinical practice with patients with chronic medical conditions. In contrast, the chapters in Part III provide a detailed discussion of this approach with 10 specific chronic medical conditions.

II

COGNITIVE–BEHAVIORAL THERAPY STRATEGIES

As noted previously, cognitive–behavioral therapy (CBT) is the most commonly practiced therapeutic approach applied to chronic medical conditions (White, 2001). CBT and related strategies are also commonly used with clinical challenges often encountered in working with medical patients such as treatment noncompliance (Blackwell, 1997).

Part II consists of four chapters that focus on four clinical challenges that often occur when working with chronic medical patients: illness denial, noncompliance, symptom exacerbation, and spiritual and life meaning issues. CBT strategies targeted to these challenges are described and illustrated with case material and extended transcriptions of representative sessions. Because psychotherapists and psychologists working in primary care settings, particularly family medicine clinics, have the opportunity to become involved with patients' spouses and other family members, some of the discussion and case examples in these chapters illustrate how to collaborate with family members to optimize patient health and well-being.

3

ILLNESS ACCEPTANCE INTERVENTION STRATEGY

A major stumbling block in the medical treatment of individuals with chronic illness is illness denial. *Illness denial* refers to individuals' unwillingness to acknowledge and accept that they have a chronic disease and the impact that disease state has on them (Fennell, 2003). Needless to say, illness denial is a major cause of treatment nonresponsiveness, particularly noncompliance or nonadherence with a prescribed treatment regimen. On the other hand, *illness acceptance* is associated with positive treatment outcomes (White, 2001). This chapter introduces the concepts of illness denial and illness acceptance. Both concepts are described in the context of a phase model of chronic illness. It then offers a focused cognitive–behavioral therapy (CBT) intervention that can engender the shift from illness denial to illness acceptance. This intervention and process are illustrated with a case study and session transcription.

ILLNESS DENIAL AND CHRONIC ILLNESS

Receiving the diagnosis of a chronic illness can be devastating to both the patient and family members. A not uncommon response to bad news is denial. Illness denial is a coping strategy to negate the reality of the situation (Falvo, 2005). In the case of chronic illness, individuals may deny that they have a medical condition by avoiding prescribed or recommended treatment or by denying the physical, social, or occupational implications of the disease. In the early course of the illness, such denial can be beneficial because it allows individuals time to adjust to the painful realization that their lives may never be the same. However, when denial persists, it effectively prevents individuals from achieving the optimal benefit from medical treatment and from learning more adaptive coping skills. The unfortunate end result is that their condition may worsen and their symptoms may be exacerbated (Falvo, 2005). Furthermore, health care providers may respond ambivalently or negatively to individuals they likely perceive as noncompliant or "problem" patients.

Illness denial can also affect others, particularly family members and coworkers. Denial may take the form of hiding one's diagnosis from family members or refusing to follow a prescribed medication and diet regimen. For example, the reluctant patient's child care responsibility is neglected or performed poorly, leading to potential harm to a child. Denial could also manifest itself in hiding one's illness from a work supervisor and coworkers. For instance, a recently diagnosed diabetic becomes seriously hypoglycemic and passes out while working on an assembly line, leading to the inadvertent injury of a coworker.

ILLNESS DENIAL AND ACCEPTANCE
AND THE PHASES OF CHRONIC ILLNESS

Chronic illness is the subjective experience of a chronic disease. Characteristic of chronic illness is its variability in terms of symptoms and course. This variability can be confusing for health care professionals and may complicate both the treatment relationship and the treatment process (Sperry, 2006b). Despite this variability, researchers have been able to articulate the experience of adjustment to a chronic disease from the client's perspective in terms of stage or phase models (R. Cox, 2003; Danielson, Hamel-Bissell, & Winstead-Frey, 1993). Fennell (2003) has described a heuristic model of chronic illness that involves four phases.

> *Phase 1: Crisis.* The onset of illness triggers a crisis for which individuals seek relief through medical diagnosis and treatment, spiritual help, or substance abuse. Family, colleagues, friends, and caregivers may respond with disbelief, revulsion, and rejection. In this phase, the basic task is to deal with the immediate symptoms, pain, or trauma associated with this new experience of illness.

Phase 2: Stabilization. A plateau of symptoms is reached, and individuals become more familiar with their illness. Individuals attempt to carry on their pre-illness activity level, which overtaxes them and contributes to relapses and ensuing feelings of upset and failure. The basic task of this phase is to stabilize and restructure life patterns and perceptions.

Phase 3: Resolution. Amidst plateaus of symptoms and relapses, individuals come to understand and accept that they have an illness with identifiable patterns and to learn others' responses to it. They also begin to realize and accept that their pre-illness sense of self will not return. In this phase, the basic task is to develop a new self and to seek a personally meaningful philosophy of life and spirituality consistent with it.

Phase 4: Integration. Despite plateaus and relapses, individuals are able to integrate parts of their old self before the illness into their new self. In this phase, the basic task is to find appropriate employment if able to work, to reintegrate or form supportive networks of friends and family, and to integrate their illness within a spiritual or philosophical framework. It also means achieving the highest level of wellness possible despite compromised or failing health status. Accordingly, *integration* means coming "to experience a complete life in which illness is only one aspect" (Fennell, 2003, p. 9).

FROM ILLNESS DENIAL TO ILLNESS ACCEPTANCE

Not every individual with a chronic illness manages to journey through all four phases. As Fennell (2003) pointed out, many chronically ill individuals get caught in a recurring "loop" and cycle between Phase 1 and Phase 2 wherein each crisis produces new wounding and destabilization. Such crises tend to be followed by a brief period of stabilization and, without intervention, a new crisis invariably destabilizes the system again. A primary reason for such looping is illness denial. Although some individuals quickly come to acceptance of their illness, most do not, at least initially. However, with appropriate focused interventions, chronically ill individuals can be assisted in breaking this recurring cycle and moving to Phases 3 and 4. Without such interventions, chronically ill individuals typically find themselves either perpetually in crisis or in an endless loop between the crisis and stabilization phases. Each period of stabilization recalls the pre-illness "normal" life. Individuals want to deny that a permanent change has occurred, and frequently spouses, family members, and friends want to deny it as well. Unfortunately, the illness experiences they suffer offer little or no incentive for accepting the illness as a permanent condition and learning to cope with it. Thus, when these individuals first experience a remission of their symptoms, they often feel a false sense of relief and are usually anxious to return to their pre-illness lifestyle. Inevitably, they also feel pressure from others to return to their former level of activities. Predictably, this results in their behaving in ways that actually promote a relapse and thereby loop them back to the crisis phase (Fennell, 2003).

INTERVENTIONS THAT FACILITATE ILLNESS ACCEPTANCE

CBT and other psychotherapeutic interventions can help chronically ill individuals who are in denial of their illness shift to acceptance of their illness. This goal can be accomplished in several ways. However, in my experience it can best be accomplished by focusing on issues involving illness perceptions, relationship issues, or grief issues, either separately or on two or more of these issues together.

In the first instance, the intervention can focus on modifying illness perceptions (Sperry, 2007). Illness denial is often associated with illness perceptions or representations that are distorted or inaccurate. For example, White (2001) found that individuals with denial of diabetes commonly hold beliefs such as "'people with diabetes never have any fun' and 'people with diabetes need amputations eventually'"(p. 163). Furthermore, individuals with acceptance-related problems often have premorbid beliefs characterized by an external locus of control (White, 2001). Illness acceptance becomes easier when interventions associate the individual's medical conditions with more positive illness perceptions and greater levels of self-efficacy with regard to self-management. Accordingly, providing clients accurate information and helping them revise their illness perceptions as well as fostering client self-efficacy are major goals of CBT interventions.

In the second instance, this intervention can focus on relationship issues wherein the spouse of the chronically ill individual does not accept the other spouse's medical condition and expects that life can somehow remain the same. Typically, the chronically ill spouse will attempt to meet that expectation and attempt to "be the same person" they were premorbidly. Because this is not possible, conflict eventually arises, which may lead to separation and/or divorce (Fennell, 2003).

In the third instance, the counseling intervention can assist individuals to grieve the loss of their pre-illness sense of self and lifestyle activity level. An individual in Phases 1 and 2

> often refuses to accept the idea that the pre-illness life is gone and hence refuse to acknowledge any permanents losses. By Phase 3, however, they know the old life and the pre-illness self will never return. Their grief is profound, and in Phase 3 many will, with support, choose to engage it

intentionally because it is difficult, if not dangerous for them to suppress it. (Fennell, 2003, pp. 276–277)

The following case example illustrates the second instance.

CASE EXAMPLE

Patty and Tim have been married for 8 years and have been experiencing relational difficulties for the past 18 months. This coincided with Patty's diagnosis and the beginning of her treatment for systemic lupus erythematosis (SLE). It is noteworthy that her diagnosis was made during a medical evaluation by a rheumatologist 3 years earlier. The couple had hoped to adopt a child and were in the final stages of the process when she began experiencing unbearable joint pain. Since the diagnosis of SLE was made, plans for the adoption were put on hold and SLE appeared to take center stage in their lives. Even though her doctors told her she had a milder form of the disease, Patty intermittently experienced severe joint pain and headaches, along with chronic fatigue. Most of the time she had little energy to do even routine chores, and it soon became clear that continuing with her professional work was becoming all but impossible. She no longer felt she could handle the administrative duties of her job, and she had taken a leave of absence 2 years before and had not gone back. She could still do basic things such as fixing meals and light cleanup, but not much more. Nevertheless, there were days when she felt energetic enough to think she was actually getting better and would set out to take on tasks she had easily accomplished in the past. Inevitably, she would overdo it and exacerbate her condition. Although relational discord had occurred occasionally before the diagnosis, it predictably had increased as Patty's symptoms worsened and were exacerbated by various demands in the home and in the relationship. Although Patty had largely accepted her illness, Tim had not. On the one hand, he accepted the doctor's assessment that SLE would limit Patty's functioning, but on the other hand, he expected that she would continue to do many things for him that he had become accustomed to in the past. Her submissive style and lack of assertive communication only seemed to compound matters.

The couple was referred by Patty's physician for couples therapy to a psychologist experienced in working with SLE patients. The psychologist recognized that Patty's illness not only impaired her functioning but magnified the influence of her personal style of submissiveness on relational dynamics, which predictably negatively impacted her and Tim's functioning as a couple. The psychologist had two therapeutic goals. The first was to increase the couple's understanding of their personal and interpersonal dynamics and the interplay and impact of SLE on them as individuals and as a couple. Accomplishing this goal presumably would lead to increased illness acceptance for both Tim and Patty. The second goal was to modify their relational pattern vis-à-vis the challenge of the chronic illness they both faced. Because of its effectiveness with similar health-related cases, he chose to begin the therapeutic process with the nine-step interview strategy. The following transcription describes the application of this approach during their fourth conjoint session.

Therapist: It's good to see the two of you again. How have things been going lately?

Tim: [*silence*] . . . I guess Patty is expecting me to take the lead. But I would really like it if she would take the lead and respond to your question.

Therapist: I hear you, Tim. You don't feel that the responsibility for responding should be yours alone, and you wish that Patty would take the initiative sometimes.

Patty: Okay . . . I'll start off. What happened is that Tim came home from work, and he was in a bad mood. I guess he must have had a hard day at work. Whatever it was, he was grousing about dinner. Earlier I had decided not to cook and hoped that we might go out for a change. After all, I had a little more energy than usual that day, which doesn't happen much since I've been down with this SLE. I had spent a few hours cleaning the house that afternoon, and I was starting to drag and my joints had really become inflamed. Typical when I overdo it. My medication doesn't help at times like that, and I was too fatigued to cook dinner. He told me he was hungry and tired and wondered why dinner wasn't ready.

Therapist: What did this mean to you, Patty? What were you thinking?

Patty: I suppose I thought that I when I'm not feeling well that I shouldn't have to cook a meal. But I also knew better than to presume we'd go out to eat without asking him first. I also thought that he seldom appreciates the housework I do when I'm feeling well or really badly. I also assumed he was angry with me for being inconsiderate of the hard day he probably had at work and that he was tired. This made me feel guilty. So I immediately apologized for not being considerate and started to put together a quick meal. But I let him know by the tone of my voice that I was upset and I started tearing up, just on the verge of crying. Doesn't he remember and care that I have a serious chronic illness?

Therapist: What actually happened?

Patty: Tim became frustrated that I was upset, and we got in an argument. He had no idea what was happening inside me. We ended up ordering take-out and ignored each other the rest of the evening.

Therapist: What did you expect to happen?

Patty: I wanted him to hug me and talk to me when he got home, and then I wanted to relax and go to our favorite restaurant. I really wanted some recognition of the work I did around the house and for him to accept that I can't do as much as I used to before this SLE. To be perfectly honest, I wanted to have a romantic evening with him.

Therapist: Did you get what you expected?

Patty: No. I absolutely didn't get what I wanted.

Therapist: Tim, what's your take on what happened the other evening?

The therapist has done a brief situational analysis from Patty's perspective. Now he turns to Tim and gets his view of the situation, including his interpretations, behaviors, and the desired and actual outcomes. Tim stated that he got home and Patty was lying on the couch, and because there was no dinner on the table he went and got take-out food. When he got home, they started arguing. Tim's interpretations were as follows: Patty got upset again for no reason. He couldn't read her mind. He didn't need her to start a fight after he had a long, hard day at work. His behaviors were as follows: To say nothing and to go and get Chinese food. He watched the evening news. His tone of voice may have been a bit gruff, but he wasn't upset with her. He didn't say much to her the rest of the evening, His desired outcome was to come home after a hard day at the office, have a good meal, and take it easy for the rest of the evening, and it didn't really matter if they ate out or stayed home. The actual outcome was that they got into an argument and he went to sleep frustrated and angry.

Therapist: Did you get what you expected and wanted?

Tim: No. Absolutely not.

Therapist: It sounds like both of you wanted to spend a relaxing evening together. What I also learned is that Patty wanted you to appreciate the work she did around the house, especially when it triggered so much pain and fatigue, and to acknowledge that because of her SLE she can't do as much as before. And Tim expected Patty to tell him directly her preference for dinner, whether it was to eat at home or go out.

Tim: She never tells me what she wants. Instead, she gets upset and leaves me clueless. I wouldn't have objected to going out to eat, but I didn't know what she wanted.

Patty: You were so irritable and gruff that I assumed you were mad at me for not having dinner ready the minute you got home. You didn't even notice that I was in pain from spending half the day cleaning. You know that doing that usually exacerbates my SLE.

Therapist: It seems that you are both still feeling frustrated with the way this turned out. I'd like to process this situation with you, with the hope of coming up with some alternate interpretations for it. [*pause*] Tim, you wanted to come home, have dinner with Patty, and settle in for the night, is that right?

Tim: Yes. But I also wanted her to tell me she was in pain and her plans for dinner, rather than getting her feelings hurt for no reason.

The therapist now proceeds to therapeutically process Tim's interpretations and behaviors and helps him articulate alternative ones which are more likely to achieve his desired outcome.

Therapist: Let's take a closer look at these interpretations. First, you thought or concluded that she was upset again for no reason. Did that interpretation help you or hurt you in terms of getting what you wanted?

Tim: [*pause*] Well, I guess it hurt me. I assumed she was being unreasonable and noncommunicative, and that just made me angry.

Therapist: Can you think of another interpretation that might have helped you get what you wanted?

Tim: I don't know. Maybe I could have concluded that she was upset and probably had a reason for it, which means I should try to find out what's wrong. That would have helped me because I wouldn't have become so angry, and maybe we could have talked calmly about things rather than argue.

Therapist: Fine. Let's look at your second interpretation. You said that you didn't appreciate her picking a fight with you for no reason. Did this interpretation help you or hurt you?

Tim: That one really hurt me because I was assuming that she was the one who was being unreasonable and that I had nothing to do with her feeling bad. I guess I was being selfish because I was irritable and angry about my bad day at the office. Maybe if I had been more sensitive and observant of her fatigue and pain— and the clean house—I wouldn't have hurt her feelings. That would have avoided the argument. [*pause*] And, I guess I can't get used to the idea that she has a degenerative disease.

Therapist: That she has a chronic disease is an important recognition, Tim, and we'll come back to that. Now with regard to your behavior, you said that your tone of voice was unpleasant when you got home. Is that correct?

Tim: Yes. [*pause*] I think I follow what you're getting at. I guess it hurt me because it probably made her think that I was angry with her. Maybe I should have made it clear that I wasn't upset with her right as soon as I got home, instead of the way I treated her.

Therapist: Great. You also said that you picked up some take-out and then ignored her for the rest of the evening.

Tim: Yes, and that hurt me because it hurt her feelings even more, which made everything worse. If I hadn't been so stubborn and had talked to her about it, we might have resolved it within a few minutes instead of ruining the whole evening.

Therapist: Would changing this behavior also have helped you achieve your other expectation, which was for her to tell you what she wanted?

Tim: Interesting. Maybe it would have helped. But ultimately that would really depend on her. I guess that may not be a realistic expectation.

Therapist: I can understand that you want her to feel comfortable telling you what she wanted, but it may be an unrealistic goal for you because it relies on her behavior, which, as you know, is beyond your control. Can you think of a related but more realistic expectation?

Tim: Yeah. I guess it would be that I wouldn't dump my own bad mood on her. That would probably make it much easier for her to tell me what she needs and wants.

Therapist: That follows. I could anticipate that the alternatives you came up with might help you achieve this.

Tim: Sure, I can too.

The therapist now turns to Patty and processes her material and helps her articulate interpretations and behaviors that are more likely to achieve her desired outcome.

Therapist: Patty, in this situation, you wanted to go out to dinner with Tim and then spend a nice evening together. You also said that you wanted him to acknowledge your SLE pain when you exerted yourself cleaning the house. Is this right?

Patty: I suspect it is.

Therapist: The first interpretation you gave was that you really should have known better than to plan to go out without first asking Tim. Did this thought help you or hurt in terms of getting what you want?

Patty: [*pause*] It did hurt me because it made me feel like I had to ask permission from him instead of just telling him that I would like to go out to dinner. I guess a better interpretation would have been to think that he would be tired from a hard day at the office and would probably enjoy eating out somewhere.

Therapist: That sounds reasonable. Your second interpretation was to assume that he must be angry with you. Did this help or hurt you in terms of getting what you wanted?

Patty: It definitely hurt because my own feelings were hurt when I thought he was angry. If I had just thought that he might have had a bad day and his irritability and moodiness had nothing to do with me, I probably wouldn't have gotten so upset.

Therapist: Sure. Your third interpretation was that Tim didn't even care about all the time and resulting pain from cleaning the house. And, if he did, it would probably show his acceptance of your chronic disease. Is that accurate?

Patty: Uh hmm. This one hurt me. In addition to not getting what I wanted, I ended up feeling really bad and upset. Instead, I should have thought that he just walked in the door and probably didn't have a chance to even notice the cleaning that I had done or my pain and fatigue. Then, I would not have been so upset, and maybe he wouldn't have gotten so frustrated and we could have had a nicer evening together.

Therapist: Will this new interpretation help you with your expectation, which was for him to acknowledge and accept that you have a chronic disease?

Here the therapist does some reality testing by asking Patty to consider if her alternative interpretation is likely to have its intended effect.

Patty: It might, but I can't really make him accept my lupus no matter what I do. So maybe it's not a realistic expectation.

Therapist: Patty, what would it be like for Tim to accept your chronic, degenerative medical condition? Be as specific as you can.

Patty: For Tim to accept my lupus, it would mean a lot of things. Probably, the main thing is that he would stop expecting me to be the same person I was before . . . like I was during our engagement and early marriage.

Therapist: Can be you be more specific?

Patty: He would accept that I don't have the energy and stamina I used to have, which means it's no longer easy to clean the whole house like I used to. And when I try, like I did the other day, I get so wiped out, I'm so fatigued and in pain, I can't do anything but lie down, take extra pain medication, and rest on the bed or the living room couch.

Therapist: What else would it mean for him to accept your medical condition?

Patty: He would ask if I needed help with taking care of the house. I've thought it might be nice to have a cleaning service come in once a week or so, but I've been reluctant to talk with Tim about it.

Therapist: Why is that?

Patty: Because I expect he'll say it's too expensive. . . . It's so frustrating . . . [*tearing up*] . . . I feel trapped between being sick and wanting to be the wife he wants me to be. And that I want to be for him. But I can't be that anymore . . . [*crying*].

Tim: Oh Patty, I don't want you be sad and in so much pain. It's hard to see you crying like this. . . . I guess I really hope against hope that things could be the way they used to be when we were first married. You were so energetic and full of life . . . [*pause*]. . . . It does help to keep my head in the sand. I know I need to start accepting that things are different now. . . . You're right, I can't expect you to overextend yourself with cleaning and preparing meals . . . I'm really sorry. . . . We can afford a cleaning service. Let's arrange it as soon as we can. . . . We can work something out about meals, too [*Patty nodding her head*].

The session continues as the therapist summarizes and frames "illness acceptance" as a function of more direct communications, recognition of each others' needs, and the challenge couples face when both spouses work collaboratively in dealing with a chronic degenerative disease like lupus.

CASE COMMENTARY

As in the case of Patty and Tim, illness denial is not an uncommon treatment issue in health-focused counseling. This case illustrates the use of the cognitive–behavioral analysis approach, focusing on the relationship issue wherein Tim's denial of Patty's SLE complicated Patty's own acceptance of her illness. Although Patty's lack of assertive communication with Tim appears to have been a contributing factor, increasing Patty's assertiveness was only one factor in increasing illness acceptance.

CONCLUDING NOTE

Achieving a sufficient degree of illness acceptance is a prerequisite for effective health care. To the extent that acceptance problems exist, not only is treatment compliance an issue but so also is the viability of the therapeutic alliance itself. Three different therapeutic strategies were described for dealing with illness denial. Fortunately, CBT interventions, and CBASP in particular, can be effective in increasing illness acceptance.

4

COMPLIANCE ENHANCEMENT

Patient treatment noncompliance is one of the most vexing challenges facing health care providers who work with the chronically ill. Treatment noncompliance is common: Medication noncompliance rates range from 50% to 75% of patients; the rates are even higher in patients with chronic medical conditions. Treatment noncompliance is also very problematic: Approximately 125,000 patients with treatable ailments die each year in the United States because of failure to take their medication properly (O'Connor, 2006). The reality is that most patients "find it difficult to make major lifestyle changes or to use medications consistently over long periods of time, and thus few patients are fully compliant with physicians' recommendations" (Becker, 1989, p. 416).

Compliance, also referred to as *adherence*, can be defined as the extent to which a person's behavior, such as keeping appointments, taking medications, or making lifestyle changes, coincides with medical or therapeutic advice. Statistics on noncompliance and its long-term consequences stagger the imagination. It is estimated that only one fourth of individuals with hypertension are under treatment, and only about one half of those actually control their blood pressure because only two thirds use enough medication (Becker, 1989; Blackwell, 1997). Psychologists and psychotherapists who deal with health-related and lifestyle change in their practice are no strangers to the phenomenon of compliance. There are a number of strategies for enhancing patient compliance in a psychological or psychotherapeutic setting. It is noteworthy that family compliance counseling is used in primary care settings, particularly in family medicine residency clinics. Central to this strategy is partnering with family members of noncompliant patients to enhance compliance. This chapter focuses on using family dynamics to enhance treatment compliance. A focused cognitive–behavioral therapy intervention strategy for increasing compliance within a family context is described and illustrated.

TREATMENT COMPLIANCE

Over the past 50 years, clinicians and researchers have endeavored to increase treatment compliance by attending to various factors believed to be key to increasing compliance. Early efforts to enhance compliance focused on the treatment regimen and health provider instructions, whereas later efforts focused on client–provider relationships and then patient representations and perception of their illness and expectations of treatment (Blackwell, 1997). Table 4.1 reflects various treatment-related factors and compliance enhancement strategies.

More recently, the focus has shifted to the influence of family dynamics. Families can be underinvolved or overinvolved in the treatment process, either of which can undermine compliance with treatment. If underinvolved, they may not support the client sufficiently, whereas if overinvolved, they may limit the client's exercise of personal responsibility. Furthermore, disturbances in the family or in the client's relationship with the family can significantly impact a client's compliance. Even in the absence of family dysfunction, client–family interaction patterns can undermine compliance, such as when a resentful client refuses to comply to spite his or her partner, or when family members may undermine a client's compliance with a weight management regimen by giving gifts of candy, teasing the weight-reducing client, or continuing to use off-limit ingredients such as salt and sugar in preparing meals (Doherty & Baird, 1983).

The terms *family compliance counseling* and *family-oriented compliance counseling* were used by Doherty and Baird (1983) to describe the process of involving the family to foster compliance in order to enhance health status and lifestyle change. They insisted that an adequate understanding of compliance involves the "therapeutic triangle," consisting of the health care provider, the client, and the client's family, and that compliance emerges in a cooperative therapeutic alliance or system from which the client derives information, support, and resources needed to adhere to an agreed-on treatment regimen. Doherty and Baird stated that the main purposes of family compliance counseling are (a) to educate client and family about the disease

TABLE 4.1

Treatment Enhancement Strategies

Noncompliance factors	Compliance enhancement strategies
Treatment regimen	Identify and eliminate factors such as complex regimens and inconvenience by use of pillboxes and reminders, patient education, and so on.
Context	Identify and deal with external treatment-interfering factors such as medication costs, travel, work demands, and so on.
Patient	Identify and deal with "difficult" personality dynamics and related factors.
Clinician–patient relations	Foster better collaboration between clinician and patient, including involvement of case managers.
Illness representation	Identify and modify treatment-interfering illness representations.
Family dynamics	Partner with family members using family compliance counseling interventions.

and treatment regimen, (b) to provide a forum for client and family members to share their emotional reactions and concerns about the disease and regimen, and (c) to facilitate an agreement among family about how the client will be supported in adhering to the treatment program. In addition, they offered a six-step process for conducting family-oriented compliance counseling. The approach they described is primarily psychoeducational. In the following sections, a psychotherapeutic strategy is offered that can be used alone or in conjunction with their approach.

A FOCUSED COGNITIVE–BEHAVIORAL INTERVENTION STRATEGY FOR ENHANCING COMPLIANCE

Unlike clients who present themselves for conventional individual, couple, or family therapy, medical clients may not be as receptive to conventional psychotherapeutic treatment strategies that are longer in duration and less focused (Sperry, 2006b). The therapeutic interviewing strategy advocated for use in enhancing treatment compliance derives from the cognitive behavior analysis system of psychotherapy (McCullough, 2000), which was designed to target chronic depression and that I have modified for use with medical conditions (Sperry, 2005). Whereas other therapeutic approaches tend to assist clients in coping with or working through past and present conflicts, this interviewing strategy encourages clients to work toward achieving what they want or desire to happen in their lives. It fosters collaboration as therapist and client work together to achieve therapeutic goals. Clinicians can use this basic therapeutic strategy to process situations and issues as they arise in any therapeutic context, whether it is a single, unscheduled 10- to 15-minute encounter or scheduled sessions that are part of ongoing therapy.

CASE ILLUSTRATION

Jessica has been referred to Jon Perry, a psychotherapist who practices in an outpatient medical clinic of a local hospital. He specializes in counseling medical clients who are not responding adequately to their treatment regimen for any number of reasons, including compliance issues. Perry has been effective in using a straightforward interview strategy with such clients and their families. He typically works with clients for one to three sessions. Jessica is a stay-at-home mother who has been married for 10 years, and she and her husband Zack have two children. She was diagnosed with diabetes mellitus, Type II, about 3 months ago and was begun on a diabetes diet plan to control her blood sugar. At the same time, she started the clinic's weight management program with the goal of losing 25 pounds. The hope was that with regular monthly medical monitoring and the weekly weight group, she could get down to and maintain her target weight. Achieving and maintaining both diet and weight could significantly reduce the likelihood that she would need insulin injections and slow the progression of her chronic illness. After 6 weeks, she had lost a total of nearly 14 pounds but then started regaining weight. Although Jessica could provide no explanation for the gain, her physician suspected compliance was the issue and arranged for Perry to meet with her. They met for a brief session and arranged for a follow-up meeting to include her husband. The following transcription picks up about 10 minutes into that session. Prior to this, Jessica described how disappointed she was with her weight gain, even though she attended the weight management group meetings religiously and followed the diet pretty closely. Perry asked her to describe what it was like when she relapsed. She teared up and said it was awful and she was so frustrated.

> *Therapist:* I hear your frustration, Jessica. Can you describe a recent situation that illustrates it?
>
> *Jessica:* Well, I was really excited about my progress in the weight management program. I was getting really close to making my target goal by losing another 6 pounds in the past 2 weeks. I told Zack that this time I really felt like celebrating. He said great, let's go out for the evening. I said great, and was hoping it would for dancing, but he took me to his favorite Italian restaurant. Then, he wanted to order for both of us. And he orders pasta. After the waiter took our order, Zack berated me for flirting with the waiter. I said I was only being friendly. Then we got into a fight and I was so mad, I didn't say another word, and when the food came I just stuffed myself. It was 2 days before we started talking

	again, and by then I had gained back about 5 pounds in those 2 days.
Therapist:	What did this mean to you? What were your thoughts or interpretations?
Jessica:	That I just wanted to go out dancing, not out to eat. Doesn't he know I'm on a low-carbohydrate diet and shouldn't be eating pasta?
Therapist:	I hear you. And what other thoughts might you have had?
Jessica:	I was thinking what's he trying to do, undermine all the progress I've made? He's always just so jealous when I talk to other men.
Therapist:	So what did you do, what were your behaviors?

Perry has already elicited two of Jessica's operative thoughts or interpretations and attempts to elicit operative behaviors.

Jessica:	I was hurt that he ordered food I shouldn't be eating. And I was so angry when he said I was flirting, and I wouldn't say anything more to him. Also, and I'm embarrassed to say it, I stuffed myself.
Therapist:	What were you hoping would happen that evening?
Jessica:	I just wanted to enjoy my success at losing weight and spend a romantic evening with my husband.
Therapist:	What actually happened?
Jessica:	I didn't get to go dancing, and I stuffed myself and probably gained back most of the weight I lost.
Therapist:	Did you get what you expected?
Jessica:	No. No, I absolutely did not get what I wanted.

Perry has now completed the situational analysis for Jessica, and begins the same process with Zack by eliciting his interpretations and behaviors as well as desired and actual outcomes. Briefly stated, Zack's interpretations were that Jessica didn't tell him directly what she wanted him to do. She should have known that he is poor at mind reading. She shouldn't flirt, especially in front of him, because it drives him crazy. Weight management causes more trouble than it's worth. His behaviors were to order food both of them used to enjoy. He got angry and told her not to flirt anymore. He spent the rest of the evening silently fuming. His desired outcome was to enjoy dinner and spend a quiet evening together with her. The actual outcome was that his plans didn't materialize and his evening was ruined.

Therapist:	Did you get what you expected and wanted?
Zack:	Not at all.

Therapist: It seems that both of you wanted to celebrate Jessica meeting her target goal. What I also heard is that Jessica wanted Zack to recognize that to celebrate, she didn't want to eat a big feast but rather go dancing. And Zack expected Jessica to tell him directly how she wanted to celebrate since he's not a good mind reader.

Zack: Sometimes she just zones out and then gets upset. I guess I wouldn't have objected to going dancing after we had eaten something. But I didn't know what she wanted.

Jessica: You make up your mind so fast, and you seemed to have forgotten that I'm on a weight management program to control my diabetes. You know I don't want to have to take pills and insulin shots.

After getting their consent to proceed, Perry now turns to processing their unhelpful interpretations and behaviors and encourages them to come up with more helpful interpretations and behaviors that are more likely to achieve their desired outcomes. He begins with Zack and then follows the same process with Jessica.

Therapist: It's clear that you are both still feeling frustrated with the way this turned out. I'd like to analyze this situation with you, with the hope of coming up with some alternate interpretations for it. Would that be all right with you? [*both nod affirmatively*] Zack, you wanted to celebrate Jessica's success by taking her to eat and spend a quiet night alone with her. Is that right?

Zack: Yeah, but I also wanted her to remind me that doing the Italian food wasn't a good way to celebrate. I didn't make the connection that she wanted to go dancing to help her keep fit and maybe even lose some more weight. I admit, sometimes I'm a little dense.

Therapist: Let's look closer at your interpretations. The first one is that she doesn't tell you directly what she wants you to do. Did that interpretation help you or hurt you in terms of getting what you wanted?

Zack: I guess it hurt me. It's true that she doesn't tell me stuff and I'm terrible at mind reading.

Therapist: Can you think of another interpretation that might have helped you get what you wanted?

Zack: I could have thought, "Ask her how she'd like to celebrate." Especially since she brought up the idea of celebrating in the first place.

Therapist: How would asking that have helped you get what you wanted?

Zack: I guess it would have led to a conversation in which we could have talked about the pluses and minuses of different ways to celebrate. You know, going out for a big feast versus going dancing or doing something else.

Therapist: That's good. Let's look at your second interpretation. You said she shouldn't flirt, especially in front of you. Did this interpretation help you or hurt you?

Zack: It really did hurt me because every time it comes up, it never gets resolved. I guess I'm overly sensitive—and maybe jealous. I really don't want to lose her.

Therapist: What do you mean, "lose her"?

Zack: Well, now that she's lost a lot of weight, I see guys giving her the eye. And I don't like it at all.

Therapist: Your other interpretation was that Jessica's weight program was for the birds and that it causes trouble. Did that help you or hurt you get what you wanted?

Zack: It seems to have made things worse. I guess I'm worried that the more she loses weight she'll be more attractive to others and who knows what will happen. [pause] I don't want her to lose interest in me and turn to someone else.

Therapist: Yes. I'll come back to that later. But let's look at your behaviors first. Did ordering the pasta for her help or hurt in getting you what you wanted?

Zack: Looking at it now it's obvious that it hurt me. I just didn't make the connection, and she didn't say anything. It seemed like the right thing to do at the time.

Therapist: How about getting angry and telling her not to flirt anymore. Did that help you or hurt you?

Zack: Well, it hurt. I'm starting to see that things get worse when I'm so sensitive—she would say I was being jealous. And facing her silent treatment is just like being rejected.

Therapist: Like being rejected?

Zack: Nothing good comes out of it. [pause] It just occurred to me that what I most fear happening is what I'm actually causing to happen.

Therapist: How is that?

Zack: When she doesn't tell me and I don't ask her what she wants, she seems to give other people—particularly guys—more attention. Then, when I tell her to stop flirting, she reacts by giving me the cold shoulder. I really feel rejected. Maybe that's why

I'm so sensitive to her losing weight. When she was heavier she was probably less attractive to others. So I'm not keen on her doing this weight management program. Bummer.

Therapist: I hear that. It seems that there is a pattern: As you're less attentive to her needs—that is, you don't ask her what she wants or expects—she may be more responsive to those who give her attention. And so far, to the extent that she loses weight in this diabetes–weight management program, you experience it as a loss to you, and so you view the program as a source of trouble rather than helping her regain and maintain her health. [pause] So what alternative might there be to getting angry and telling her not to flirt?

Zack: Well, maybe it all goes back to being more proactive and finding out what she's thinking and what she wants rather than assuming that if she doesn't say anything that everything is all right and I can just make decisions for us both. If I'm more attentive and ask her, it will probably make it much easier for her to tell me what she needs and wants.

Therapist: I think it might. [turning to Jessica] Jessica, in this situation, your first interpretation was that you didn't want to go out to eat but to go dancing. Is this right?

Jessica: Yes.

Therapist: Did this thought help you or hurt in terms of getting what you want?

Jessica: [pause] Sure seems like it did hurt me because it made me feel like I had to go along with his dinner plans instead of just telling him that I really wanted to go dancing. I guess a better interpretation would have been to be more assertive and say what was on my mind.

Therapist: Sounds reasonable. Your second interpretation was that he was trying to sabotage your success by ordering you a high-carbohydrate pasta dinner. Did this help or hurt you in terms of getting what you wanted?

Jessica: It definitely hurt because I know he really likes that pasta dish, and I also used to like it a lot—before going on this program. I guess I thought I would hurt his feelings if I said that what I really needed was just a small high-protein meal and then some exercise, like dancing.

Therapist: Yes. Your third interpretation was that Zack is always jealous when you talk to other men. Is that accurate?

Jessica: Right on. And it hurt because I've no intention to leave Zack or have an affair or anything, but I get angry when he says that I'm flirting when I'm just being friendly and he starts attacking me as being unfaithful. I really love him, but I can't take that attacking so I just back off and don't give him any attention until things cool down, which is usually the next day or so. I didn't know until just now that he feels rejected by me. That's never been my intention. And it hurts me that he doesn't have more faith in me. Maybe, when he starts to say I'm flirting with others that I could think I don't have to say anything or defend myself, but rather I can use it as a cue to smile and start paying more attention to him.

Therapist: How could this alternative interpretation help you?

Jessica: It could show that I really care for him, and it would probably short-circuit his being defensive and feeling rejected. It'd also help me feel less lonely and misunderstood.

Therapist: That follows. Let's look at one of your behaviors. You said you were angry and hurt and then you stuffed yourself. Did that help or hurt you?

Jessica: It hurt because I went back into my emotional eating pattern. That night I did splurge but fortunately didn't gain back all the weight I lost. But it was a setback.

Therapist: What alternative behavior might you have employed?

Jessica: What I learned in my weight management group is to use those two negative feelings, anger and hurt, as cues to move away from food, take a walk, take some deep breaths, and clear my head. Those things have worked for me already in other situations that haven't involved Zack. Now, I need to do them when I'm with him.

Therapist: Sounds realistic. [pause] Jessica, is there anything that Zack said that you'd like to speak to or comment on?

Jessica: I think I mentioned it already. I didn't know that you felt so rejected when I gave you the silent treatment. And I never got the sense that you really wanted me to succeed in this diabetes–weight management program. When you said that as I succeeded in losing weight you felt even more jealous and rejected, well, it makes more sense to me. [pause] Isn't there some way for me to lose weight and reduce the progression of my diabetes without you feeling so bad?

Therapist: Zack, is there anything that Jessica said that you'd like to speak to or comment on?

Zack: Yes. It's really reassuring to hear that you really love me and want to stay with me. This has been tough talking about this stuff but it has been helpful. [pause] And I'm really in favor of you remaining in the diabetes program and getting healthier.

CASE COMMENTARY

This case highlights the reality of the treatment compliance triangle, that is, that one or more family members can make the difference between compliance and improved health outcomes or noncompliance and reduced health outcomes. In this example, Zack's role—particularly his interpretations and behaviors—in the triangle was critical in understanding Jessica's noncompliance. By using this cognitive–behavioral strategy, the therapist was able to engage both Zack and Jessica in the collaborative process of reviewing a critical situation in a nondefensive and helpful manner.

CONCLUDING COMMENT

Compliance remains a formidable challenge for all health care providers, including health psychologists and psychotherapists. Because family dynamics can impact a client's compliance with a treatment regimen for both medical conditions and lifestyle change, a case was made for use of family-oriented compliance counseling. After briefly noting a psychoeducational approach to family-oriented compliance counseling, a cognitive–behavioral strategy to accomplish similar outcomes was described and illustrated with a session transcription. I provide a final caveat: Noncompliance is a complex and multifaceted phenomenon, and because patients are different, it should not be surprising that some patients respond well to certain compliance enhancement strategies (noted in Table 4.1) and not to others. The point is that more than one strategy may be indicated and that clinicians should be familiar with all of these strategies.

5

SYMPTOM REDUCTION

Americans experience a variety of bothersome medical symptoms, often on a regular, ongoing basis. Such symptoms include fatigue, allergies, lower back pain, joint pain and stiffness, acid indigestion, headaches, and insomnia. These symptoms may or may not be related to chronic diseases, but they are commonplace. For instance, 86% of adults queried reported experiencing at least one bothersome symptom every 4 to 6 days (Verbrugge & Ascione, 1987). More specifically, 80% of adults have reported being troubled by lower back pain over the course of their lifetime, and 25% said they had experienced such back pain in the recent past (Loney & Stratford, 1999). The climbing rates of claims for workers' compensation and permanent disability suggest that Americans are also increasingly disabled by their symptoms. Although there was no increase in injuries and back disease, the number of disability claims for lower back pain increased at 14 times the growth of the population between the years 1963 and 1994 (Robertson, 1995). For most of the sufferers, no serious medical condition was identified to explain these symptoms.

It is ironic that despite having access to reputedly the best medical care in the world, Americans have found standard medical treatments to be relatively ineffective in providing relief for such symptoms. There are a number of possible reasons for this, not the least of which is that the expertise of conventional Western medicine lies in the treatment of physical disease rather than in the amelioration of illness. *Illness* is defined as the subjective experience of a disease state, and symptoms reflect the experience of illness (Sperry, 2006b). Another way of saying this is that although symptoms can be produced by disease states, they are also produced by an individual's expectations, beliefs, moods, and life experiences as well as sociocultural context and family dynamics.

Fortunately, some psychotherapeutic interventions can effectively reduce or even eliminate the symptomatic distress associated with chronic illnesses and conditions. This chapter begins by describing key psychological and intrapsychic dynamics as well as relational and family dynamics that can engender medical symptoms. Then it describes a focused cognitive–behavioral therapy (CBT) intervention strategy that can effectively control and even eliminate such symptoms. Case material illustrates this intervention.

PSYCHOLOGICAL AND INTRAPSYCHIC DYNAMICS

Several factors or forces account for the increasing numbers of Americans who experience significant symptomatic distress when there is apparently no structural or medical explanation for their joint pain, fatigue, allergic reactions, and headaches. These forces are sociocultural, economic, medical, psychological or intrapsychic, and interpersonal and family factors. The first three forces are beyond the scope of this chapter and will not be discussed. This section briefly discusses three psychological factors, and the subsequent sections describe interpersonal and family dynamics forces. The three psychological forces are symptom expectation, symptom amplification, and symptom attribution. As noted in the discussion that follows, each is intimately related to the other two.

Symptom Expectation

An *expectation* is an anticipatory belief about something. In providing extensive coverage to medical conditions, accidents, and birth defects, the mass media has increased the average American's medical knowledge considerably such that even individuals with no personal experience of a motor vehicle accident, for example, are aware of the causes and severity of structural damage and symptoms and the disability and compensation associated with so-called "whiplash" injury. With this knowledge comes increased expectation manifested as vigilance about symptoms, prompting some individuals to interpret normal bodily sensations as abnormal and to react to such sensations with affect and cognitions that intensify and amplify the symptoms.

Symptom Amplification

Symptom amplification involves focusing attention on a symptom and reacting with intense alarm and worry, and individuals who readily amplify symptoms are called *symptom amplifiers*. Symptom amplification typically results in some degree of dysfunction as well as a reluctance to relinquish the symptoms. Individuals may amplify symptoms for sociocultural, economic, medical, intrapersonal, or interpersonal reasons. The opposite reaction is *symptom minimization*. This response is noted in individuals who delay reporting serious symptoms to their physicians, who deny illness, or who fail to adhere to a medical regimen. Attention to a symptom amplifies it, whereas distraction minimizes it (Barsky & Borus, 1999).

Symptom Attribution

Symptom attribution refers to the process of attaching or linking causality between a symptom and an accident or medical conditions. For example, as an accident victim becomes hypervigilant for symptoms, symptom attribution is a natural result given the commonly held expectation for chronic and more bothersome symptoms. Thus, any vague sensations following even a fender bender—such as tightening, heat, or tingling in the neck or shoulders—may be attributed to the accident itself in the form of a whiplash injury. In other words, the individual links the symptoms to whiplash and concludes that these sensations are evidence of a serious injury. Furthermore, when symptoms are attributed to a serious disease rather than a more benign cause, such as overwork, lack of sleep or exercise, or other minor stressors, the expectation is that serious conditions exist that can be life threatening, and thus symptoms tend to be amplified.

RELATIONAL AND FAMILY DYNAMICS

Relational and family dynamics can strongly influence a patient's perception and expression of medical symptoms. With regard to relational or interpersonal dynamics, it has been noted that talking about one's symptoms with another person can result in the symptom becoming either better or worse for both parties, depending on the communication process itself. Verbal cues can effectively communicate demands for how others should feel about and respond to the symptom bearer. Furthermore, symptoms become ways of communicating something to another person with body language rather than with words. Nonverbal communication cues such as grimacing, limping, or rubbing a body part can effectively communicate a silent demand for assistance, emotional support, sympathy, or even guilt. For example, a partner may be reluctant to ask his significant other for a back rub, but he has learned that a back rub and undivided attention and sympathy can be obtained from the significant other simply by grimacing and saying that his spinal stenosis is acting up again. In short, symptom expression can be a subtle or not so subtle way of asking for or demanding help or special considerations in interpersonal relationships.

Family dynamics play a central role in the so-called "psychosomatic family" (Minuchin, Rosman, & Baker, 1978), in which an individual family member, usually an adolescent, has a diagnosed medical condition, often diabetes. These individuals have inadvertently learned that when their medical condition flares up and requires hospitalization, they can get their parents who were about to separate or divorce to stop fighting and come together to care for them. In short, the individual's medical symptoms serve as the nonverbal communication that holds the family together when previous attempts by the child to influence other family members through verbal communication have failed (Minuchin et al., 1978).

A COGNITIVE–BEHAVIORAL THERAPY INTERVENTION STRATEGY FOR SYMPTOM REDUCTION

Even though standard medical treatment offers little or no relief to individuals with bothersome symptoms for which there is no structural basis or medical explanation, emerging research suggests that many, if not most, individuals can be helped with specialized interventions (Barsky & Ahern, 2004; Clark et al., 1998; Nakao et al., 2001). A six-step strategy provides a useful protocol for physicians and behavioral health professionals to systematically address such symptoms. The first five steps can be managed and monitored by a physician, and the sixth typically involves a referral to a therapist or psychological consultant. The steps are as follows:

1. Rule out the presence of a diagnosable medical disease;
2. identify symptoms that could reflect the presence of a psychiatric disorder;
3. build a collaborative alliance with the patient;
4. set the goal of treatment as the identification and alleviation of factors that amplify and perpetuate symptoms; and
5. provide limited assurance. (Barsky & Ahern, 2004; Barsky & Borus, 1999)

Obviously, these five steps are not CBT strategies or interventions per se, but if these strategies are insufficient to reduce symptomatology, Step 6 is prescribed. It involves cognitive behaviorally oriented interventions targeting medical symptom reduction (Barsky & Borus, 1999). These focused CBT strategies help individuals cope with symptoms by reexamining their health beliefs and expectations as well as exploring the impact of assuming the sick role and stressors on their symptoms. Research has found these CBT strategies to be very effective in reducing symptomatic distress (Barsky & Ahern, 2004; Clark et al., 1998; Nakao et al., 2001). These focused strategies can provide alternative explanations for symptoms, restructure faulty beliefs about disease processes, modify treatment expectations, and offer effective coping techniques like distraction and focused attention (Barsky & Borus, 1999). Unlike medical and technological interventions such as spinal manipulation and transcutaneous electrical nerve stimulation units (often called "TENS units"), which foster a passive posture for the symptomatic individual, cognitive–behavioral strategies stimulate individuals to assume an active role in the treatment process.

CASE STUDY

Sandy is a 53-year-old married woman with a 7-month history of lower back pain. She is referred for medical symptom reduction treatment to a clinical psychologist affiliated with her physician's clinic. Sandy lives with her husband and describes her marriage as "very good before all this back pain stuff started." Until recently, she had been in good health and denies any previous psychological treatment or treatment for alcohol or other drug use. She attributes the onset of her back pain to reaching up for a box on a closet shelf. She described feeling a "pulling" in her lower back, which she thought nothing about until 2 or 3 days later when "the pain was so bad I couldn't get out of bed." Sandy was subsequently treated with a conservative medical regimen: analgesics, heat, and bed rest for about 2 months. Because it "didn't do much," she asked for and began a course of physical therapy on which she remained until the time of the health counseling consultation. She'd been an accountant for about 21 years. After using up her accumulated sick leave, her supervisor began pressuring her to return to her job or resign and seek disability.

During the course of a comprehensive assessment, the psychologist learned that Sandy was a symptom amplifier and had attributed her symptoms to a serious back condition that she expected would eventually require surgery "since none of these other treatments are working." The psychologist also learned that Sandy's sister was getting remarried and that when Sandy was reaching for the present that she was going to send to the bridal shower— it was on the top shelf in the closet—she was "struck by this God-awful pain in the back." Needless to say, Sandy has a conflictual relationship with her younger sister, whom she considers a "tramp and a screw-up." She said she had "absolutely no intention of giving tacit approval to my sister's behavior by going to the shower or wedding." Still, she believed that she would be roundly criticized by other relatives if she didn't at least send a present and offer an excuse for not going. Presumably, being bedridden with back pain would be an acceptable excuse. During the initial evaluation, Sandy saw no connection between her back pain, her conflicted feelings about her sister, and the excuse that being bedridden offered.

A contract was made to meet for six treatment sessions focusing on symptom reduction. The psychologist's plan for the first session was to briefly assess 13 key clinical markers of her illness profile (cf. Sperry, 2006b) and then to begin the symptom reduction process. Basic to this process was a CBT-based strategy for eliminating behaviors and thoughts that reinforced her pain symptoms. The transcription picks up about 25 minutes into the first 50-minute session.

Sandy: My husband has been pretty unhappy lately. It's been a big adjustment for him over these past several months. When I try to talk about it, he just shrugs it off and say things are okay, but I know they're not. He's been trying to help out my daughter with some of the household chores I used to do. Lately, he's been preparing dinner. He really isn't much of a cook and doesn't like having to do it. I really don't want him to resent me for it.

Therapist: Can we talk more about it and see what we can come up with?

Sandy: Yes, I'd like that.

Therapist: There's a helpful way I've found of analyzing situations and the behaviors and beliefs that make us feel better or worse. It's the ABC approach. "A" stands for "antecedent," or the circumstances that trigger certain "beliefs and behaviors," which are the "Bs." For example, when an individual's back is really achy and stiff (A), she might think that cooking dinner was impossible because it would only make her pain worse (belief), and so she lies down on the couch and complains to her husband how bad she feels (behavior). "C" stands for "consequences," which are the results of her Bs. In this example, her husband offers to do the laundry without any help from her. So instead of doing something that might distract her from that achy pain and stiffness, she lies down on the couch, feeling awful and complaining. Now compare that with an alternative situation with the same woman. She feels her back getting stiff and achy (A). She asks her husband to help her with the laundry and talks about pleasant things (B; behavior), because she knows (B; belief) that focusing on her pain and complaining about it only makes it worse. Her mood improves and her back pain is less noticeable because she focused on cooking and pleasant conversation (C). As a result, she feels more satisfied and more in control. On top of that, the laundry gets done and she and her husband both feel a little better about their relationship. So I propose that we apply the ABC method to the situation you brought up about your husband now doing dinner preparation on weekdays. Are you willing to give the method a try?

Sandy:	I am.
Therapist:	Fine. Would you describe the situation around dinnertime when you're alone with your husband? In other words, what is the "A" or antecedent?
Sandy:	Things have gotten worse since my daughter's work hours were switched from first to second shift a week ago. Now, she'll only be able to cook on weekends, so he's trying to cover the weekday meals by himself. It's a stressor for him. I'm not very mobile with my back, so going out to a restaurant isn't very feasible—nor can we really afford going out or even ordering take-out for most meals all the time. Anyway, the "A" is probably that it's a half hour before dinnertime and my back is really achy and stiff, and I've got no desire to cook or do anything else.
Therapist:	So you're in pain and you don't feel up to doing anything, especially preparing a meal. Let's look at the first "B," your beliefs or interpretations about the situation. What were you thinking about this situation?
Sandy:	I was thinking that if I exerted myself in any way, my pain would only get worse.
Therapist:	That makes sense. What other thoughts might you have had?
Sandy:	That I hate being in these circumstances. My life is totally controlled by this back pain. It's messing up my relations with my daughter and husband, and they could get fed up and abandon me. [pause] It's just not fair.
Therapist:	Let's look now at the other "B," your behaviors. What did you do in the situation?
Sandy:	Well, I turned on the heating pad on and laid down on the living room sofa. I turned off the TV, because I couldn't stand the noisy chatter. I started feeling really awful and depressed. Then I started crying, and my husband, who had just come home from work, asked what was wrong. I told him: "Guess—it's my back again." I told him how bad I felt and that there was so much work to do around the house and nobody to do it. He asked if he should prepare a tray of the kind of food I like, and he'd bring it to me when I calmed down.
Therapist:	Then what happened, what was the outcome, called the actual "C" or consequences?
Sandy:	He brought me the tray, and I ate. Actually, I just picked at the food. He said he had eaten something by himself in the kitchen. Then he went to his workshop to work on his hobbies, leaving me in pain and alone on the sofa. Not only was my back worse, but I felt bad that my husband ate by himself and then abandoned me by going to his workshop.

Therapist:	What would you have liked to have happened, that is, your desired "C," consequence or outcome?
Sandy:	Well, I would have liked to have had no pain and to have enjoyed a pleasant meal and evening with my husband.
Therapist:	Did you get what you wanted?
Sandy:	[*long pause*] Not by a long shot.

The psychologist has completed a situational analysis including interpretations, behaviors, and outcomes and will now proceed to therapeutically process them.

Therapist:	Okay. Let's look back at your beliefs and behaviors to see if they were helpful or hurtful in getting what you wanted. Did your thoughts, "My life is totally controlled by this back pain" and "It's just not fair," help or hurt you in getting your desired consequence?
Sandy:	It didn't help.
Therapist:	Makes sense. If you believe that you're totally controlled by your pain, you won't be motivated to try to make efforts to do things that might help, such as distract yourself from the pain. What about your thoughts, "It's messing up my relations with my daughter and husband, and they could get fed up and abandon me" and "It's just not fair"? Do those thoughts help or hurt?
Sandy:	They obviously didn't help. They just made me feel more pain and more out of control and less cared for.
Therapist:	Good. How about your behaviors? Did lying on the couch and crying help or hurt you?
Sandy:	I would have thought it would have helped, but it didn't, because I ended up feeling bad. No, it didn't help.
Therapist:	What about telling your husband that there was so much work to do around the house and nobody to do it? Did that help or hurt?
Sandy:	It hurt. He probably offered to make me some food because he felt guilty. But then he ate by himself and left me alone and sought refuge with his hobbies instead of spending time with me.
Therapist:	Sure. Now let's go back over this situation to see if you could have thought or done anything differently to get what you wanted. I'm not trying to tell you what you should want, and I'm not suggesting that you must do what others want you to do. The assumption is that certain beliefs and behaviors make us feel either better or worse, and we just have to focus on picking

the ones that make us feel better. So, what beliefs or thoughts would be more likely to get you the consequence or outcome you wanted?

Sandy: I'm not sure. [*pause*]

Therapist: How about, "Focusing on something negative like my pain, and then complaining about it, only makes the situation worse, so I should focus on something positive"?

Sandy: Yes, I really think it would help. That's what my doctor says: "Distract yourself by attending to something that you like and the pain won't seem as intense." But it's hard to think those things. I probably should distract myself like that, but I don't. I keep thinking how unfair having this chronic pain is.

The psychologist notes Sandy's comment about unfairness but chooses not respond to it at this time. It is probably a core schema for Sandy, and the psychologist will come back to it at a more opportune time in a subsequent session.

Therapist: I know it's hard for you, and that's why you've come for counseling. But there is good news. If you regularly practice the strategy that we're talking about now, eventually you'll come to think and do things that will help you get what you want in those situations. Your thoughts are like reflexes, and you automatically think them every time you get in a situation where you're experiencing pain. If you keep practicing distracting thoughts, in time they will become helpful automatic thoughts and replace the hurtful thoughts. [*pause*] So, now let's look at your behaviors. What behaviors might have been more helpful in getting what you wanted?

Sandy: I could have asked my husband to help me with making a light supper. I could have suggested some easy-to-prepare food items and maybe done something that wasn't too straining like pour some ice tea. We both like ice tea during the summer.

Therapist: Great. What might you have done instead of complaining about your pain?

Sandy: I could have started a conversation about something we both enjoy talking about, or I could have asked him about the most interesting thing that happened to him while he was at work.

Therapist: So how would helping your husband make a light dinner and starting a pleasant conversation have helped you get what you want?

Sandy: It's becoming clearer to me now that positive distractions help focus me on something besides my pain, so I don't feel the pain as much, if at all. And I know my husband really enjoys spending time with me talking about pleasant things. [*pause*] And I'm seeing how uncomfortable he is when I let him know about my pain. He immediately makes some excuse, and leaves as soon as he can.

Therapist: What we've been discussing is a strategy for decreasing your pain while increasing your control and satisfaction as well as improving your relationship with your family. When someone is sick for a while, other family members take over some or many of that individual's roles and responsibilities. Take the family responsibility we've just discussed—preparing meals. You've already said that you relinquished cooking responsibilities to your husband because of your pain condition but are now motivated to take them back. The strategy involves letting your family know your plan to gradually resume cooking and other family functions that are important to you. Then, at a slow and steady pace, regain control of that activity. For example, you might begin by preparing one meal a week to start, a simple dinner, and then asking a family member to do the clean-up afterward. Then, as you start noticing that your pain doesn't get worse and your energy increases, you'll be proving to yourself that preparing meals is not harming your health. The positive consequence will be that you will take back more responsibilities, which will result in greater control and satisfaction and better family relations. How does that sound to you?

Sandy: Great! It makes a lot of sense that I'll only really get beyond this pain and feel better and family relations will improve when I take back—slowly take back I guess—[*laughs*] control over roles and responsibilities that are important to me. [*pause*] Yes, I need to do it. I can do it.

CASE COMMENTARY

By the sixth session, Sandy experienced significant symptom reduction and was sufficiently pain free to gradually return to normal activities. She subsequently continued in individual therapy for 15 additional sessions that focused on issues with her sister that appeared to have precipitated the pain syndrome. The therapeutic work addressed her core schemas of unfairness, self-righteousness, and criticalness using both schema-focused and narrative therapy interventions. The successfulness of this initial symptom-reduction intervention and the subsequent psychotherapy sessions were, in part, due to the treatment occurring in the primary care clinic. Had she been referred to a therapist practicing outside the clinic, it is likely that Sandy, like many other individuals who identify themselves as medical patients rather than as psychotherapy clients, would not have followed up with the referral.

CONCLUDING NOTE

This case illustrates how a CBT strategy can be used in working with mind–body issues, particularly in medical symptom reduction when family dynamics are involved. Because 30% or more of adults experience pain and other symptoms that do not appear to have a structural basis and thus tend to be relatively nonresponsive to conventional medical treatment, counselors and other mental health professions can provide significant symptom reduction using focused conceptualizations and interventions such as those described in this chapter.

6

SPIRITUALITY AND LIFE MEANING

Life meaning issues routinely surface during the course of individual therapy for patients attempting to cope with a chronic medical condition (Griffith & Griffith, 2001). Life meaning concerns are commonly expressed with questions such as "Why did this happen to me?" "Is there a reason for living now that I'm becoming progressively disabled?" "Why all this pain and suffering?" "Where is God when I need him?" In fact, there is a predictive pattern of life meaning issues that clients face in coming to terms with such an illness. Being aware of this pattern can greatly aid psychologists and psychotherapists working with such patients, just as it is important to know about the patient's spirituality and religious coping strategies. Furthermore, having an effective strategy for processing such issues can increase both clinical outcomes and client satisfaction. This chapter begins by distinguishing religion and spirituality and describing the predictable pattern of spiritual issues that arise in working with individuals who are experiencing chronic illness. A phase model of such issues is presented. Then, a focused cognitive–behavioral therapy (CBT) intervention strategy that has much promise for therapeutically processing such issues is introduced. Finally, this therapeutic intervention is illustrated with a case study and session transcription.

RELIGION AND SPIRITUALITY

It is common for the terms *spirituality* and *religion* to be distinguished. Spirituality involves one's deepest desire or longing and the way one responds to it (Rolheiser, 1999). This longing is both unsatisfiable and hardwired in the core of our being. As such, everybody, including the cognitively impaired, experience it, albeit to varying degrees of intensity. Whereas *religion* involves searching for significance through the sacred, *spirituality* is the way people "think, feel, act or interrelate in their efforts to find, conserve, and if necessary, transform the sacred in their lives" (Pargament, 1999, p. 12). Spirituality is not something on the fringes of life, nor is it an option that only a few pursue or want to process in psychiatric treatment. Rather, everyone has a spirituality that is reflected in everyday thoughts, feelings, and actions (Sperry, 2001). In this chapter, religion is mostly described in terms of "religious beliefs," whereas spirituality is mostly described in terms of "spiritual practices" that include activities such as prayer, meditation, fasting, and so on. Spirituality is important to patients with chronic medical conditions because it provides perspective that allows them to find meaning and hope in their inevitable suffering.

LIFE MEANING ISSUES AND THE PHASES OF CHRONIC ILLNESS

For many, the experience of chronic illness engenders a host of life meaning issues and crises, almost always involving a reconsideration of their core values and religious beliefs. The types of crises and issues and the manner in which they are experienced is dependent largely on religious upbringing and other cultural factors, and their urgency tends to be driven by the extent to which the disease is life threatening or disability provoking (Sperry, 2006b). Accordingly, it is essential to understand patients' religious beliefs. Furthermore, research indicates that the nature and expression of life meaning issues follows a predictable pattern, a pattern that reflects the phase of the patient's chronic illness. On the basis of this research, Fennell (2003) described four phases reflecting the experience of chronic illness. These phases range from denial to integration, with specific meaning issues and crises predictably characteristic of each phase. These specific life meaning issues are summarized here.

Phase 1

Fear of God's punishment and abandonment are central spiritual characteristics of Phase 1. The urgency and lack of control that chronically ill individuals experience over their physical and psychological well-being tend to manifest themselves in somewhat primitive religious and spiritual beliefs.

To the extent to which individuals believe they are bad for being ill and cannot change their situation or fix themselves, they may believe that God has abandoned them; that there is no God at all; or that God is a punishing angry and avenging being who levies bad fortune—particularly under the guise of illness—as a sign of deserved punishment. On the other hand, those who are atheists may experience deep existential dread and despair and conclude that they have no reason to continue living. The end result for both believers and nonbelievers is deep grief (Fennell, 2003).

Phase 2

Although fear of God's punishment and abandonment characterize Phase 1, in Phase 2 those who are believers may no longer believe that God is punishing them but rather that he has turned his attention away from them. It is not surprising that the experience of chronic illness draws many back to spiritual practices, often to religious affiliations that have highly structured beliefs and hierarchical practices. Often, this behavior reflects the conviction that their former state of health will be returned if only they perform prayers and practice rituals sincerely and over a long enough period of time. Their assumption is that God will—or must—reward their efforts. On the other hand, other individuals will reject the god of their past and seek more satisfying spiritual meaning and connections with like-minded individuals and settings who treat them empathically and understand their suffering (Fennell, 2003).

Phase 3

Of all the phases, Phase 3 involves the most serious life meaning undertaking as people with chronic illness attempt to develop a new self and identity. In this phase, chronically ill individuals search for an explanation for their illness, even though that explanation may be that it occurred randomly and without any divine or other intention. During this time, these individuals seek a genuine sense of purpose for their lives. It is a purpose that they can become committed to as they undertake the task of forging a new self, a self that reflects their experience of chronicity without denial, anger, pleas, demands, or regrets. It is not surprising that when they realize that the tenets of their prior religious beliefs seem inauthentic or inadequate to their new conception of self, they seek out new spiritual resources and affiliations (Fennell, 2003).

Phase 4

In this phase, individuals move beyond the search for a sense of meaning of Phase 3 to a search to find meaning in all their relationships and all their daily activities. That is, in this phase, it is not the innate value of an activity that concerns chronically ill individuals but rather the activity's overall place and meaning in their existence. Their heightened awareness makes them demand more from everything they do. Even though they may have to live with pain and limitations, they now believe that whatever they do will be meaningful (Fennell, 2003).

The clinician's task is to understand patients' life meaning concerns and underlying religious beliefs and to help them reframe such concerns so that they can cope and to come to terms with their medical condition. To accomplish this, clinicians must have some degree of understanding of a number of religious beliefs, many of which may be different from their own. An excellent resource in gaining this understanding is *The Handbook of Psychotherapy and Religious Diversity* (Richards & Bergin, 1999). Although not specifically focused on chronic medical conditions, this book reviews the tenets of the world's major religions in a distinctly clinical context. *Spirituality-Oriented Psychotherapy* (Sperry & Shafranske, 2006) addresses different approaches and strategies, including CBT, for dealing with spirituality and religious issues.

RELIGIOUS COPING STRATEGIES

Awareness of the patient's religious beliefs and spirituality allows the clinician to accommodate such beliefs in the case conceptualization, particularly the patient's struggle to find meaning and establish balance in their personal lives and in the inevitable changes that occur in their relationships with others (Lomax, Karff, & McKenny, 2002). More specifically, religious beliefs and spirituality can be important factors contributing to a patient's ability to cope with the various challenges associated with experiencing chronic illness. Research on religious coping and its clinical application appears to offer considerable value to those working with chronic medical patients.

An early study of religious coping strategies in chronic medical conditions used the three-item Religious Coping Index, which includes an open-ended item on coping as well as specifically asking the degree to which one uses religion or spirituality as a means to cope (Koenig, Larson, & Larson, 2001). When administered to hospitalized military veterans and patients in an academic hospital, 20% of veterans and 42% of the academic hospital patients spontaneously reported that religious beliefs and practices were "most important" to enable coping. Seventy percent of veterans and 90% of the academic hospital patients endorsed "moderate" use of religion to help cope in general, and 55% and 75%, respectively, indicated religion was used more than a "large extent" to cope with illness. In both self-rated and observer-rated depression scores in the veteran population, religious coping was inversely correlated with depressive symptoms. More interesting, the extent of the use of religion to cope predicted lower depressive scores 6 months later in a follow-up study of 201 readmitted patients.

The degree to which religious coping strategies are effective or harmful for individuals has been studied extensively by Pargament and colleagues (Pargament & Brant, 1998; Pargament, Koenig, & Perez, 2000; Pargament, Koenig, Tarakeswar, & Hahn, 2001, 2004). In research examining the relationship between different religious coping strategies and psychological adjustment to a variety of health stressors and trauma, some strategies were found to be healthy whereas others appeared to be harmful. Helpful or positive coping strategies included perceptions of spiritual support and guidance, congregational support, and attributions of negative life events to the will of God or to a loving god. Negative coping strategies such as spiritual discontent, either with a community or with God, and perceiving negative life events as God's punishment were related to poorer outcomes (Pargament & Brant, 1998).

To effectively measure religious coping strategies, Pargament and colleagues developed the Religious/Spiritual Coping Inventory (RCOPE), a comprehensive self-report tool (Pargament et al., 2000). The RCOPE incorporates a variety of subscales representing various purposes of religion and has been found to correlate well with measures of physical, emotional, and spiritual health in samples of both relatively young healthy college students as well as a sample of elderly hospitalized patients. Factor analysis indicates that subscales distinguish both positive as well as negative religious coping strategies. A longitudinal study using the RCOPE and its short version, the Brief RCOPE, was used to explore religious coping and changes in medical, psychological, and spiritual health in a sample of medically ill hospitalized patients over a 2-year period. Negative religious coping strategies in the form of spiritual discontent and demonic reappraisal predicted greater mortality in these patients, independent of variables related to demographics, physical and mental health, and church attendance (Pargament et al., 2001). In a related study, positive religious coping strategies predicted increases in stress-related growth, spiritual outcomes, and cognitive functioning at follow-up, whereas negative coping methods predicted declines in spiritual outcomes and quality of life as well as increased depressed mood and decreased independence in daily activities (Pargament et al., 2004). It is interesting to note that some of the negative religious coping methods were related to improvements in health measures as well as declines in other measures, suggesting that the relationships between spiritual coping and health care outcomes are more complicated than initially envisioned. Accordingly, although some forms of religious coping may be protective and healthy, other forms of religious coping may contribute to poor spiritual and health outcomes (Pargament et al., 2001).

Furthermore, religious beliefs and spirituality can sometimes be a source of suffering and distress. For example, in a study of African American women who had experienced an abusive relationship, many described being disappointed by the advice of clergy who recommended that they remain in the relationship or try harder to be a "good wife" (Potter, 2007).

CASE EXAMPLE

Maria is a 49-year-old woman from Cuba who has been married to Pedro for 31 years. They have four grown children who live in the community. Maria was diagnosed with a progressive form of multiple sclerosis (MS) about 5 years ago. For the past 3 years, she has needed the assistance of a walker to get around, especially outdoors. Bladder control has been a problem for her on a few occasions. She is most embarrassed by this and has subsequently become more reluctant to venture out in public. She was referred to Denise Romero, a psychotherapist, by her neurologist because of increasing marital conflict in a relationship that otherwise appeared to be supportive and satisfying and because of feelings of abandonment by God. After her initial evaluation, Romero indicated that she would like to meet for a couple of sessions with both Maria and her husband. Maria and Pedro both agreed to this plan.

During their second conjoint session, Maria described a difficult situation that had "really unglued" her. The therapist completed a biopsychosocial assessment as described in chapter 2, this volume, to process the situation. In response to Step 1, she learned that Maria and Pedro had gone to services at their Presbyterian church on Sunday, even though Maria reported feeling sad and tired. Pedro had convinced her that getting out would boost her spirits, and he reminded her that their minister's sermon would surely cheer her up as it had on several previous occasions. They went. Maria was, in fact, very inspired by their minister's sermon and could not wait to speak with him afterward. Unfortunately, a long line of parishioners quickly formed to speak with him also, and Maria found herself standing with her walker in the parking lot separated from the minister and others waiting to talk with the minister by an inclined driveway that she could not easily surmount. So she just stood there, angry, despondent, and "unglued." The following interpretations or thoughts were elicited:

> The minister doesn't care about me. He's too wrapped up talking with healthy, well-bodied people.
>
> God seems to be absent when I need him the most. It's like he abandoned me.
>
> Pedro is a jerk. He should have gotten the minister to come over to greet me.

The following behaviors and feelings were elicited:

> I just stood on the side in my walker and watched others gather in the welcoming line for the minister.

> I didn't say anything to Pedro about my desire to talk to our minister. I got increasingly angry and started to feel neglected and abandoned.

Her desired outcome was to tell the minister how much his sermon had meant to her and to ask him to visit her to discuss pressing spiritual concerns. Her actual outcome was "I was stood up. Neither God nor the minister—nor even my husband—responded to me." The session transcription picks up at this point.

Therapist: Did you get what you wanted?

Maria: Not at all.

Therapist: Let's look back at your beliefs and behaviors to see if they were helpful or hurtful in getting what you wanted. Did your thought, "The minister doesn't care about me. He's too wrapped up talking with healthy, well-bodied people," help or hurt you in getting what you wanted?

Maria: It hurt. It sure didn't help me.

Therapist: That makes sense. If you believe that he doesn't care and is only interested in healthy people, you might not be very motivated to make the effort to make contact with him. What kind of thought or interpretation of the situation could have helped you get what you wanted?

Maria: Maybe thinking, "Other people also thought his sermon was so good and helpful that they wanted to talk to him too. It doesn't have anything to do with whether they're healthy or sick. After all, I hear he regularly does pastoral visits to those who are in the hospital or housebound all the time."

Therapist: How would that thought have been helpful to you?

Maria: Because it wasn't so negative and judgmental, and I would have been more inclined to make a determined effort to make sure that he would talk to me even if I had to call and make an appointment for him to visit me at home.

Therapist: That follows. Wonderful. What about the thought, "God seems to be absent when I need him the most. It's like he abandoned me"? Did it help or hurt?

Maria: Well, it hurt, and it made me feel more disconnected and unloved. It's very embarrassing to say that I've had such negative thoughts about God. I don't know where it came from. I've really felt pretty connected to him in the past

Therapist: Thoughts about being abandoned by God are not at all uncommon for individuals dealing with a debilitating illness like MS. And yes, it can be embarrassing and unexpected. Many others with chronic illness report experiencing that God seems to have abandoned them and no longer seems care about them anymore. This is not an uncommon experience in the beginning of their journey to make sense of their chronic illness and adjust to it. [*pause*] I seem to recall that during the first session when I asked you some questions about spirituality and your relationship to God that you had a rather positive image of God as you were growing up. [*Maria nods affirmatively*] Over the years of clinical practice, I've noticed—and published research seems to bear this out—that as individuals come to a more complete acceptance of their illness, their thoughts and images of God seem to shift to becoming more positive and helpful. It seems like you're beginning to come to terms with the reality—as difficult as it is to face—that your MS is not going away and that it will likely worsen. As your acceptance increases, it's likely that believing you've been abandoned by God will begin to fade. We can keep working on that in future sessions.

Maria: That helps me make sense of this. I really find that thought about God just too distressing. Thanks.

Therapist: You're welcome. [*pause*] What about the thought, "Pedro is a jerk. He should have gotten the minister to come over to greet me"? Did that help or hurt?

Maria: It hurt. It's not really like me to be so negative and such a nag to Pedro. [*Pedro nods affirmatively*] In some ways, when things seem to be going so wrong and I'm feeling so bad and so out of control—literally with loss of bladder control—I just want to lash out, and Pedro's the closest person around most of the time. So, he gets my wrath. [*turning to Pedro*] I'm really sorry, Pedro. I guess I wouldn't be surprised if you said you couldn't take it anymore and wanted out.

Pedro: Don't say that. I'm in this for the long haul [*laughs*]. At least for now.

Maria: I know you love me.

Therapist: Okay. Can we examine the behaviors you listed earlier, Maria?

Maria: Sure.

Therapist: Did standing on the side in your walker watching others in the welcoming line for the minister help or hurt you?

Maria: It didn't help. It actually made me feel even more helpless. I guess I should have done something.

Therapist: What else might you have done that could have helped get you what you wanted?

Maria: I could have edged myself and my walker as close as I could and called out to him, respectfully, of course, to come over to visit with me when the line was down.

Therapist: How would that have helped?

Maria: Calling out to him would have let him know that I was around and wanted to speak with him. He's a pretty conscientious guy. I'm sure he would have made the effort to make contact if he knew that I really needed to talk to him. In some ways I suppose he represents God to me. And I guess it's easy to confuse my thoughts and feelings of not being recognized and having my needs met as abandonment by both minister and God. Wow. Does that make any sense?

Therapist: Yes, it does. That's quite insightful. Thoughts and feelings about God and ministers can and do "transfer." [*Maria nods; pause*] What about not saying anything to Pedro about your desire to talk to the minister? Did this behavior help or hurt in terms of getting the outcome you wanted?

Maria: It didn't help at all. I probably should have just told Pedro what I wanted and had him go over and make sure the minister talked to me before he left. Pedro would have done it. After all, he ran over and got in the welcoming line anyway.

Therapist: Wonderful. What about getting increasingly angry and feeling neglected. Did that help or hurt?

Maria: It hurt. There seems to be some connection between my thoughts and what I feel and what I do. When I think that God and the minister are ignoring and not paying attention, I feel angry and neglected, which makes me even more powerless and feeling that my life and this illness are worse.

Therapist: Yes. There sure seems to be a connection between your thoughts and your behaviors and your feelings. It seems like when your thoughts are negative and disempowering, your behaviors and your feelings seem to have you more alone and powerless. And what's more, they hurt you in that you don't get what you want. On the other hand, when your thoughts are more positive and proactive, the alternate behaviors you came up with seem to have you much more proactive and connected to others, including God. Such thoughts and behaviors are more likely to help you get what you want.

The session continues with an analysis of Pedro's experience of the situation involving the minister. More discussion on illness acceptance ensues in this and in subsequent sessions.

CASE COMMENTARY

As with Maria, it is not uncommon for the spiritual issues of clients experiencing chronic illness to involve ministers, chaplains, or spiritual practices. This case points up how Maria's spiritual concerns about being abandoned by God are consistent with the first phase of the experience of chronic illness (Fennell, 2003). Maria was reasonably psychologically minded and exhibited some capacity for insight in this session. The focus of this session was to clarify her issues and increase her coping capacity, both religious and relational.

Furthermore, because Maria reported a reasonably healthy image of God as well as positive experiences with ministry personnel and those involved with her religious upbringing, it was sufficient to process her presenting spiritual concern using this approach in a brief and focused manner. This focus was illustrated in this session as well as in two subsequent sessions that more directly focused on assisting her in increasing her acceptance of her MS. Subsequent sessions could then focus on issues related to subsequent phases. On the other hand, had there been an early history of abuse or neglect involving religious training or personnel or both, which are likely to be reflected by a negative image of God, much more intensive therapy might have been indicated.

CONCLUDING NOTE

Increasingly, clinicians are expected to help their clients deal with life meaning issues and spirituality in the course of treatment. Because life meaning issues are prominent for individuals experiencing chronic medical illness, it is likely that psychologists and psychotherapists would do well to become familiar with the kinds and patterns of meaning issues with which clients are likely to present. In this regard, an understanding of the phase model briefly described in this chapter can be invaluable. Although there are various ways of processing spiritual and meaning issues, the modified cognitive–behavioral analysis model described and illustrated here is particularly useful and valuable in clarifying such issues and increasing coping capacity.

III

INTEGRATIVE TREATMENT
PROTOCOLS

Part III of this book describes 10 common chronic medical conditions that clinicians are likely to encounter. Each chapter consists of four sections: (a) a description of the illness, (b) treatment considerations, (c) a detailed protocol for assessment and treatment, and (d) an illustrative case example.

In describing the medical conditions, I first provide a general overview, followed by the epidemiology and subtypes of the medical condition, and then discuss some of the causal factors that have been hypothesized or supported by research. Where data exist, I also include information on gender, age, ethnicity, and socioeconomic status as it pertains both to epidemiology and to onset and experience of the illness. The final topic in this first section is prognosis.

In the section on treatment considerations, I look at illness perceptions, assessment considerations, treatment targets, and various treatment interventions as they pertain specifically to the disease in question. I focus in particular on those elements that have received research support with regard to the particular illness. Therefore, the subtopics in this section may differ slightly from chapter to chapter.

Each chapter concludes with an integrative treatment protocol in which all of the background information that has been described in earlier parts of the chapter is summarized, followed by what is specifically recommended in terms of a biopsychosocial assessment, resulting in a patient profile. This is followed by an assessment to identify patients who may be at higher risk either in terms of symptom severity and relapse or in terms of comorbid conditions, including psychiatric ones. An assessment of these elements results in a biopsychosocial illness profile for a particular patient.

The "Intervention Planning" section of the protocol alerts the clinician to the effect of such factors as severity of symptoms, comorbidities, and risks that affect the choice of interventions. Typically, patients with moderate and severe symptoms (e.g., higher levels of chronic pain) may require more intensive and combined treatments than patients with milder symptoms. Similarly, it is important to assess the course or trajectory of the chronic disease. Some disease processes take a progressive debilitating course, whereas others follow a course that is mild and relatively stable with only occasional periods of exacerbation. To tailor treatment to the patient, the clinician needs to be able to accurately note course, progression, and impact of the disease at the time the patient seeks or is referred for treatment and throughout the course of the psychological intervention. There are also various factors that increase a patient's risk for treatment failure, which I describe where applicable. These may include, for example, onset of symptoms at an early age, symptom severity, low socioeconomic status, and family history. By considering all of these factors, the clinician will be best able to select, combine, and sequence interventions to optimize treatment.

The "Intervention Implementation" section summarizes the psychological interventions most effective in treating both physical symptoms (e.g., anticipatory nausea in patients undergoing chemotherapy) and psychological symptoms (e.g., depression, anxiety) that are most likely to occur in a particular chronic illness. This section also summarizes the medical treatments that are typically used for the disease in question.

The "Intervention Monitoring" section describes the steps needed to ensure that the clinician is aware of the patient's disease state as well as to ensure the psychological treatment is on track. There are biomarkers for medical conditions that range from lab tests to biopsies. I describe those that the clinician is most likely to find useful (e.g., blood pressure readings in hypertension, staging in cancer, blood tests for long-term glucose control in diabetes). There are many more behavioral markers the clinician will find useful in specific illnesses, such as patient self-rating scales (e.g., SUDS), clinician rating scales, and patient diaries and logs.

A brief case example concludes each chapter. These illustrate how elements of the profile are used to assess and treat a patient with the given medical condition.

7

ARTHRITIS

Arthritis is a medical condition involving damaged joints resulting in persistent pain. It is a complex disorder that comprises more than 100 distinct conditions and can affect individuals at any stage of life. Two of the most common forms are osteoarthritis (OA) and rheumatoid arthritis (RA). Both have different causes, risk factors, and effects on the body, yet they often share a common symptom: persistent joint pain. The joint pain of arthritis can appear as hip pain, knee pain, hand pain, or wrist pain as well as joint pain in other areas of the body. Any part of the body can become inflamed or painful from arthritis. Some arthritic conditions can result in debilitating, even life-threatening, complications or can affect other parts of the body, including the muscles, bones, and internal organs. Joint pain, stiffness, and/or swelling for more than 2 weeks suggest a diagnosis of arthritis. The biopsychosocial perspective has provided a unique insight into this disease and illness as well as combined and integrative treatments that can reduce its physical, psychological, and interpersonal effects.

The following sections present basic background on chronic pain as a disease and illness followed by a detailed discussion of various psychological and biopsychosocial treatment intervention options. This discussion includes both clinical and research findings. The chapter concludes with an integrative treatment protocol and a case example illustrating the protocol.

EPIDEMIOLOGY

Both OA and RA and other *rheumatic*, that is, joint, conditions affect nearly 40 million Americans, which is about 1 of every 6 individuals. Approximately 50% of people over the age of 70 have OA, and 1% of the general population has RA (Keefe et al., 2002). As the nation's population ages, arthritis is expected to affect 60 million people by 2020.

Although prevailing myths have portrayed arthritis as an inevitable part of aging that can only be endured, effective interventions are available to prevent or reduce arthritis-related pain and disability. Although the human cost is incalculable, the economic cost for 1992 alone was estimated to be $64.8 billion. OA has the distinction of being the largest single cause of disability in the United States.

TYPES OF ARTHRITIS

Osteoarthritis

Osteoarthritis is a degenerative disease of a joint that results from wear and tear. The pressure of gravity causes physical damage to the joints and surrounding tissues resulting in pain, tenderness, swelling, inflammation, and even diminished joint functioning as well as limited movement. In the beginning, OA is noninflammatory, and its onset is subtle and gradual, usually involving one or only a few joints. The joints most often affected are the knees, hands, and spine. The main risk factor for OA is aging. Additional risk factors include joint trauma, obesity, and repetitive joint use.

OA alters the hyaline cartilage and causes loss of the articular cartilage of the joint as well as irregular growth to the connecting bone structures. This disease begins asymptomatically before age 40, and after age 40 nearly everyone experiences some pathological changes in their weight-bearing joints. Although men and women are equally affected by it, the onset is sooner in men. Pain is the earliest reported symptom and is increased by exercise and relieved by rest. Morning stiffness lasts 10 to 30 minutes and lessens with movement. As the disease progresses, joint motion decreases, and tenderness and grating sounds—called *crepitus*—appear. As articular cartilage is lost in the joint, ligaments become lax. Ligaments that effectively supported the joint before the disease progressed now become lax or loosened, resulting in the joint becoming less stable and increasing the risk of complications, such as fractures if the individual falls. Pain and tenderness are experienced arising from the changes in the ligaments and tendons. OA progresses slowly, and the daily pain is generally significantly less than with RA.

Rheumatoid Arthritis

Rheumatoid arthritis is an autoimmune disease that results when one's immune system mistakenly attacks the *synovium*, that is, the lining inside the joint. RA is a chronic and potentially disabling disease that causes joint pain, stiffness, swelling, and loss of joint function. Currently, the cause remains elusive; however, it is suspected that genetic factors are involved. Early diagnosis of RA can be difficult because it usually begins gradually with subtle symptoms. The majority of research related to arthritis has been on patients with RA, despite the fact that they account for only 10% of arthritis patients. Patients with RA report 42% greater daily pain than patients with OA (Keefe et al., 2002).

SEVERITY

All arthritic conditions involve pain and patterns of pain that differ among the arthritides and the location. RA is by far more severe and more progressively degenerative than OA. OA is typically worse at night or following rest. RA is generally worse in the morning. In the early stages, patients often do not have symptoms following their morning shower. In elderly people and children, pain may not be the main feature, and the patient simply moves less (elderly) or refuses to use the affected limb (children).

CAUSAL FACTORS

The causal factors in OA are not fully understood. Nevertheless, it is known that with increased age, the water content of the cartilage increases, and the protein makeup of cartilage degenerates. Repetitive use of the joints further irritates and inflames the cartilage, causing joint pain and swelling. Eventually, cartilage degenerates, and in advanced cases, a total loss of the cartilage cushion between the bones of the joints occurs, leading to further pain and limited joint mobility.

The causal factors in RA appear to have an immunologic basis (Keefe et al., 2002). Although the process is not fully understood, genetic abnormalities appear to increase the risk of developing RA. Such abnormalities increase the probability that the body's immune system will attack joint tissues. Presumably a bacterial, viral, or other foreign substance triggers this immune response.

GENDER, AGE, ETHNICITY, AND SOCIOECONOMIC STATUS

Gender

Women reported 72% greater pain than men, and women reported using more emotion-focused strategies than men. Men were more likely to experience increased negative mood the day after high pain. Women are affected 2 to 3 times more often than men (Keefe et al., 2002).

Age

Although the onset of arthritis may occur at any age, it is most often between 25 and 50 years. Age appears to be a predisposing factor for depression, with younger RA patients being significantly more likely to report depressive symptoms. Also, increased intrusion of RA symptoms led to more depressive symptoms in younger patients (Keefe et al., 2002), suggesting that younger RA patients experience depression at a lower level of intrusion and may require greater attention to any worsening of symptoms. Older RA patients who have difficulty with cognitive tasks reported much lower self-efficacy, higher pain, and worse mental health outcomes (Keefe et al., 2002).

Ethnicity

The prevalence of arthritis in adults in the United States ranges from 25% in Whites to 40% in non-Hispanic Blacks to 44% in Hispanics. Non-Hispanic Black and Hispanic older adults have reported having arthritis at a substantially higher frequency than have non-Hispanic Whites. In addition, Hispanics have reported higher rates of activity of daily living limitations than have non-Hispanic Whites with comparable disease burden (Abraido-Lanza, 2004). Further study is needed to confirm and elucidate the reasons for these racial and economic disparities in older populations (Dunlop, Manheim, Song, & Chang, 2001).

Socioeconomic Status

Multiple studies have shown that socioeconomic status is correlated with increased disability, depression, and maladaptive coping styles (Keefe et al., 2002). Given the same levels of disease severity, RA patients living in impoverished areas reported significantly poorer health and lower self-efficacy (Keefe et al., 2002). Lower levels of formal education are linked to higher mortality and morbidity (Pincus & Callahan, 1985).

FAMILY DYNAMICS

Arthritis impacts and is impacted by couple and family dynamics (Evers, Kraaimaat, Geenen, & Bijlsma, 1998). Arthritis can affect patients' spouses, and levels of distress were similar between arthritis patients and their partners. Negative or critical remarks from husbands correlated with higher ratings of pain and disability for women with RA (Griffin, Friend, Kaell, &

Bennett, 2001). Furthermore, negative spousal interaction predicted patient adjustment more than supportive interactions, and a patient's inability to meet spousal expectations seems to contribute to depressive symptoms (Bediako & Friend, 2004). Also, self-efficacy of the RA patient predicted spouses' caregiving burden and optimism (Keefe et al., 2002). Finally, among patients with RA, higher daily emotional and social support is linked to higher levels of psychological well-being and less depression (Keefe et al., 2002).

PSYCHIATRIC COMORBIDITIES

Research has indicated that depression, helplessness, and stress are important factors in explaining individual differences in response to the disease (Keefe et al., 2002). They represent major psychiatric comorbidities.

Depression

Depression is common among arthritis patients and influences overall adjustment to arthritis, particularly in RA patients (Fifield et al., 2001; Keefe et al., 2002). Some 15% to 17% of RA patients have reported depressive symptoms, and those who were depressed reported significantly poorer functioning and more arthritis-related physician visits and hospitalizations (Katz & Yelin, 1993). Disease activity and arthritis-related physical limitations have been found to predict depression in patients with RA. Depression has predicted a moderate to large amount of variance in physical and psychological disability, even controlling for disease status (Keefe et al., 2002). Furthermore, arthritis patients with a prior history of major depression are more likely to report higher levels of current pain (Keefe et al., 2002).

Learned Helplessness

Appreciating the role of learned helplessness is particularly important in RA, which is characterized by flare-ups that can be severe and unpredictable (Callahan, Cordray, Wells, & Pincus, 1996). Research indicates that learned helplessness mediates the relationship between RA severity and depression (T. W. Smith, Peck, & Ward, 1990). It leads to passive coping with pain and psychosocial impairment, fosters a vicious cycle, and predicts flare-ups in disease activity (Nicassio et al., 1993).

Stress

Stress is often blamed for disease flare-ups in RA patients. Although no consistent link has been found between the two, there is agreement that stress is important in understanding how patients adjust to arthritis. The relationship between stress and depression is much stronger in RA patients than in OA patients, and RA patients demonstrate more psychological and physiological reactivity to interpersonal stress than OA patients as measured by cortisol and Interleukin-6 levels (Keefe et al., 2002). OA patients have been found to be less reactive to interpersonal stress than patients with RA (Keefe et al., 2002).

PROGNOSIS

Given that it a progressive and disabling condition, the prognosis of RA is guarded to poor for most patients. On the other hand, the prognosis for OA is often more hopeful. Because RA is not curable, much of the focus of clinical research has been on reducing pain, increasing social support, enhancing adjustment, and avoiding or delaying disability (Krol, Sanderman, & Suurmeijer, 1993).

TREATMENT CONSIDERATIONS AND INTERVENTIONS

Psychological factors that affect pain and disability have been noted in patients with arthritis (Keefe et al., 2002). Considerable research has also focused on social factors. Research on such components of adjustment can help clinicians tailor treatment to particular patients. Illness representations, self-efficacy, and emotional regulation and coping styles are factors that can influence a patient's response to treatment and thus should be considered in planning tailored treatment.

Illness Representations

Illness representations form the basis for coping efforts, treatment compliance, and emotional responses (Schiaffino, Shawaryn, & Blum, 1998). Schiaffino et al. (1998) found a dynamic relationship between illness representations and illness experience. Patients with RA who believed their arthritis "to be curable and, to some extent, 'their own fault' reported higher levels of depression" (p. 267). This finding is consistent with research on learned helplessness and perceived control, in which self-blame occurs when best efforts fail. Because such illness representations and related beliefs are depressogenic and interfere with treatment, they must be therapeutically examined, challenged, and modified with cognitive–behavioral therapy (CBT) or other psychotherapeutic interventions.

Self-Efficacy

Self-efficacy is a useful construct in understanding and predicting pain and disability in patients with arthritis. When self-efficacy is found to be low and illness representations were internal and global, patients experienced more depression (Keefe et al., 2002). Self-efficacy predicts perception of controlled pain stimuli and ability to ignore pain stimuli (Keefe et al., 2002). Further, self-efficacy is related to coping self-statements and negatively related to catastrophizing (Keefe et al., 2002). Keefe et al. (1990) found that increases in pain-coping skills training was correlated with self-efficacy as well as immediate and long-term outcomes. In recognition of its clinical value, new guidelines for arthritis pain management emphasize the development of self-efficacy (Simon et al., 2002).

Emotional Regulation and Coping Styles

Individuals have different ways of coping with their illness, and researchers have attempted to identify such styles. Four distinct styles of emotion regulation have been noted in arthritis patients. They are ambiguity, control, orientation, and expression (Van Middendorp et al., 2005). Two of these styles, ambiguity and orientation, have been found to be correlated with poorer psychological well-being, whereas the other two, expression and control, are associated with favorable functioning for patients with RA.

A more traditional way of classifying coping styles is active versus maladaptive coping. Different styles of coping show different relations to positive and negative affect; although active coping was only related to positive affect, maladaptive coping was related to both increased negative affect and decreased positive affect (Keefe et al., 2002). It has been found that active coping predicts positive affect whereas affective regulation is correlated to negative affect (Affleck, Urrows, Tennen, & Higgins, 1992; Hamilton, Zautra, & Reich, 2005).

PSYCHOEDUCATIONAL INTERVENTIONS

Self-management appears to be an important part of the treatment regimen. Usually this involves a patient education component in which information about the disease and its manifestation and progressive course is provided. This can be accomplished by face-to-face contact, phone contact, or computer programs or written materials. In addition, such strategies as exercise; relaxation training; and skill training in cognitive pain management, problem solving, and social skills can be incorporated. These strategies can be learned over a period of weeks in a classroom, small group, or individual context. Typically, cognitive strategies such as cognitive pain management focus on reframing the individual's way of thinking about the disease and in modulating the chronic pain component. Because of the significant psychological component, counseling or referral for psychotherapy may be indicated.

Individuals with OA benefit from CBT protocols focused on teaching pain coping skills. Including spouses in pain coping skills appears to be an effective approach, improving not only pain and self-efficacy but also marital satisfaction. Treatment should target individuals scoring high on denial and anxiety. Brief therapy can be used with persons with mild or moderate OA, whereas longer therapy is indicated for those with severe illness and those anticipating surgery.

A growing body of evidence indicates that optimum adjustment in RA involves coping efforts that focus on daily illness control that helps patients deal with the unpredictability and lack of control associated with RA (Chaney et al., 1996; Keefe et al., 1997). Chaney et al. (1996) also reported that self-management treatment packages for RA that include information on the nature of arthritis, cognitive techniques for appraising physical symptoms, and self-management skills appear to reduce depressive symptoms, pain, joint inflammation, and utilization of health care services and to result in increased social and physical activities for patients.

A meta-analysis of randomized controlled trials involving psychoeducational interventions for RA found that they can improve outcomes but that effect sizes were similar to those for nonsteroidal anti-inflammatory drugs (NSAIDs; Astin, Beckner, Soeken, Hochberg, & Berman, 2002). Astin et al.'s (2002) systemic review included interventions such as relaxation, biofeedback, CBT, and stress management. They found that these approaches were useful adjuncts to standard medical management, providing a small but statistically significant effect for pain, functional disability, depression, coping, and self-efficacy. They concluded that such interventions decrease pain and disability and may affect disease activity and that the critical mediator of improvement in health status was self-efficacy and coping (Astin et al., 2002).

Pain Coping Skills Training

Pain coping skills training has proven useful in reducing arthritis-related pain and disability (Keefe et al., 2002). Pain coping skills training includes education about biopsychosocial pain mechanisms and three pain coping skills: attention diversion skills, activity-based skills, and cognitive coping strategies. This coping skills training has been effectively used with patients alone (Keefe et al., 1990) and, even more effectively, with the participation of patients' spouses (Keefe et al., 1996).

Spousal involvement resulted in significantly lower levels of pain, psychological disability, and pain behavior and higher scores on measures of coping attempts, marital adjustment, and self-efficacy than patients who received patient education and social support (Keefe et al., 1996).

Arthritis Self-Management Program

Barlow, Turner, and Wright (1998) reported on the use of the Arthritis Self-Management Programme (ASMP) in the United Kingdom. ASMP was delivered over 6 weeks in 2-hour weekly sessions with course content including information about arthritis, an overview of self-management principles, exercise, pain management, depression, nutrition, and communication with family and health professionals. The study participants experienced a small but significant reduction in pain at 4 months and again at 12 months, with neither disease duration nor comorbidity influencing outcomes. These outcomes were reported for both OA patients and RA patients.

COGNITIVE–BEHAVIORAL THERAPY

Among other treatment targets, CBT is particularly useful in modifying treatment-interfering illness representations. Controlled studies have documented the efficacy of CBT protocols for managing pain in individuals with OA and RA (Keefe & Caldwell, 1997). These protocols and the associated research literature are extensive and attest to the clinical value of CBT in the treatment of chronic illness. Of particular note is that data indicate that tailoring treatment to patient characteristics may be a way to optimize CBT effectiveness, particularly in RA patients (Evers, Kraaimaat, van Riel, & de Jong, 2002).

Osteoarthritis

One of the most effective CBT interventions for OA is pain coping skills training, which was described previously. This intervention involves cognitive coping strategies in addition to attention-diversion skill training and activity-based skill training and can be delivered to patients individually or with the participation of their spouses (Keefe et al., 1990, 1996). It is also important to address thinking errors and use cognitive restructuring when indicated.

Rheumatoid Arthritis

In their study of cognitive–behavioral interventions for women with RA, Sinclair and Wallston (2001) found that patients with higher scores on psychological and physical well-being scales improved far more than women who entered with low or moderate scores. Also, they reported that women on the extreme ends of the maladaptive coping spectrum improved most as a result of the intervention.

An important study has demonstrated the effectiveness of CBT in RA and that it can be optimized by applying early, customized treatments to patients at risk. A randomized controlled trial with tailor-made treatment modules was conducted among patients with relatively early RA, that is, duration of less than 8 years, who had been screened for psychosocial risk profiles. All participants received standard medical care from a rheumatologist and rheumatology nurse consultant. Patients in the CBT condition additionally received an individual CBT treatment with two of four possible treatment modules. Choice of treatment modules was determined on the basis of patient priorities, which resulted in most frequent application of the fatigue module followed by the negative mood, social relationships, and pain and functional disability modules. Results indicated that CBT had beneficial effects on physical, psychological, and social functioning. Specifically, fatigue and depression were significantly reduced, as was helplessness. Active coping and medication compliance also increased in contrast to the control condition (Evers et al., 2002).

OTHER PSYCHOTHERAPEUTIC INTERVENTIONS

By itself, psychotherapy does not appear to have the viability of CBT and other treatments. Nevertheless, for some patients psychotherapy may be an option as a single treatment or as an adjunct. A few psychotherapy studies have been reported. In one, weekly analytically oriented psychotherapy—for a median duration of 3.3 years—was provided to 15 patients with RA. Six patients were reported to have achieved significant and continuous improvement in psychological and physical well-being during and after treatment. In another 5 patients, similar improvements took place over a period of 1 to 2 years. However, when childhood trauma issues were addressed, these 5 patients relapsed, and the course of their disease became more variable. In 4 patients, the connections between psychic state and the course of the joint disease were more varied throughout the psychotherapy. The researchers contended that the probability of the study outcome being due to chance alone was small, especially given that RA is a chronic progressive disease (Lindberg, Lindberg, Theorell, & Larsson, 1996).

Exercise

Exercise can be a useful adjunct in the treatment of OA. Research indicates that appropriate exercise, that is, within the limits of normal joint motion and comfort, does not predispose to OA. Passive exercise during acute inflammation to prevent contracture should be used with care and within pain limits, and active exercise is important for range of motion and muscle retention during periods without inflammation.

However, joints with preexisting injury are at increased risk of developing OA with repetitive loading and immoderate exercise. Thus, an exercise prescription is not indicated in arthritic patients with preexisting injury. Patients with arthritis can derive a number of benefits from a thoughtful and closely monitored exercise program (D. Hoffman, 1993).

MEDICAL TREATMENT

Medical treatment includes medications to reduce inflammation, pain, and swelling as well as physical therapy and exercise. Rehabilitation techniques are also used to prevent dysfunction and decrease the severity or duration of disability. It is interesting that psychological factors are more strongly associated with disability than the disease process itself.

Osteoarthritis

Treatment for OA includes rehabilitation techniques focused on preventing dysfunction and disability and decreasing severity. Primary treatment considerations include the stage and magnitude of tissue changes, the number of joints involved, the pain cycle, the cause of pain (biomechanical defects or inflammation), and the patient's lifestyle. Patient education—about the nature of the problem, prognosis, importance of cooperation, and optimal physical fitness—may also be beneficial. Patients should continue employment and physical activity. Exercise and daily stretching are critical for healthy cartilage and range of motion.

Rheumatoid Arthritis

For RA, complete bed rest for short periods may occasionally be prescribed during the most active painful stage of severe disease. Splints may be useful for local joint rest, but range of motion and exercise as tolerated are important. Attention to good nutrition is also important. Medications, such as salicylates and NSAIDs, are important for pain management and anti-inflammatory effects, but attention should be given to gastrointestinal tolerance. Corticosteroids are the most dramatically effective short-term anti-inflammatory drugs; however, their clinical benefit for RA often diminishes with time.

MEDICATION

First-line drugs are used to treat the inflammation and pain associated with OA and RA. Aspirin and other NSAIDs, such as ibuprofen (e.g., Motrin, naproxen, Naprosyn, diclofenac, and Voltaren), have immediate analgesic and anti-inflammatory effects and are considered to be relatively safe. Second-line drugs used for treatment of RA include hydroxychloroquine, gold, penicillamine, azathioprine, sulfasalazine, and methotrexate. These drugs can control symptoms and appear to delay progression of the disease. However, they can also cause severe adverse effects, and their effectiveness seems to diminish over time. NSAIDs are usually taken concurrently with the slower acting second-line drugs.

COMBINED TREATMENT

Like other chronic illnesses, combined and integrated treatment is essential in arthritis. A common example of combined treatment involves the use of two medications. In more advanced cases of arthritis, a second drug is added that has a synergistic effect with the first, resulting in a more effective outcome. An increasingly common treatment combination includes medication, psychoeducational interventions, exercise, and CBT.

Integrative Treatment Protocol: Arthritis

1. Key Background Information	
Pathology	Medical condition involving damaged joints with persistent pain.
Epidemiology	Affects 1 of 6. Ostearthritis (OA) affects 65% of older adults, whereas rheumatoid arthritis (RA) affects about 5% of the total population.
Types	OA: More common—nonsystemic, some damage to weight-bearing joints, pain and tenderness, and slowly progressive. Onset by age 40, most have it by age 70. RA: Less common—systemic and immunological; significant and progressive joint destruction. Onset: between ages 25 and 50.
Severity	RA is considerably more severe and more progressively degenerative than OA.
Causal factors	OA: age and repetitive use eventually lead to cartilage degeneration. RA: presumed that genetic abnormalities foster immunological response, which is triggered by a bacteria, virus, or other foreign substance.
Gender, age, ethnicity, and socioeconomic status (SES)	OA: female:male = 1:1; RA: female:male = 2.5:1, with women reporting 72% greater pain than men. Lower SES associated with poorer health; lower education levels linked to higher morbidity and mortality.
Psychiatric comorbidities	Depression: RA—predicts poorer functioning and more arthritis-related medical visits and hospitalizations, more pain and physical limitations. RA Psychodynamics: High need to control self and others, masochistic but rebellious; deep-seated rage, which stimulates production of the biomarker (rheumatoid factor).

Family dynamics	High support linked to higher levels of well-being and mobility and less depression. Spousal criticalness linked to pain and disability.
Prognosis	Poor for RA; good to guarded for OA.

2. Biopsychosocial Assessment

Patient profile	From interview and observation and Revised Illness Perception Questionnaire (IPQ-R; Moss-Morris et al., 2002) assessment: IPQ-R factors, especially illness perceptions, explanations, treatment expectations; severity of symptoms and functional impact; capacity, previous change efforts, and readiness for change; and personality style or personality disorder and family and cultural factors.
Illness profile	Identify higher risk arthritis patients: • younger with greater disease or RA with depressive symptoms, • those with consistently high levels of pain, • those with spouses who are critical or nonsupportive about disease, • patients whose arthritis interferes with performance of valued roles, • patients with a history of depression or any major affective disorder, • those of lower SES, and • those alone or lacking a consistent support system.

3. Intervention Planning

Patient profile	Illness representation: A common belief is that OA and RA are curable but are the patient's fault; these illness beliefs are depressogenic, hinder treatment, and need to be therapeutically addressed.
Illness profiles	Disease or illness type goals: • RA: increase coping, slow progression, increase perceived control; more intensive and combined interventions needed. • OA: decrease severity and prevent dysfunction and disability.
Coping style	Active, adaptive style is related to positive mood and decreased pain; maladaptive style is related to negative affects.
Self-efficacy	Predicts patient's perception of pain and ability to ignore it; also related to coping self-statements and catastrophizing thoughts.
Activity level and range of motion	Relatively sensitive biomarkers of disease prevention and progression.
SES and social support	Predictors of depression, symptom severity, disability, and treatment response.

4. Intervention Implementation

Psychoeducational interventions (OA and RA)	Meta-analyses show that relaxation, stress management, and biofeedback, when used as adjuncts to standard medical treatment, slightly improve outcomes in impacting pain levels, functioning, depression, self-efficacy, and coping.

(continues)

Pain coping skills training	Proven to reduce pain and disability. Includes information, attention diversion skills, activity-based skills, and cognitive coping strategies.
Cognitive–behavioral therapy (CBT)	Generally beneficial in modifying problematic illness representations with cognitive restructuring and/or positive reattribution, treatment-interfering thoughts or behaviors, and interpersonal conflicts and support issues. RA: Focus on pain-coping skills, interfering illness representations, and cognitive restructuring. OA: Focus on teaching pain-coping skills and realistic cognitive appraisal of pain, tailoring treatment to patient characteristics optimizes CBT effectiveness.
Other psycho-therapies	OA: When indicated, shorter term dynamic therapy for mild to moderate OA, with longer term therapy for more severe OA; focus on interfering illness beliefs, relationships. RA: Dynamically oriented interventions focused on interfering illness beliefs and psychodynamics, for example, rage and issues arising from increasing physical disability.
Medication	First-line drugs for OA and RA are analgesic and anti-inflammatory agents, for example, nonsteroidal anti-inflammatory drugs (NSAIDs). Second-line drugs for RA include hydroxychloroquine, gold, penicillamine, azathioprine, sulfasalazine, and methotrexate.
Exercise	OA: Encourage daily exercise and stretching to increase and maintain range of motion and promote cartilage healing. RA: Encourage passive exercise during acute flare-ups to prevent contractures and encourage active exercise for range of motion and maintenance of muscle mass during noninflammatory periods.
Combined treatment	As with most chronic illnesses, the more severe the symptoms and functional disability, the more multifactorial and combined treatment are essential.

5. Intervention Monitoring

- Review patient's log of symptoms and functional impairment.
- Track session-to-session progress with regard to compliance, pain and other symptom reduction, and functionality, such as activity level and range of motion.

CASE OF ANGELA J.

Angela J. is a 62-year-old married Hispanic woman who has been self-treating her OA for some 6 years without much relief. In fact, her disease has progressed to the point that she can barely get out of bed in the morning without assistance. Like many of her friends, she has been taking an over-the-counter herbal remedy, glucosamine-chondroitin. Her daughter, a nurse, had been after her for some time to "stop playing doctor" and consult with a rheumatologist at the arthritis clinic of a local hospital where the daughter works. Angela met with physician Julius Aurellio, who diagnosed her with

OA with mild spinal stenosis, which probably accounted for her morning back pain and swelling.

What concerned him even more was that Angela appeared to be moderately depressed. She admitted that she did feel sad, had lost interest in some of her favorite hobbies, had trouble falling asleep, and was more irritable. Aurellio gave her a prescription for an NSAID and wanted her to try an antidepressant but she refused. After Aurellio expressed his concern about her depressive features, she agreed to a consultation with the practice's psychological consultant, Renee Ramirez. Ramirez met with Angela that same day and undertook a biopsychosocial evaluation. After identifying Angela's illness representations, she completed a mental status exam and found that although Angela was somewhat depressed, she denied suicidal ideation and a plan.

During her years of practice, Ramirez had become aware of the phenomenon of arthritis patients having conflicting "cure–control" and "cause" beliefs, that is, that their condition is curable but it is their fault they are arthritic because of overactivity, poor diet, lack of exercise, and so on. The result of such conflicting beliefs is an increasing sense of helplessness and depression. Her experience has been that treating the depression directly with medications, CBT, or other psychotherapies is usually insufficient to effect symptomatic relief. Rather, the conflicting illness beliefs need to be therapeutically examined, challenged, and modified. If this is not done, neither the depression nor arthritis pain can be effectively treated because these beliefs will continue to interfere with the treatment of either.

Accordingly, Ramirez engaged Angela in a brief course of CBT in which these conflicting beliefs were processed. At the same time, Angela began pain-coping skills training with a psychology intern. Because the clinic had found that patients profit significantly more from the program if their spouse is involved, Angela's husband, Jaime, participated in the training with her. Within 2 months, Angela's pain and depression had diminished and the dose of her NSAID was reduced. A follow-up plan was set in which she would continue to be monitored by Aurellio every 2 months and would check in with Ramirez in 6 months.

8

ASTHMA

Asthma is a chronic respiratory disease characterized by reversible airway obstruction and airway responsiveness to a variety of irritants. It is typically accompanied by tissue inflammation, mucus congestion, and constriction of the smooth muscles in the airways. Although there is great variability in symptomatology, an asthma attack begins with spasms of wheezing, coughing, and shortness of breath. Tightness or pressure in the chest may also be present. The course of this disease is highly variable, depending on the individual's unique symptoms, triggers or precipitants of symptoms, health status, and capacity for self-management of this condition. Thus, it should not be too surprising that nearly 75% of emergency room admissions for asthma are avoidable (Pleis & Lethbridge-Cejku, 2006). Asthma is closely linked to allergies, and most individuals with asthma also have allergies. It is not surprising that children with a family history of allergy and asthma are more likely to have asthma (Bloom & Cohen, 2007). Furthermore, approximately 40% of people with asthma fail to use appropriate symptom management strategies when their symptoms worsen. Upwards of 60% of people with asthma are poor at judging the extent of *dyspnea*, which is subjective difficulty or distress in breathing (Pleis & Lethbridge-Cejku, 2006).

The following sections present basic background on asthma as a disease and illness followed by a detailed discussion of various psychological and biopsychosocial treatment intervention options. This discussion includes both clinical and research findings. The chapter concludes with an integrative treatment protocol and a case example illustrating the protocol.

EPIDEMIOLOGY

The prevalence of asthma in the United States is about 5% among adults and 10% among children, although the incidence appears to be increasing. That means that about 20 million Americans have been diagnosed with asthma, and of these, nearly 9 million are children (Bloom & Cohen, 2007). Morbidity and mortality increase disproportionately among the indigent in inner city areas. Approximately 25% of people with asthma experience severe symptoms (Pleis & Lethbridge-Cejku, 2006). Of these, the majority are women, ethnic minorities, those with the least education, smokers, and those receiving care from nonspecialists. Asthma is the leading cause of hospitalization among children and is responsible for more absenteeism from school than any other chronic illness (Bloom & Cohen, 2007).

SEVERITY

The severity of this disease state varies widely. As noted earlier, approximately 25% of asthmatics experience severe symptoms (Pleis & Lethbridge-Cejku, 2006). Compared with those with mild to moderate asthma, those with severe symptoms also tend to have less of an understanding of the asthma, its clinical manifestations, and the means to control asthma attacks. Most commonly—in at least 50% of cases—asthma sufferers experience a reaction within seconds after exposure to a trigger, and this reaction continues for approximately 1 hour. There is also a delayed reaction that begins 4 to 8 hours after exposure that lasts for hours or even days.

CAUSAL FACTORS

Airflow obstruction and airflow hyperresponsiveness are signature features of this disease. These reactions are related to various causal factors: airway edema, acute bronchoconstriction, chronic mucus plugs, and/or changes in the lung itself. More specifically, airway obstruction is due to a combination of factors, including spasms of airway smooth muscles, edema of airway mucosa, increased mucus secretion, and infiltration of the airway walls. The end result is an "asthma attack." It is hypothesized that the eosinophilic inflammation response that occurs in asthma may be the result of cytokine production associated with stress (Lehrer, Feldman, Giardino, Song, & Schmaling, 2002).

Historically, asthma was considered one of the classic seven psychosomatic illnesses along with peptic ulcer, hypertension, colitis, cardiac arrhythmia, neurodermatitis, and hyperthyroidism (Alexander, 1950). It was believed that asthma was caused by repressed feelings in a biologically predisposed individual. Although most no longer consider asthma to be a psychosomatic illness or a behavioral disease, there is evidence indicating that stress and other psychological factors may be triggers or exacerbants rather than causes of asthma. More specifically, behaviors such as crying and screaming and psychological factors such as failed expectations or relational stress can trigger asthma symptoms. Lehrer et al. (2002) have published a comprehensive review of the research regarding psychological aspects of asthma.

GENDER, AGE, AND ETHNICITY

Gender and Age

Ten percent of children and adolescents suffer from asthma. It is more frequent among boys and male teens than females. However, among adults, asthma is more frequent in women. It is noteworthy that the incidence of asthma is increasing among children and that the risk of underdiagnosis and undertreatment of asthma is higher in children from ethnic minority groups (Davis, Kreutzer, Lipsett, King, & Shaikh, 2006).

Ethnicity

Although asthma affects people of all races, African Americans are more likely than Caucasians to be hospitalized for asthma attacks and to die from asthma. In a study by Davis et al. (2006), the prevalence of asthma among African Americans was roughly twice that of Caucasians. Asthma in Hispanic subgroups ranged from 13.2% for Mexican Americans to 22.8% for Puerto Ricans and 23.0% among Cuban Americans. Lifetime asthma diagnosis among 11 Asian American subgroups ranged from 10.9% among Korean Americans to 23.8% among Filipino Americans (Davis et al., 2006).

PSYCHIATRIC COMORBIDITIES

Comorbid psychopathologies are known to exacerbate asthma and decrease quality of life (Lehrer et al., 2002). Lehrer et al. (2002) have also noted that family disorganization is another exacerbant. More specifically, anxiety, depression, and panic attacks are the most common comorbid conditions experienced by asthma patients.

Anxiety

Individuals with asthma appear particularly likely to experience anxiety (Lehrer et al., 2002). These patients seem to have decreased physical and emotional functioning, including poorer asthma control. Anxiety symptoms appear to result in respiratory effects consistent with acute asthma exacerbation (Lehrer et al., 2002). The relationship appears to be reciprocal in that an emotional state can trigger asthma or can be triggered by asthmatic responses (York, Fleming, & Shuldham, 2006).

Depression

There is growing consensus among researchers over an increased prevalence of depression among patients with asthma, despite variable reports ranging from 1% to 45% (Opolski & Wilson, 2005). Depression appears to contribute to respiratory consequences consistent with asthma, whereas contentment is related to effects that relieve airway constriction (Opolski & Wilson, 2005). Depression may also play a role in asthma self-management. It has been established that depressed patients with chronic illness are 3 times more likely to be noncompliant with regard to medical treatment (Opolski & Wilson, 2005). The bidirectional association between depression and asthma can result in a deteriorating cycle.

Panic Attacks

One of the most commonly studied negative emotions in asthma is panic (Carr, Lehrer, & Hochron, 1995). The incidence of panic disorder among patients with asthma is statistically significant: Approximately 10% of asthma patients meet criteria for panic disorder (Lehrer et al., 2002). Panic disorder patients report 7 times more physician visits and twice as many lost work days as the general population (Carr et al., 1995). An excessively high panic response, such as rapid breathing, can lead to hyperventilation-induced asthma exacerbation that can then result in overuse of asthma medication and decreased effectiveness. It was found that among people with asthma, dyspnea may predict panic better than catastrophic thinking (Carr et al., 1995).

Panic can elicit respiratory effects that replicate asthma exacerbations (Lehrer et al., 2002). This relationship was the subject of a study by Carr, Lehrer, Hochron, and Jackson (1996) in which airway impedance responses to psychological stressors were evaluated. The authors concluded that panic disorder results in a chronic state of preparedness that promotes hyperventilation. They speculated that panic symptoms may be adaptive in patients who have asthma because patients with low asthma-related panic have increased asthma mortality. It was further suggested that reduction of panic symptoms may be contraindicated in asthma patients with acute distress and that asthma symptoms in patients with comorbid panic disorder should be closely monitored during treatment for panic symptoms (Carr et al., 1996).

PROGNOSIS

With proper treatment and treatment compliance, almost all asthma patients can become free of symptoms. Some patients will actually outgrow their asthma. This depends largely on age of onset and level of severity. Approximately 50% of children with mild asthma will have no symptoms by the time they reach adolescence. However, approximately 25% of children with a history of asthma by age 7 continue to wheeze at age 33, indicating that their asthma continues (Bloom & Cohen, 2007).

Asthma does, however, often recur in adulthood. Children with more severe asthma are less likely to be free of symptoms when they get older. Recurrence of wheezing after prolonged remission during late adolescence was strongly associated with atopy and cigarette smoking. Asthma that develops in adulthood can be associated with long-term exposure to specific triggers, such as chemicals or pollution, and can sometimes be greatly improved if the triggers are avoided (Strachan, Butland, & Anderson, 1996).

TREATMENT CONSIDERATIONS AND INTERVENTIONS

Psychological factors clearly influence the experience of asthma as a trigger and exacerbant as well as response to treatment. Social and cultural factors also influence the experience of asthma. Clinicians would do well to consider these factors in planning and implementing psychological treatment interventions. Specifically, they should focus on illness representations, coping styles, self-efficacy, and perceptual accuracy as factors that can influence a patient's response to treatment and thus should be considered in planning tailored treatment.

Illness Representations

Illness representation has become one of the most promising factors in asthma treatment and is a key considerations in both the medical and psychological treatment of asthma. An individual's constellations of perceptions and beliefs about a particular disease—understanding of it and its symptoms, cause, time or illness duration, impact or consequences, curability, and ability to control it—is referred to as *illness representation*. Illness representations in asthma tend to be sensitive predictors of treatment compliance. The following studies demonstrate the link between these representations and medication compliance.

Medication noncompliance in asthma patients was predicted by beliefs about the necessity of medication and concerns about its potential adverse effects and by negative perceived consequences of illness. Sociodemographic and clinical factors explained little of variance in compliance, whereas illness perceptions and treatment beliefs were substantial independent predictors (Horne & Weinman, 2002). In a similar study, current compliance with inhaler use was predicted by age, gender, and certainty about asthma status (i.e., identity, beliefs about causes, and beliefs about cure control). Age, beliefs about cure control, and beliefs about the duration of one's asthma significantly predicted intention to comply with medication treatment in the future (Jessop & Rutter, 2003). A study by Byer and Myers (2000) examined the relationship among illness representations, beliefs about medication, and compliance with medication in a primary care sample of 64 asthma patients. Multiple regression analyses revealed that the number of inhaler prescriptions was significantly associated with patient beliefs about the necessity for their asthma medication and external cause as well as belief in long illness duration and high morbidity. Furthermore, self-reported compliance was significantly associated with patient beliefs about the necessity of their asthma medication and strong identity (Byer & Myers, 2000).

PSYCHOEDUCATIONAL INTERVENTIONS

Self-management is a key component of effective asthma management (Sudre, Jacquemet, Uldry, & Perneger, 1999). It involves at least two goals. The first goal is to assist these individuals in self-managing their asthma at home and in working through treatment adjustment in response to changes in their symptoms. Patient education is a necessary prerequisite for effective self-management. It includes basic facts about asthma, the role of quick-response and long-term-control medications, correct use of metered-dose inhalers, strategies for decreasing environmental exposure, a plan for reducing acute episodes, and the benefit of involvement of family and significant others in the treatment process. Equally important is the second goal, which is the development of the asthmatic's skills, judgment, and confidence necessary for engaging in self-management activities and for collaborating with health care providers.

Asthma Education

One of the most common interventions with asthma patients is education and psychoeducational care. Devine's (1996) meta-analysis of 31 published studies found methodological weaknesses but concluded that education and relaxation-based behavioral interventions were correlated with improved clinical outcomes in adults with asthma.

Hicks and Harris (2001) suggested that because asthma education programs increase knowledge but do not decrease morbidity, further research is needed to resolve the discrepancy between patients' knowledge and actual behavior. In their randomized controlled trial, Vazquez and Buceta (1993) found that asthmatic children who participated in a self-management group did increase their self-management behaviors but had no corresponding increase in health status. On the other hand, children who were in the relaxation training group or the control group neither increased self-management behaviors nor experienced any improvement in health status.

Symptom Perception Training

Many patients fail to effectively discern changes in their airways, which can lead to near-fatal attacks. Researchers have found that with perceptual feedback training, patients are able to improve their perceptual accuracy and improve clinical outcomes (Lehrer et al., 2002). When patients who experienced a severe exacerbation in the previous year participated in an action plan that involved home peak-flow monitoring, they were able to reduce their emergency visits (Lehrer et al., 2002). There is value in helping patients who overperceive their symptoms or experience disproportionate discomfort. However, Lehrer et al. (2002) cautioned that decreasing the discomfort of asthma symptoms in patients may result in increased risk of severe illness if patients fail to heed important early warning signs.

Relaxation Training

Relaxation therapy has been accepted as a valuable part of asthma self-management. A systematic review of all available published randomized controlled trials on relaxation training and asthma concluded that there was a lack of evidence for the efficacy of relaxation therapies for asthma management (Huntley, White, & Ernst, 2002). Another systematic review of available research concluded that relaxation training did have a small but inconsistent effect on asthma and that relaxation may be very beneficial in preventing stress-induced asthma (Lehrer et al., 2002). Given the link between strong emotion and respiratory effects, there may be a role for relaxation on mitigating states of extreme anxiety to prevent asthma exacerbation.

Written Emotional Expression Exercises

Recently, research has been reported on the health benefits of disclosure of psychologically traumatic experience through writing. This approach is referred to as *written emotional expression exercises*. In one study, asthma patients were asked to write down their thoughts and feelings about traumatic experiences, and significant improvements in forced expiratory volume in the first second (abbreviated as "FEV_1") were found, even after a 4-month follow-up (Smyth, 1998).

COGNITIVE–BEHAVIORAL THERAPY

Typically, cognitive–behavioral therapy (CBT) is useful and effective in modifying automatic thoughts, intermediate beliefs, and maladaptive schema. In addition, there are a number of specific treatment targets for CBT interventions with asthma. A particularly important target is modifying treatment-interfering illness representations. Other treatment-interfering factors that can be treatment targets for CBT with asthma patients include procrastination, difficulty focusing, and relational issues.

C. J. Ross, Davis, and MacDonald (2005) tested a CBT-based 8-week group treatment program for adults with asthma and coexisting panic disorder. Although the treatment group initially demonstrated improvement in panic frequency, general anxiety, and morning peak expiratory flow, only the panic disorder outcomes were sustained during 6-month follow-up. It is interesting that even participants who were not panic free at the end of the study exhibited significant decreases in pretreatment panic frequency (C. J. Ross et al., 2005). Although quality of life was not improved, the study demonstrated improvement in panic symptoms of patients with asthma using group CBT (C. J. Ross et al., 2005).

Opolski and Wilson (2005) reported on a study by Grover et al. of 10 asthma patients assigned either to a control group that received asthma medication or an experimental group that received CBT, including asthma education, muscle relaxation, behavioral techniques, cognitive restructuring, and coping skills as well as asthma medication. Although the control group did not experience significant changes, the experimental group reported significant decreases in asthma symptoms, anxiety, and depression, along with increased quality of life.

OTHER PSYCHOTHERAPEUTIC INTERVENTIONS

Hypnotherapy

Hypnotherapy has long been used with asthma patients. Unfortunately, there is relatively little published research on its efficacy. One controlled study of hypnosis in the treatment of children with asthma found symptom improvement but not increased pulmonary function, decreased visits to the emergency room, and fewer missed school days (Kohen, 1995). A critical review of the literature on hypnosis and asthma concluded that hypnotherapy can be beneficial, particularly for asthmatics who are highly hypnotizable (Hackman, Stern, & Gershwin, 2000).

Family Therapy

Given the large number of children and adolescents with asthma and the role of family dynamics, it should not be too surprising that family therapy is an often-used intervention. Two controlled studies (Gustafsson, Kjellman, & Cederbald, 1986; Lask & Matthew, 1979) found that family therapy can lead to improvement in asthma symptoms in children with severe asthma and in families exhibiting interpersonal difficulties that impede a complex medical protocol. It may well be that family therapy is most beneficial for families in which interpersonal problems interfere with the complex medical regimen of children with severe asthma (Lehrer et al., 2002).

MEDICAL TREATMENT

Effective medical treatment usually involves a management protocol. It consists of assessing the severity of the illness, controlling environmental factors to avoid or minimize triggering symptoms or exacerbations, using medication to manage exacerbations and reverse and prevent airway inflammation, using patient education and self-management methods, and monitoring the course of therapy. The goal of conventional medical treatment is fourfold: (a) to prevent chronic symptoms, (b) to maintain pulmonary function as close to normal functioning as possible, (c) to minimize the need for emergency room visits and hospitalization, and (d) to avoid the adverse effects of treatment.

Recovery from asthma is typically defined as movement into the normal range of pulmonary function. Needless to say, even small improvements can be clinically significant. It should be noted that at the present time, the focus of conventional medical treatment is entirely on disease management rather than on cure. Conventional medical treatment focuses on four treatment targets: (a) providing medications to control inflammation and prevent chronic symptoms, (b) providing medications to treat asthma attacks when they occur, (c) avoiding asthma triggers, and (d) monitoring peak flows.

MEDICATION

There are two general types of asthma medications for long-term control as well as quick relief of symptoms. *Anti-inflammatory* drugs prevent asthma attacks on an ongoing basis. Corticosteroids are an important type of anti-inflammatory medication for asthma patients. They reduce swelling and mucus production in the airways. As a result, airways are less sensitive and less likely to react to triggers. *Bronchodilators* relieve asthma attacks and symptoms by relaxing the muscle bands that tighten around the airways. This action rapidly opens the airways and clears mucus from the lungs. As a result, breathing improves.

Management of asthma has improved with use of inhaled or systemic corticosteroids, leukotriene modifiers, and beta$_2$-agonists (Hunt, 2001; Stoloff, 2005). Adherence and self-management are particularly important in asthma control (Hunt, 2001). This includes an "asthma action plan" for the patient and avoidance of triggers (Hunt, 2001).

COMBINED TREATMENT

Combined or integrated asthma treatment includes all four of the conventional medical treatment targets plus lifestyle modification and psychoeducation described above. At a minimum, it includes monitoring daily asthma symptoms in an asthma diary and avoiding both physical and psychological asthma triggers.

Integrative Treatment Protocol: Asthma

1. Key Background Information	
Pathology	Asthma is a chronic respiratory disease characterized by reversible airway constriction and increased airway responsiveness. Airway tissues are inflamed, and mucus congestion occurs.
Epidemiology	Approximately 5% of adults and 10% of children suffer from asthma, although the incidence appears to be increasing at an alarming rate. It is enormously costly on both the personal and national levels.
Severity	Can be life threatening; approximately 25% experience severe symptoms. Seventy-five percent of emergency room admissions for asthma are avoidable: 40% of asthmatics fail to use appropriate symptom management strategies when symptoms worsen, and up to 60% are poor at judging the extent of distress in breathing.
Causal factors	Airway edema, acute bronchoconstriction, chronic mucus plugs, or changes in the lung itself cause airflow obstruction and airflow hyperresponsiveness, resulting in an "asthma attack." Asthma is no longer considered a psychosomatic disease, but psychological factors influence its course, treatment, and compliance.
Gender, age, ethnicity, and socioeconomic status (SES)	Asthma is more frequent among boys and male teens than females, but among adults asthma is more frequent in women. It affects all races, but African Americans are more likely to be hospitalized and to die from asthma. Incidence is high among Hispanic subgroups, particularly Puerto Ricans and Cuban Americans; it is even higher among Korean Americans.
Psychiatric comorbidities	• Anxiety: Anxiety exacerbates asthma and decreases the quality of life of asthma patients. They can have decreased physical and emotional functioning, including poorer asthma control.

	• Panic disorder: Approximately 10% of asthma patients suffer from panic disorder. They report 7 times more physician visits and twice as many lost work days as the general population. Panic disorder results in a chronic state of preparedness that promotes hyperventilation.
	• Depression: There is increased prevalence of depression among asthma patients. Depressed asthma patients are 3 times more likely to be noncompliant with regard to medical treatment. Panic and depression may elicit respiratory effects that replicate asthma exacerbations.
Prognosis	With proper treatment and treatment compliance, nearly all people who suffer from asthma can become symptom free.

2. Biopsychosocial Assessment

Patient profile	From interview and observation and Revised Illness Perception Questionnaire (IPQ-R; Moss-Morris et al., 2002), assess the following:
	• IPQ-R factors, especially illness perceptions, explanations, and treatment expectations;
	• severity of symptoms and functional impact;
	• capacity, previous change efforts, and readiness for change; and
	• personality style or disorder and family and cultural factors.
Illness profile	Identify higher risk asthma patients:
	• those with life-threatening asthma or frequent flares, especially those failing to perceive symptoms as they develop;
	• those with emotional- or stress-induced asthma;
	• those with psychiatric comorbidities such as anxiety, panic disorder, and depression;
	• those with unstable or dysfunctional family situations;
	• those with noncompliance or difficulty using home peak-flow monitoring; and
	• those with noncompliance or difficulty using an inhaler.
Laboratory tests	Forced expiratory volume in the first second (FEV_1), the standard measure of respiratory functioning.
Asthma symptom diary	Review patient's diary of symptoms, triggers, time of day, severity, and emotions.

3. Intervention Planning

Patient and illness profiles	Illness representation: plan for modifying treatment-interfering representations, if applicable.
Disease/illness type goals	• Symptom perception training: Because severe asthma attacks can be life threatening, initial focus should be on increasing perceptual accuracy of airway changes, that is, symptom perception training, and proper use and compliance with inhalers and medications. Then focus can shift to improving self-efficacy and family functioning and decreasing comorbidities.
	• Functional capacity: With self-management a key component of patient success, emphasis should be on patient education and adherence to increase functionality.

(continues)

4. Intervention Implementation	
Psychoeducational interventions	Asthma education is correlated with improved clinical outcomes. Education programs increase knowledge but do not appear to decrease morbidity.
Symptom perception training	Training to more accurately perceive airway changes, which reduces the likelihood of fatal consequences and emergency room visits; uses peak-flow monitoring.
Relaxation interventions	Because strong emotions lead to respiratory difficulty, relaxation reduces extreme anxiety and prevents asthma exacerbation.
Written emotional expression exercises	Disclosing psychologically traumatic experiences through writing can result in lower FEV_1.
Cognitive–behavioral therapy (CBT)	Individual: Beneficial in modifying treatment-interfering behaviors and cognitions, particularly illness representations. Group: Groups that included asthma education, muscle relaxation, behavioral techniques, cognitive restructuring, and coping skills significantly benefited asthma patients. CBT groups also showed improvement in panic symptoms of patients with asthma.
Medication	Standard treatment focuses on (a) medications to control inflammation and prevent chronic symptoms (anti-inflammatories), (b) medications to treat asthma attacks when they occur (bronchodilators), (c) avoiding asthma triggers, and (d) monitoring peak flows.
Combined treatment	Combined or integrated asthma treatment includes all four of the conventional medical treatment targets plus lifestyle modification and psychoeducation. At a minimum it includes monitoring daily asthma symptoms in an asthma diary and avoiding both physical and psychological asthma triggers.

5. Intervention Monitoring

- Review patient's asthma symptom diary.
- Track FEV_1 lab values in patient's chart.
- Track session-to-session progress with regard to compliance, symptom reduction, and functionality.

CASE OF PATTY R.

Patty R. is a 24-year-old recently divorced woman with a 9-year history of asthma. The divorce was painful, and her asthma worsened. Currently, she is living alone and "not seriously dating anyone." Six months before, after a few years of college, she decided to "dump academics and do something real." Soon afterward, she convinced her younger sister to become her business partner and open a floral shop in a upscale suburban mall. Patty found that being a small business owner was exhilarating, and she "adored" working with wealthy customers. The only problem seemed to be exposure to pollen and various other allergens in the shop. Needless to say, she quickly found she had hay fever, and this allergic condition complicated her asthma and led on two occasions to full-blown asthma attacks and emergency treatment at a local hospital. Prior to this time, her asthma was reasonably well controlled on medication and an inhaler, but now it was poorly controlled. Her internist, Robert Westerman, proceeded to prescribe medications to control her allergies, but Patty did not like the side effects. She was referred to an allergist who suggested a desensitization treatment, but Patty balked at the prospect of "being stuck with needles every week for years and years." Patty was now missing 2 to 3 days of work a week, and her sister was feeling the burden of running a new business without a partner. Not sure how to proceed, Westerman referred her to his colleague, Janet Walters, a psychologist specializing in chronic respiratory illnesses, to deal with Patty's much more challenging chronic health condition.

Walters undertook a biopsychosocial assessment that included the IPQ-R, and on the basis of this assessment began working on engaging Patty in a tailored treatment process. She noted that Patty was only partially accepting of her medical condition, that she rated the consequences or impact of her asthma and allergies as only minimal, and believed that she only had pretty good control over her symptoms. Patty's view of the causality of her asthma was that it was "just hereditary," and she did not make any connection to stress. In short, although her internist assessed her asthma–allergy condition as severe, Patty downplayed this, suggestive of illness denial. Patty reported that she had begun smoking at age 14, and it appears that it somehow triggered her first asthma attacks. This was diagnosed by her pediatrician, who advised her to stop smoking; on the positive side, she did so on her own. Patty admitted that her pediatrician was "gorgeous and I had a crush on him for years when I was a teen." This change effort success was duly noted by Walters. Personality-wise, a high need for attention and some other histrionic features were observed. Cultural factors did not seem operative, but it did appear that symptom exacerbation was linked to relational stressors. Divorce issues; "men problems"; and conflicts with her mother and with her business partner, her younger sister, also appeared to be exacerbants.

When queried about her health behaviors, Patty admitted that she had never really gotten the hang of using her inhaler effectively and thought it was a bother to carry around with her and that she had never disclosed this to Westerman. Although Patty's asthma was occasionally induced by stress and allergens and her internist did not consider this life threatening, it nevertheless was problematic. Accordingly, illness denial, some problematic illness representations, and noncompliance with her inhaler became main treatment targets. An equally important target was relational distress. The fact that Patty had a previous success at a lifestyle change effort (i.e., quitting smoking) and was able to easily engage with both individual and group sessions suggested a good prognosis would be moderate to high for this therapy.

Intervention consisted of individual CBT sessions focused on increasing illness acceptance and modifying her illness representations. They also processed residual relational issues from her divorce and current relational issues with male companions, her sister, and her mother. Aware of how her histrionic dynamics could interfere with treatment, Walters framed her feedback to engender her collaboration. Patty also participated in one of her CBT groups that focused on symptom perception training, psychoeducation, and relaxation and mindfulness. That Patty was able to keep a diary of symptoms and triggers and learn—in a group session—to use an inhaler effectively suggested that she was sufficiently engaged in the treatment process. Within 4 months, Patty's condition was stabilized, and a plan for quarterly follow-up was made.

9

CANCER

Cancer, or *malignancy*, refers to any of the more than 100 diseases characterized by excessive, uncontrolled growth of abnormal cells that invade and destroy other adjacent tissues and can *metastasize*, that is, spread to other regions of the body. Cancer can develop in any tissue of any organ at any age. Early symptoms include fatigue, weight loss, fevers and night sweats, cough, bloody stools or change in bowel habits, and persistent pain.

Various factors appear to influence type and prevalence of cancer. These include gender, geography, and ethnicity, to name a few. So where prostate cancer, lung cancer, and colon cancer are more common in American men, breast cancer, lung cancer, and colon cancer are more common in American women. Certain cancers are more common in particular geographic areas. For example, although gastric cancer is very common in Japan, it is relatively rare in the United States. This difference suggests that diet may play a significant role in cancer prevalence.

This chapter describes information and research data on cancer and its treatment. It then selectively summarizes information relevant to making decisions about the psychological treatment of cancer in an integrative protocol, and then illustrates the use of this protocol with a case example.

EPIDEMIOLOGY

Cancer is the second leading cause of death and causes 25% of all deaths, an estimated 550,000 U.S. deaths in 2000 (American Cancer Society, 2005). Each year, more than 1.2 million Americans are diagnosed with cancer. It is estimated that 8.4 million Americans alive today have a history of cancer and that about 1,200 people die from cancer each day. In 2006, 1.4 million people were expected to be newly diagnosed with cancer, with 564,830 cancer deaths estimated for Americans (American Cancer Society, 2007). Because survival rates are rising, the number of people surviving cancer is increasing, creating a significant population of cancer survivors—those who have finished treatment and those who are currently undergoing treatment. Approximately 10.1 million Americans with a history of cancer were alive in January 2002, and approximately 64% of adults diagnosed with cancer today will be alive in 5 years (American Cancer Society, 2005). It has been estimated that the overall cost to the U.S. economy for cancer in 2005 was $209.8 billion.

TYPES

Each body organ is composed of different types of tissue, and most cancers arise in one of three main types—epithelial, connective, or blood-forming tissue. *Carcinomas* are cancers that occur in epithelial tissues and account for approximately 90% of human cancers. *Sarcomas*, which account for less than 2% of all cancers, originate in connective tissues. *Leukemias* develop in blood cells, and *lymphomas* originate in the lymphatic system. Combined, these cancers account for the remaining 8%.

Cancers are further identified according to the type of cell affected. Cancers that originate from *squamous* cells, that is, flat, scale-like cells found in epithelial tissue, are called *squamous cell carcinomas*. *Adenomatous* cells are glandular or ductal cells, and carcinomas that originate in these cells are called *adenocarcinomas*. Furthermore, sarcomas that develop in fat cells are called *liposarcomas*, whereas those that develop in bone cells are called *osteosarcomas*.

SEVERITY

The severity of cancer is specified by grade and by stage. Because staging varies from cancer to cancer, the staging of prostate cancer is illustrated here.

Grading

Grade, called a *Gleason grade*, indicates how different the cancer cells are from normal cells. Gleason grade ranges from 1 (low) to 5 (high). Low

Gleason grades and scores generally indicate slow-growing cancer. High grades and scores indicate a cancer that is likely to grow aggressively.

Staging

Staging is the assessment of the size and location of the cancer; it is used to plan appropriate treatment. There are two different systems used to stage prostate cancer. In the more traditional A-D staging, Stage A is considered to be early cancer because the tumor is located within the prostate gland and is not felt during a digital rectal exam (DRE). In Stage B, the tumor is considered to be within the prostate and can be felt during a DRE. In Stage C, the tumor has spread outside the prostate to some surrounding areas but not to lymph nodes or other organs. In Stage D, the cancer has spread or metastasized to nearby lymph nodes and to distant sites. The newer tumor, nodes, and metastases (TNM) staging takes into consideration tumor stage (T) and whether the cancer has spread to lymph nodes (N) and metastasized (M) to distant sites in the body. Tumor stage is assessed on a scale of 1 to 4. Tumors graded T1 are confined to the prostate gland but are so small that they cannot be felt during a DRE or detected during ultrasound. T2 prostate cancer is confined to the prostate, but it is large enough to be detected during a DRE. T3 and T4 prostate cancers have expanded beyond the prostate into surrounding tissues. Lymph node involvement is graded on a scale of 0 to 3. N0 (N zero) means that the cancer has not spread into the lymph nodes. The cancer is considered N1, N2, or N3, depending on the number and size of lymph nodes involved. Metastasis is rated 0 or 1. M0 (M zero) means no metastasis has occurred; M1 indicates metastasis to a distant location.

GENDER AND ETHNICITY

Gender

Over the course of a lifetime, men are reported to have a 1 in 2 chance of being diagnosed with cancer, whereas the rate for women is estimated to be 1 in 3 (American Cancer Society, 2005). Van't Spijker, Trijsburg, and Duivenvoorden (1997) found that in studies of women with cancer, the participants reported less depression and anxiety than participants in studies of both men and women or only men. Further, younger patients had higher rates of depression, anxiety, and overall psychological distress than older patients, possibly because of the unexpectedness of this severe illness so early in the life cycle. The meta-analysis by Rehse and Pukrop (2003) of 37 randomized controlled trials (RCTs) on the effects of psychosocial interventions on the quality of life of cancer patients found that men benefited from intervention more than women, and they speculated that this was due to women typically being more "psychologically adjusted" and being more comfortable seeking social support (Rehse & Pukrop, 2003, p. 183). They also theorized that it is acceptable in Western culture for women to ask for help but less so for men.

Ethnicity

Ethnicity can influence not only the incidence and severity of cancer but also treatment utilization, treatment compliance, and response to treatment (De La Cancela, Jenkins, & Chin, 1998). Although breast cancer incidence is somewhat lower among African American women than among Caucasian women in the United States, breast cancer mortality is consistently higher among African Americans. This is due largely to the fact that African American women are often diagnosed at a later stage of the disease. Demographic and socioeconomic factors are predictors of advanced stage of the disease at time of diagnosis among African Americans. These include having low income, never having been married, having no private health insurance, delaying seeing a physician because of money, or lacking transportation. In addition, cultural beliefs predict an advanced stage at diagnosis. These cultural factors involve health care utilization, folk beliefs, fundamentalist religious beliefs, relationships with men, perceived risk or fatalism, belief in various treatments for breast cancer, and breast cancer knowledge. Not having a regular physician or seeing a physician once a year or less is highly associated with advanced breast cancer (American Cancer Society, 2005).

CAUSAL FACTORS

Researchers from Columbia University School of Public Health reported that 95% of cancer is caused by diet and environment (Perera, 1997). As with other chronic diseases in which individuals' lifestyle choices interact with their genes, cancer is in large part a controllable disease. In fact, most cancers are potentially curable if detected at an early stage. By performing self-examinations, individuals can help recognize early signs of some cancers. Diagnostic testing and therapy are essential for optimal results. When cure or reasonable management is likely, physicians should discuss all therapeutic options. Reducing the incidence of cancer requires that the behavioral and environmental factors that increase cancer risk are addressed and that screening and health counseling services are made available and accessible in the cancer's early, most treatable stages.

PSYCHIATRIC COMORBIDITIES

Individuals with cancer can demonstrate a range of emotional distress and diagnosable psychiatric disorders that can and do interfere with quality of life and treatment outcomes (Rodrigue, Behen, & Tumlin, 1994). The prevalence of these comorbidities is high. On the basis of *Diagnostic and Statistical Manual of Mental Disorders* (3rd ed.; *DSM–III*; American Psychiatric Association, 1980) diagnostic criteria, 47% of cancer patients who were evaluated with a psychiatric interview and standardized psychological tests received a *DSM–III* diagnosis. Of these, 44% were diagnosed with clinical syndrome (Axis I) and 3% with personality disorders (Axis II). Approximately 68% of the diagnoses were adjustment disorders, and 13% were diagnosed as major depressive disorders. The remaining diagnoses were split among organic mental disorders (8%), personality disorders (7%), and anxiety disorders (4%). Some 85% of cancer patients with a psychiatric condition were experiencing a disorder with depression or anxiety as the central symptom. The majority of conditions were judged as highly treatable disorders (Derogatis et al., 1983).

Some individuals with cancer demonstrate cognitive and behavioral coping responses to cancer rather than distress and poor psychological adjustment (Jarrett, Ramirez, Richards, & Weinman, 1992). Research on psychological coping found that cancer patients who reported high levels of optimism and self-esteem experienced less psychological distress and better coping than those with low levels (Stiegelis et al., 2003). However, as cancer advances and death is imminent, active coping is nearly futile (Brennan, 2001).

PROGNOSIS

In cancer, prognosis is estimated by several factors, including stage of the disease, age, general health, and response to treatment. Survival rates indicate the percentage of those with a certain type and stage of cancer who survive the disease for a specific period of time after diagnosis. Survival rates in the United States for all cancers during the period 1992 through 1999 were as follows: 64% of Caucasians and 53% of African Americans survived 5 years; the overall 5-year survival rate for all cancers was 63% (American Cancer Society, 2007).

TREATMENT INTERVENTIONS

Successful treatment of cancer requires an elimination of all cancer cells, whether from the primary site, adjacent areas, or metastases to other regions of the body. In addition to medical treatments, the value of psychological intervention is well-documented in adults with cancer. Generally speaking, group interventions continue to prove as effective as individual, if not more so, highlighting the importance of social support. The length of treatment issue remains unresolved, but the client–therapist relationship is consistently an important factor.

An Institute of Medicine report entitled "Cancer Care for the Whole Patient: Meeting Psychosocial Health Needs" recommended specific actions that health care clinicians, health plans, policymakers, and others should take to achieve this a standard of health care: that psychosocial factors must be included in comprehensive care (Tucker, 2008). Clinicians are directed to identify a patient's psychosocial needs at the initial visit, link such needs with psychosocial services, and then integrate that aspect of care into the overall treatment plan.

Although cognitive–behavioral therapy (CBT) remains tried and true, psychoeducational interventions for environmental and lifestyle modification and a host of psychotherapeutic treatments also are reportedly effective. Because of the progressive nature and course of many forms of cancer, multimodal and combination therapies are commonly practiced. Many of these noteworthy approaches with a research base are reported in the following sections.

Illness Representations

Illness representations in cancer tend to be sensitive predictors of treatment compliance, treatment outcomes, and well-being. For example, in a prospective study of breast cancer patients, illness representations—as measured by the Illness Perception Questionnaire (IPQ; Weinman, Petrie, Moss-Morris, & Horne, 1996)—were assessed. Patients' beliefs about the impact or consequences of their cancer symptoms and duration of their illness predicted their psychological morbidity after 1 year of treatment. In other words, those with chronically high distress had a year earlier indicated their negative perceptions and beliefs about their illness on the IPQ (Millar, Purushotham, McLatchie, George, & Murray, 2005).

Another prospective study assessed illness representations in cancer patients. This study looked at the role of illness beliefs and perceptions in the decision to participate in a support group for women with breast cancer. Logistic regression analysis showed that support group participation was predicted by stronger beliefs that cancer was caused by altered immunity, higher cancer-related distress, and lower avoidance tendencies. A noteworthy recommendation of this study is that support programs would do well to tailor their focus on resolving cancer-related distress rather than general anxiety or depression (Cameron et al., 2005). Similarly, a study of illness perceptions in women with increased risk of breast cancer showed significantly higher levels of cancer-specific distress than those in the comparison group (Rees, Fry, Cull, & Sutton, 2004).

Diagnosis and Screening

Typical early symptoms of cancer include fatigue, weight loss, fevers and nights sweats, cough, bloody stools or change in bowel habits, and persistent pain. Necessary to early diagnosis of cancer is a complete history and physical examination. The purpose of cancer screening and early diagnosis is to decrease cancer mortality, to allow the use of less radical therapies, and to reduce financial cost. Common screening procedures include the Pap smear for cervical cancer, breast examination and mammography for breast cancer, and the prostate specific antigen blood test and DRE for prostate cancer.

LIFESTYLE MODIFICATION

Researchers estimate that more than 60% of cancer deaths in the United States are preventable through lifestyle modification. Although there is no certain way to avoid all cancers, reducing individual risk factors significantly decreases the likelihood of contracting many forms of this devastating disease.

Smoking Cessation

The American Cancer Society (2005) has estimated that smoking causes nearly 30% of all cancer deaths in the United States, that is, approximately 166,000 cancer deaths each year. In short, all cancer deaths caused by cigarette smoking could be prevented completely by not smoking and not using smokeless tobacco. For those who already smoke, quitting will reduce the risk of developing cancer. Studies have shown that after about 10 years of not smoking, a former smoker's risk lowers to that of a nonsmoker.

Diet Modification

Next to quitting smoking, eating a healthy diet is considered an effective means of lowering cancer risk. Specific foods, that is, cauliflower; cabbage; tomatoes; soy products; and foods high in vitamins A, C, and E appear to protect against cancer. In addition, antioxidants, such as those contained in green tea, offer protection from carcinogens. Diet recommendations usually include limiting amounts of red meat, sugar, saturated animal fat, and salt (American Cancer Society, 2005).

Exercise

Low levels of physical activity have been implicated in colon cancer. Moderate activity for 30 minutes a day enhances the immune system, shortens the time food takes to move through the intestines, and alters body composition and hormone levels. Physical activity also helps avoid obesity, which is associated with an increased risk for cancers of the colon and rectum, prostate, breast, endometrium, and kidney. By maintaining a healthy weight through regular physical activity and a healthy diet, individuals can substantially lower their risk for these cancers (American Cancer Society, 2005).

Environmental Modification

Protecting the skin from the sun's rays could prevent about 80% of all skin cancers. Other modifications include drinking purified water; washing pesticides from fruits and vegetables; and reducing exposure to radiation, especially from electronic appliances such as microwaves, computer screens, and televisions. Practicing safe sex can also reduce cancer risk.

PSYCHOEDUCATIONAL INTERVENTIONS

Psychoeducational interventions are commonly used with cancer patients, and group interventions are the most studied (Monti et al., 2006). Meyer and Mark (1995) performed a meta-analysis of 62 studies of cancer patients, comparing treatment and control groups for psychosocial, behavioral, and psychoeducational interventions. Their meta-analysis on the effectiveness of psychosocial interventions for patients with cancer revealed small to moderate effect sizes for five dependent measures: emotional adjustment; functional adjustment; physical symptoms related to disease or treatment; medical outcomes; and global outcomes, which include combinations of the other four. Only the medical outcomes category proved to be statistically nonsignificant. Nevertheless, they did not find differential effectiveness for different kinds of interventions. Meta-analyses of the effect of psychological intervention on anxiety and depression found that preventative interventions had a significant effect on anxiety but not on depression (Sheard & Maguire, 1999)

Relaxation Training

The results of the meta-analysis by Luebbert, Dahme, and Hasenbring (2001) of 15 studies revealed that relaxation training significantly improved patients' depression, anxiety, and hostility.

Group-Based Cognitive–Behavioral Stress Management

A recent study conducted and evaluated research on group-based psychosocial interventions that were designed to improve quality of life in patients with prostate cancer (Penedo et al., 2006). The study found that the interventions increased quality of life and also improved personal growth and sense of meaning and enhanced interpersonal relationships. The researchers attributed this to cognitive restructuring, social support, and disclosure that led to development of a cohesive narrative. Antoni et al. (2001) researched the effectiveness of cognitive–behavioral stress management on depression and benefit finding on women with breast cancer. They found that their 10-week group intervention resulted in reduced depression and increased both general optimism and benefit finding. This finding remained significant even at 3-month follow-up. Meta-analyses found that group therapy with cancer patients was at least as effective as individual therapy (Sheard & Maguire, 1999).

Mindfulness-Based Stress Reduction

Mindfulness-based stress reduction (MBSR) is used widely with those with chronic illness who are distressed and/or having limited response to treatment. J. Smith, Richardson, Hoffman, and Pilkington (2005) reported a systematic review on the use of MBSR in cancer. They reviewed three RCTs and seven uncontrolled studies. Their analysis indicated that the intervention was linked to mood improvement, quality of sleep, and stress reduction. Furthermore, they noted that the effect was dose dependent.

Mindfulness-Based Art Therapy

A variant of MBSR is mindfulness-based art therapy (MBAT). An RCT evaluated the effectiveness of MBAT for women with cancer. It was found that women who participated in this intervention demonstrated significant decreases in markers of distress, such as anxiety and depression, and improvement in measures of mental health, general health, and social functioning. These MBAT effects appear to be diagnosis specific (Monti et al., 2006).

COGNITIVE–BEHAVIORAL THERAPY

As with most other chronic medical conditions, CBT has become a cornerstone of treatment. Research has shown a clear benefit from the use of CBT for patients with cancer (Monti et al., 2006). A main focus of CBT is in helping cancer patients modify treatment-interfering illness representations. Because fear and anxiety are commonplace, CBT interventions can be effective in enabling cancer patients to maintain control and manage the pervasive uncertainty in their lives, address avoidance issues, and ensure the most supportive environment possible (White, 2001). Some caution in choice of techniques is indicated. For example, although cognitive reframing can be useful with irrational beliefs about one's health status in the early stages of the disease, it can be problematic in advanced stages (Carlick & Biley, 2004). With such patients, especially those who tend to catastrophize, verbal reattribution is indicated (White, 2001).

OTHER PSYCHOTHERAPEUTIC INTERVENTIONS

A number of psychotherapeutic approaches have been used in the treatment of cancer. Three of these are solution-focused therapy, existential therapy, and narrative expressive therapy. They are described briefly in the following sections.

Solution-Focused Therapy

Solution-focused therapy is one of the most commonly practiced therapeutic approaches in mental health settings. It may well have promise in health-focused counseling with certain modifications. For instance, the use of the "miracle question" with cancer patients can be problematic: "Suppose you go to sleep tonight, a miracle happens, and your problems are solved. What will be different to let you know a miracle happened?" Because most cancer patients focus on the disease as the source of their problem, it is probably better to avoid the word *miracle* and focus on "the problems that brought you to counseling" (Neilson-Clayton & Brownlee, 2002, p. 6). Neilson-Clayton and Brownlee (2002) also suggested the use of coping questions to elicit exceptions from clients with regard to cancer patients because the circumstances tend to seem insurmountable. Coping questions focus on intensity—when could the problem be seen as less severe, frequent, or intense? Finally, they advocated for use of the question, "How have you kept yourself from giving up altogether?"(pp. 9–10). Their approaches should be validated empirically but may be of clinical value to psychotherapists working with cancer patients.

Existential Therapy

Because the ability to find new meaning following the diagnosis of cancer has been correlated with psychological adjustment, existential therapies have emerged in the treatment of cancer. An RCT by Lee, Cohen, Edgar, Laizner, and Gagnon (2006) found that breast and colorectal cancer patients receiving existential therapy had significant increases in self-esteem, optimism, and self-efficacy.

Narrative Expressive Therapy

Regaining a sense of coherence is beneficial to cancer patients and is created through life narratives that give meaning to the experience of cancer in their lives (Eriksson & Lindstrom, 2005; McAdams, 1993). Petersen, Bull, Propst, Dettinger, and Detwiler (2005) described an intervention approach for cancer patients based on narrative–expressive therapy to address underlying stress and to prevent posttraumatic stress disorder because this disorder is not uncommon in cancer patients. The purpose is to promote coherence, meaning making, and adaptation while also connecting patients with others.

This intervention is targeted for long-term stress and prevention of posttraumatic stress disorder in seriously ill cancer patients (Petersen et al., 2005).

Hypnotherapy

Hypnotherapy has long been used in patients with chronic illness to control various symptoms, including procedural pain. Considerable research has demonstrated the efficacy of hypnosis in controlling anxiety, pain, nausea, and vomiting in cancer patients (Genuis, 1995). When applied to procedural pain, hypnosis is typically induced by eye fixation, passive muscle relaxation, and deepening procedures (strategies for inducing a greater level of relaxation and the hypnotic state). Then patients are verbally led through a sequence of events leading up to and following the prescribed medical treatment. Resultant symptoms such as nausea or anxiety are then cue controlled by hypnotic suggestion (E. E. Taylor & Ingleton, 2003).

MEDICAL TREATMENT

The major medical modalities of treatment are surgery, radiation, and chemotherapy. Other methods include endocrine therapy for selected cancers such as breast, prostate, or liver cancer; immunotherapies; and multimodal therapy, which combines the assets of two or more of these modalities. Irrespective of the specific medical treatment offered, patients with cancer that is unlikely to be cured need to be adequately informed about the expected outcomes of particular treatments as well as the expected side effects of each. Intensive care may be needed for treatment-related complications. A discussion of surgery and radiation is beyond the scope of this chapter.

Chemotherapy is a form of cancer treatment in which drugs are used to destroy cancer cells. Chemotherapy works by inhibiting cancer cells from multiplying. In the process, healthy cells can also be harmed, especially those that divide quickly. It is this damage to healthy cells that accounts for chemotherapy drugs' side effects. Fortunately, some of these cells usually repair themselves after chemotherapy. Because some drugs work better in combination than alone, two or more drugs are often given at the same time (i.e., *multimodal therapy*). Other drugs may be used, such as endocrine therapy for selected cancers such as breast, prostate, or liver cancer. Adjunctive treatments, such as biological therapy or immunotherapies, can be used to boost the body's immune system against cancer and help repair or make new cells destroyed by chemotherapy.

COMBINED TREATMENT

Combined treatment appears to be the standard of care in cancer treatment today. From a medical treatment perspective, this typically involves the medical treatments of chemotherapy, radiation, and surgery as well as lifestyle and environmental modification. More recently, it has also included various psychological interventions. Often two or more psychological treatments are part of the regimen. Multimodal approaches were found to be more effective than medical treatment alone in a meta-analysis of 37 RCTs by Rehse and Pukrop (2003). A minimum of 12 weeks of intervention was needed for long-term effect, which the authors attributed to therapist effect and a strong therapeutic bond. The strongest effect was for structured short-term educational programs. Two combined treatment approaches are described here.

Combined Hypnotherapy and Cognitive–Behavioral Therapy

E. E. Taylor and Ingleton (2003) reported on their investigation of cancer patients in a program of hypnotherapy—including guided imagery—and CBT. After 12 sessions, patients reported increased coping, more confidence, less distress, and fewer side effects. The patients noted that CBT was valuable for helping them clarify their thoughts and behave more adaptively and that the hypnotherapy aided them in relaxing, sleeping, and coping. Finally, the guided imagery was credited with reduction of fear and side effects.

Behavioral Intervention for Cancer Treatment Side Effects

Cancer patients commonly experience the side effects of surgery and chemotherapy. Psychological treatment methods can provide some relief from such side effects. Redd, Montgomery, and DuHamel (2001) reported that multimodal approaches, that is, CBT, hypnotherapy, and adjunctive behavioral interventions, are most effective in dealing with anxiety and distress experienced as a result of cancer treatment. They also reported that hypnosis proved the most effective with procedural pain. Although CBT was just as effective with the reported pain, it did not mitigate anticipatory anxiety. Behavioral interventions were effective with anticipatory nausea and vomiting but not with postchemotherapy nausea and vomiting.

Integrative Treatment Protocol: Cancer

1. Key Background Information	
Pathology	Diseases characterized by excessive, uncontrolled growth of abnormal cells that invade and destroy other adjacent tissues and metastasize to other regions of the body.
Epidemiology	Second leading cause of death among U.S. adults (25% of all deaths). About 8.4 million people in the United States have a history of cancer, and some 1,200 die from cancer each day.
Severity	Specified by grade (Gleason 1–5) and by stage (A–D or tumors, nodes, and metastases [TNM]).
Causal factors	95% of cancers are reportedly caused by diet and environment.

Gender and ethnicity	Men appear to benefit more from psychological treatment of cancer than women. Ethnic factors influence the incidence and severity of cancer, treatment utilization, compliance, and response to treatment and can predict an advanced stage of the disease at diagnosis.
Psychiatric comorbidities	Comorbidity is high in adjustment disorders (68%), major depressive disorder (13%), organic mental disorders (8%), personality disorders (7%), and anxiety disorders (4%). Depression or anxiety as the central symptom: 85%. High optimism and self-esteem were linked to less psychological distress and better coping.
Prognosis	Five-year survival rates in the United States for all cancers during 1992 through 1999 were 63%.

2. Biopsychosocial Assessment

Patient profile	Use interview, observation, and Revised Illness Perception Questionnaire (IPQ-R; Moss-Morris et al., 2002) to assess the following: • IPQ-R factors (illness perceptions, explanations, treatment expectations); • severity of symptoms, functional impact of symptoms, and illness phase; • capacity, previous change efforts, and readiness for change; and • personality style or disorder and family and cultural factors.
Illness profile	Identify higher risk cancer patients: • younger patients; • those with high cancer-related distress, advanced disease, and/or severe pain; • those with significant and interfering treatment side effects; • those exhibiting or complaining of depression or anxiety; and • those exhibiting pessimism and low self-esteem.
Treatment diary	Patient records daily symptoms, optimism level, functional level, energy level, and success and challenges in self-management.

3. Intervention Planning

Illness profile	Plan for modifying problematic representations, if applicable.
Severity	Consider the grading and staging of the cancer in planning treatment.
Comorbidities	Consider the level and impact of anxiety, depression, headache, and treatment side effects.

4. Intervention Implementation

Psychoeducational interventions	Most common with cancer patients: • Group: as effective as individual, and can positively impact emotional adjustment, functional adjustment, physical symptoms related to disease or treatment, and medical outcomes. • Behavioral: effective with anticipatory nausea and vomiting.

(continues)

	• Relaxation: helpful with stress, anxiety, and depression. • Mindfulness: useful for anxiety; men seem to benefit from these interventions more than women.
Lifestyle and environmental modification	Focus on reducing risk of cancer with smoking cessation, diet modification, exercise, limited alcohol use, sun protection, reducing radiation exposure, and practicing safe sex.
Cognitive–behavioral therapy (CBT)	Effective in cancer treatment, particularly in modifying problematic illness representations, removing treatment barriers, improving compliance, and improving self-management and interpersonal relations.
Other psychotherapeutic interventions	• Solution-focused therapy: Modify wording of the "miracle question" and focus on "the problems that brought you to counseling." Use coping questions to elicit exceptions and focus on intensity: "When could the problem be seen as less severe, frequent, or intense?" • Existential therapy: Useful in helping patients find new meaning in being diagnosed. • Narrative expressive therapy: Can decrease underlying stress and promote coherence, meaning making, and adaptation. • Hypnotherapy: Useful in controlling various symptoms, including procedural pain. Induce trance, deepen, and then cue control by hypnotic suggestion.
Medical treatment	Main modalities are surgery, radiation, and chemotherapy.
Medication	Chemotherapy and various adjunctive drug treatments such as endocrine therapy, immunotherapy, or biological therapy.
Combined treatment	Combining one or more medical treatments with one or more psychological treatments. Side effects of chemotherapy can be treated with guided imagery combined with CBT and other behavioral interventions. The more aggressive or advanced the disease, the more likely a combined strategy will be used.

5. Intervention Monitoring

- Review patient's diary of symptoms and functional impairment.
- Track session-to-session progress with regard to compliance, symptom reduction, and functionality.

CASE OF BILL J.

Bill J. is a 69-year-old retired and widowed White man who was diagnosed with a particularly aggressive form of prostate cancer (Gleason 4; T = 3, N = 3, M = 1) 18 months ago. He had been a senior vice president of operations for a large bank until 6 months ago, when pain and treatment side effects forced him to retire. His wife died 3 years ago of breast cancer after a heroic struggle, and he continues to grieve her loss. For the past 8 months, he has experienced considerable pain and side effects from his cancer and chemotherapy treatments. Over the past year, his oncologist has tried him on a number of conventional and experimental chemotherapy protocols, which either are effective and have serious side effects or are ineffective and have no side effects.

Because the oncologist cannot offer him relief from the pain and side effects, he refers Bill to Evan Jackson, a psychotherapist with considerable experience working with cancer patients. In their initial evaluation meeting, Jackson does a complete biopsychosocial evaluation. As part of this, he elicits Bill's illness representations.

He finds that Bill believes that his timeline is short, that his cancer is incurable, and that he has little control over it. It should be noted that these beliefs are consistent with that of his oncologist and the second and third medical opinions he has received. In short, his illness representations are realistic and appropriate.

Jackson worked collaboratively with Bill and identified four treatment targets: (a) to reduce pain and side effects of the chemotherapy, (b) to improve mood and sleep and reduce stress, (c) to deal with his depression and bereavement, and (d) to assist him in finding meaning and integration in his life with cancer. Jackson then proposed the following intervention plan. First, a multimodal approach consisting of CBT, hypnotherapy, and specific behavioral interventions would be used to reduce the anxiety and distress associated with the side effects of Bill's cancer treatment. Second, mindfulness-based stress reduction would be used to improve his mood and the quality of his sleep and to reduce stress. Third, he would provide a referral for medication evaluation (presuming an antidepressant will be prescribed for his depression, the plan would be to combine the medication with CBT for both depression and bereavement issues). Finally, narrative expressive therapy would be used to promote coherence, life meaning, spirituality, and wellness such that his experience of cancer can be better integrated into his life and family narrative. Bill was agreeable to it and treatment began in earnest.

10

CARDIAC DISEASE

Cardiac disease, also called *heart disease*, is a common term that refers to diseases and conditions affecting the heart and its vessels. *Cardiovascular disease* (CVD) is a technical term referring to a collection of diseases and conditions that can have widespread effects on patient health. It consists of two main types: diseases of the heart (*cardio*) and diseases of the blood vessels (*vascular*). Cardiac disease is the leading cause of death in adult men and women and is a major public health concern in the United States. Psychological intervention with cardiac conditions has long been associated with successful cardiac treatment.

The following sections present basic background on cardiac disease and illness followed by a detailed discussion of various psychological and biopsychosocial treatment intervention options. This discussion includes both clinical and research findings. The chapter concludes with an integrative treatment protocol and a case example illustrating the protocol.

EPIDEMIOLOGY

Coronary artery disease (CAD) is the most common type of cardiac disease. It is estimated to affect one in three adults in the United States and is the leading cause of death in both men and women. In 2003, nearly 500,000 deaths were attributed to CAD (American Heart Association, 2006). On the positive side, heart attack mortality rates in the United States have been declining over the past 10 years. Nevertheless, patients with chest pain account for nearly half of all referrals to cardiology clinics (Bass & Mayou, 1995).

TYPES OF CARDIAC DISEASE

Some of the more common cardiac diseases and conditions are briefly described.

Coronary Artery Disease

CAD occurs when coronary arteries, the vessels that supply blood to the heart muscle, become hardened and narrowed because of the buildup of cholesterol and other material, called *plaque*, on their inner walls. As the plaque increases in size, the insides of the coronary arteries get narrower, and less blood can flow through them. Eventually, blood flow to the heart muscle is reduced, and because blood carries much-needed oxygen, the heart muscle is not able to receive the amount of oxygen it needs. Reduced or cut-off blood flow and oxygen supply to the heart muscle can result in angina and myocardial infarction (MI).

Angina

Angina is chest pain or discomfort that occurs when the heart receives an insufficient supply of blood. It is a symptom of CAD rather than a separate disease entity. The three types of angina are stable, unstable, and variant or Prinzmetal's angina.

Myocardial Infarction

Also called *heart attack*, an MI happens when a blood clot develops at the site of plaque in a coronary artery and suddenly cuts off most or all blood supply to that part of the heart muscle. Cells in the heart muscle begin to die if they do not receive enough oxygen-rich blood. This can cause permanent damage to the heart muscle. Over time, CAD can weaken the heart muscle and contribute to heart failure or arrhythmias.

Heart Failure

Heart failure, commonly referred to as *congestive heart failure*, is a condition of ineffective heart pumping such that vital organs get insufficient blood, resulting in such signs and symptoms as shortness of breath, fluid retention, and fatigue. Congestive heart failure results when heart failure has led to fluid buildup in the body.

Arrhythmia

Arrhythmias are changes in the normal beating rhythm of the heart. Some arrhythmias are relatively benign, whereas others can be life threatening.

Coronary Heart Disease

Coronary heart disease (CHD) refers collectively to both diseases of the coronary arteries and their resulting complications, such as chest pain, MI, and scar tissue caused by an MI. Unlike CAD, which affects only the coronary arteries, CHD, like MI, affects the heart muscle.

Atherosclerosis and Arteriosclerosis

Atherosclerosis refers to hardening of the arteries, and *arteriosclerosis* refers to narrowing of the arteries, both caused by accumulation of plaques and other substances. This hardening and narrowing can result in chest pain or a heart attack.

Hypertension

Commonly known as *high blood pressure*, *hypertension* is the excessive force of blood pumping through blood vessels and is the most common form of CVD. It can cause stroke and heart failure. It is also one of the most preventable and treatable types of CVD. Chapter 14 of this volume focuses entirely on hypertension.

Stroke

A *stroke* is a sudden loss of brain function that occurs when blood flow to the brain is interrupted—*ischemic stroke*—or when blood vessels in the brain rupture—*hemorrhagic stroke*. This interruption of blood flow causes the death of brain cells and loss of function in the affected areas.

GENDER, AGE, AND ETHNICITY

Gender

For some time, it has been known that women's experience and reporting of symptoms of CAD and heart attacks are somewhat different than men's, sometimes leading to diagnostic delays. Several studies also have reported differences between men and women relating to cardiac treatment. Lemos, Suls, Jenson, Lounsbury, and Gordon's (2003) replication study indicated that traditional gender-stereotyped tasks were assumed earlier among female patients and without regard for resulting cardiac symptoms. Women reported that the inability to perform domestic tasks produced both distress and guilt (Lemos et al., 2003). In addition, research indicates that women who continue to perform strenuous gender-stereotyped tasks may be placed at greater cardiac risk (Lemos et al., 2003). The referral of patients to rehabilitation programs also appears to be influenced by gender. The overview study conducted by Sotile (2005) indicated that women were less likely to be referred to cardiac rehabilitation programs despite the existence of convincing evidence for potential patient benefit.

Age

The risks for CAD are known to increase with age. The case study investigated by Whooley (2006) found that aging also increases the risk for psychological illness such as depression, with CVD and major depression the two leading causes of disability worldwide. Age may also be a factor in the ability of the patient to participate in rehabilitation programs that can benefit quality of life (Sin et al., 2004).

Ethnicity

Diet, genetics, health beliefs, and behaviors are key considerations in both risk factors and the expression of cardiac disease among various ethnic groups. More than one quarter of Mexican Americans have some form of cardiac disease. Compared with other groups, African Americans appear to have the highest rates of cardiac disease, which includes CAD, stroke, high blood pressure, and heart failure. Those of South Asian descent are at high risk for cardiac disease, but those of Japanese descent are at low risk. Historically, Native Americans had very low incidence and prevalence of cardiac disease, but today cardiac disease is the leading cause of death in this group.

COMORBIDITY—MEDICAL

CVD remains a chief concern for population health, especially regarding the increased occurrence of diabetes, obesity, and stroke in the general population, known risk factors for CVD (American Heart Association, 2006).

COMORBIDITY—PSYCHIATRIC

Several comorbidities are associated with CVD. These include stress, anxiety, depression, and anger, which are common in cardiac patients and have been shown to negatively influence recovery from heart disease (Rozanski, Blumenthal, Davidson, Saab, & Kubzansky, 2005; Sotile, 2005). In addition, psychosocial risk factors such as high levels of hostility, social isolation, and chronic marital and family conflict can adversely affect patient adherence to treatment (Rozanski et al., 2005; Sotile, 2005).

Stress

Conflict in close relationships, stress, and coping with heart disease can hamper quality of life and physical functioning and be detrimental psychologically to CAD patients. A prospective study found that these psychosocial variables are closely associated during hospitalization for CAD and in follow-up periods (Brummett et al., 2004).

Anxiety

Studies have found that anxiety has a variable affect on cardiac patients. Hughes et al.'s (2004) prospective study found that anxiety was associated with younger patients, people with high cholesterol and triglyceride levels, ethnicity (White), and patients who were surgically managed with coronary artery bypass. The presence of social support was also associated with lower anxiety levels. The role of spirituality in ameliorating the effects of anxiety was also a subject of investigation. Religious practice was associated with a lower anxiety level in patients, but when the relationship of religious practice and social support was eliminated during analysis, it was the social support that mediated the effects of anxiety (Hughes et al., 2004).

Depression

Depression is a factor for one in five patients with coronary heart disease and one in three patients with congestive heart failure (Whooley, 2006). Depression has been revealed to have strong physical and emotional affects on cardiac patients (Suls & Bunde, 2005). The long-term effects of depression can cause deficits in patient vitality and emotional flexibility (Rozanski et al., 2005). Investigators used multi-orthogonal analyses to examine the separate and cumulative effects of such emotions on patient well-being (Kubzansky, Cole, Kawachi, Vokonas, & Sparrow, 2006). Meta-analysis demonstrated that patients with depression were less likely to adhere to treatment recommendations, and although some studies have demonstrated that depressed patients benefit from both pharmacological and physical therapies (Sotile, 2005; Suls & Bunde, 2005; Whooley, 2006), it is curious that meta-analyses have not demonstrated that alleviating patient psychological distress improves adherence to treatment (Rozanski et al., 2005). Rozanski et al. (2005) and Kubzansky et al. (2006) found that depressed patients manifest higher resting heart rates and diminished heart rate variability along with other autonomic nervous system dysfunctions. Depression was also associated with hypercortisolemia, which can cause the suppression of growth and reproductive hormones, and decreased bone mineralization. Hypercortisolemia can promote additional risk factors for cardiac patients by encouraging central obesity, insulin resistance, and diabetes (Rozanski et al., 2005).

Depression is also associated with increases in inflammatory proteins such as C-reactive protein, interleukin-6, and tumor necrosis factor (Rozanski et al., 2005). In addition, Rozanski et al. (2005) determined that the full spectrum of the pathophysiologic effects of depression has not been extensively investigated and requires further study.

Anger

The overlap between negative emotions such as anger, anxiety, and depression implies that patients with a disposition toward negativity may have an additional risk factor for adverse health outcomes (Suls & Bunde, 2005).

More specifically, anger, hostility, and attitudinal negativity are risk factors for negative health effects from cardiovascular reactivity, which is associated with increased risk for MI and the onset of angina symptoms (Sotile, 2005). Chen, Gilligan, Coups, and Contrada (2005) found that if the patient perceives a supportive social environment, there are moderating effects on cardiovascular reactivity. In addition, multiple-regression analysis indicated that the personality of the patient is interdependent with social environmental risk factors (Chen et al., 2005).

IMPLANTED CARDIOVERTER DEFIBRILLATOR

The physical effects of treatment methods can also influence a patient's psychological well-being. Sears, Kovacs, Azzarello, Larsen, and Conti (2004) found that patients with implanted cardioverter defibrillator (ICD) devices experienced high levels of anxiety, even panic, regarding the shock experience. These feelings came to dominate the patients' psychology, and as a result, the person's quality of life was affected (Sears et al., 2004).

SOCIAL FACTORS

The social context of cardiac patients plays an important role in their ability to recover and reduce additional risk factors. Spirituality has often been considered an important method of deriving social support for people with cardiac disease. However, research findings have emphasized social support as a more important mediator for reduced anxiety than religious practice alone (Hughes et al., 2004). The social aspects of organized religions may help to explain the beneficial effects for patients, distinct from clinical studies that separated religious practice and social support. Patient adherence to treatment recommendations can also be adversely influenced by a lack of effective social support. The results of the Normative Aging Study by Kubzansky et al. (2006) suggest that a strong inverse relationship between educational levels and negative emotion found in the study may also indicate the contribution of sociocultural factors to the promotion and maintenance of negative emotional states.

PROGNOSIS

One half of men and 63% of women who die of cardiac disease do not experience angina or other warning symptoms prior to their fatal attacks. Two thirds of patients who have suffered a first heart attack, however, do not take the necessary steps to prevent another. Estimates are that about 30% of fatal attacks and most subsequent surgeries could be avoided with healthy lifestyle changes and by compliance with medical treatments (American Heart Association, 2006). Clinical findings confirm differences in the prognosis for men and women with heart disease. It has been reported that women have a 56% greater risk for early mortality following an MI than men (Marrugat, Antó, Sala, & Masiá, 1994).

TREATMENT CONSIDERATIONS AND INTERVENTIONS

Patients with cardiac disease frequently have physical and psychological morbidity, and the quality of life of CAD patients is often hampered by concomitant feelings of depression, anxiety, anger, and stress. The psychological needs of cardiac patients can be addressed with a variety of treatments.

Cardiac rehabilitation, including psychosocial interventions, is increasingly recommended as beneficial to patients (Sotile, 2005). Evidence increasingly supports tailored interventions such as lifestyle change, exercise therapy, psychosocial treatments, and medication. In addition to cardiac medication, psychotropic drugs such as antidepressants and anxiolytics can improve clinical outcomes for patients with cardiac disease (Rozanski et al., 2005; Sears et al., 2004; Sin et al., 2004; Suls & Bunde, 2005).

Furthermore, cardiac patients require multiple levels of treatment, and patients appear to benefit from access to a variety of clinical professionals, including cardiologists, psychologists, physical therapists, and nurses. The biopsychosocial approach to cardiac rehabilitation has been studied extensively, and convincing evidence exists that incorporating multidisciplinary care would prove beneficial for both patients and physicians (Sotile, 2005).

Two key clinical considerations in planning treatment interventions with cardiac patients are cardiac rehabilitation programs and illness representations. Given the predictive value of illness representation measures such as the Illness Perception Questionnaire (Weinman, Petrie, Moss-Morris, & Horne, 1996) and the Revised Illness Perception Questionnaire (Moss-Morris et al., 2002) with regard to treatment compliance and success in cardiac rehabilitation programs, it is essential that such measures be routinely used with all cardiac patients.

Illness Representations

An individual's constellations of perceptions and beliefs about a particular disease—understanding of it and its symptoms, cause, time or illness duration, impact or consequences, curability, and ability to control it—is referred to as illness representation. Illness representations in cardiac disease tend to be sensitive predictors of treatment compliance, treatment outcomes, and well-being. Research with cardiac patients indicates that illness representations predict the course of cardiac illness, self-efficacy, participation in a cardiac rehabilitation program and return to work, and treatment compliance.

In a study of illness representations and their correlates in CHD, men attributed the cause of their CHD more often to risk behaviors and their own attitudes and behaviors whereas women believed that stress was the cause of their CHD. Women also perceived more symptoms associated with CHD but reported less severe consequences. CHD severity was the most important illness representation. Stronger perceived competence was related to weaker illness identity, stronger control and cure, and less severe consequences (Aalto, Heijmans, Weinman, & Aro, 2005).

Another study assessed illness representations and self-efficacy in patients with CHD. A longitudinal design was adopted with predictor variables and dependent variables—general self-efficacy, diet self-efficacy, and exercise self-efficacy—and demographic and illness characteristic effects. These were measured in 300 patients while they were in the hospital and 9 months following discharge. Questionnaires measured four illness representation components (identity, consequences, timeline, and control/cure), outcome expectation for diet and exercise, and self-efficacy (general, diet, and exercise).

The same measures were collected 9 months later. Results showed that the relationship between illness representation components and self-efficacy changed over time and that consequence and timeline were significantly related to self-efficacy measures initially; however, symptom and control/cure were the variables that were significantly related to self-efficacy measures 9 months later. After statistically controlling for individuals' baseline self-efficacy measures, demographics, and illness characteristic effects, it was found that symptom and control and cure made significant contributions to exercise, diet, and self-efficacy, respectively, 9 months later. In short, this research found a significant relationship between illness representations and self-efficacy (Lau-Walker, 2006).

A third study examined whether cardiac patients' initial perceptions of their MI would predict subsequent attendance at a cardiac rehabilitation course, return to work, disability, and sexual dysfunction. The study found that when patients believed that their illness could be controlled or cured, it predicted their subsequent attendance at a cardiac rehabilitation. On the other hand, the belief that their illness would last a long time and have serious consequences was associated with a longer delay before returning to work. A strong illness identity was significantly related to greater sexual dysfunction at both 3 and 6 months (Petrie, Weinman, Sharpe, & Buckley, 1996). Finally, another study based on the premise that intentional noncompliance to prescribed treatment leads to poor clinical outcomes in heart failure patients examined the relationship between patients' and spouses' or partners' illness representations of the symptoms, cause, timeline, consequences, and control of heart failure and the patients' compliance behavior. Congruence between patients and spouses or partners in perceptions was investigated to determine if congruence or lack of congruence affected patients' adherence behavior. The Illness Perception Questionnaire and the Adherence Estimation Questionnaire (Fox, 2001) were used to determine illness representations and adherence estimation in a sample of 60 older adult heart failure patients and their spouses or partners. Patients' and spouses' or partners' perceptions of symptoms and the latter's perceptions of the timeline for heart failure were significantly related to patients' adherence behavior. The addition of the spouses' or partners' illness representations to the patients' illness representations explained 52% of the variance in patients' adherence behavior. A significant linear relationship was not found between the amount of congruence between patients and spouse's or partners and patients' adherence behavior. However, patient adherence increased when patients and spouses or partners were congruent in perceptions of control of heart failure (Fox, 2001).

Cardiac Rehabilitation

Cardiologists and other clinicians have a vital role in screening for psychological risk factors and in referring patients to appropriate specialists and cardiac rehabilitation programs, when indicated (Rozanski et al., 2005). Such programs have an important part to play in treatment for certain patients. There are existing facilities for the rehabilitation of cardiac patients in most states. In addition, 46 states have societies affiliated with the American Association of Cardiovascular and Pulmonary Rehabilitation to assist in locating facilities for specific patients (Sotile, 2005).

PSYCHOEDUCATIONAL INTERVENTIONS

Self-management interventions have been found to be beneficial in educating patients on the nature of cardiac disease, the types of rehabilitation available, medications to help address psychological conditions such as depression, cardiac technologies such as ICD, and exercise therapy (Sears et al., 2004). Patients should also be apprised of the importance of adhering to guidelines regarding the resumption of activities and responding meaningfully to cardiac symptoms (Lemos et al., 2003).

Psychosocial interventions can be used to reduce multifactorial risk factors and psychosocial risk factors (Rozanski et al., 2005). The findings of Hughes et al.'s (2004) targeted approach indicate that reductions in anxiety associated with social support may be beneficial for cardiac patients (Rozanski et al., 2005).

Smoking Cessation

Because of the negative impact of cigarette smoking on cardiovascular functioning, clinicians should encourage efforts to quit smoking (Whooley, 2006)

COGNITIVE–BEHAVIORAL THERAPY

Cognitive–behavioral therapy (CBT) has been confidently recommended for patients with cardiac disease (Whooley, 2006). In addition, Sears et al. (2004) found that CBT resulted in less depression, anxiety, and psychological distress among ICD patients. Whooley (2006) found that close monitoring of patients during therapy is critical to treatment effectiveness. CBT intervention has also been associated with improvement in psychosocial risk factors. Among other treatment targets, CBT is particularly useful in modifying treatment-interfering illness representations.

Because CBT has become the psychological treatment of choice for cardiac problems, it should not be surprising that a number of treatment programs and protocols for specific cardiac problems have developed in the past 2 decades. Four of these areas of clinical practice and research are briefly noted in this section.

Cognitive–Behavioral Therapy and Arrhythmias

Patients who survive life-threatening arrhythmias often experience psychological reactions that respond well to CBT (White, 2001). Receiving an ICD device may be lifesaving for the patient, but they may experience high levels of anxiety and even panic in response to the defibrillator-generated shock that is triggered by an arrhythmia. There is a growing literature in the cognitive conceptualization and treatment of both arrhythmias and ICD-induced anxiety and panic (Dunbar & Summerville, 1997). In working with those with ICDs, the identification of misinterpretations—for example, "Oh no, I'm going to be shocked again"—can be effectively addressed with verbal reattribution strategies (White, 2001). Education about ICD technology and preparing patients for shock occurrence appears to be a significant component of therapy (Sears et al., 2004). Furthermore, Sears et al. (2004) proposed that exposure therapy may be a useful adjunct in working with ICD patients.

Cognitive–Behavioral Therapy and Angina

Angina is typically triggered and exacerbated by both stress, strong emotions, and physical exertion and results in chest pain and shortness of breath. Decreased activity level and fear of returning to work are common patient reactions to chest pain and are usually related to the illness representation and misconception of "taking it easy." Accordingly, a fine-grained assessment of these triggering factors is essential to effective treatment. A review of recent angina episodes should include trigger; duration; medication use; reaction of patient and significant others; cognitions; and mediating factors such as activity levels, avoidant behavior, and so on. Exercise is often avoided if the patient associates it with angina, and physical deconditioning ensues, which is problematic because it lowers the angina threshold (Lewin, 1997). Because angina is associated with anxiety, neuroticism, Type A behavior, and heightened levels of somatic awareness (White, 2001), these factors should also be assessed and inform the clinical formulation. CBT is helpful in modifying thoughts and illness perceptions related to angina and decreased activity.

Cognitive–Behavioral Therapy and Noncardiac Chest Pain

There are some cardiac patients whose symptoms are mediated more by psychological factors than cardiac factors (Bass & Mayou, 1995). The main therapeutic challenge with these patients is to elucidate the precise manner in which psychological variables influence their symptom experience. In a controlled trial, CBT was shown to be effective for these noncardiac chest pain patients in both research and hospital outpatient settings (Mayou et al., 1997). This assessment includes life experiences, beliefs, thoughts, emotions, and behaviors that influence and activate cardiac symptoms in the absence of cardiac pathology. Such information is vital to both a clinical formulation and CBT intervention plan.

Cognitive–Behavioral Therapy and Cardiac Rehabilitation

Cardiac rehabilitation helps patients to better understand and make a commitment to treatment regimens, make major changes in health behaviors, modify illness perceptions and health beliefs, and lower cardiac risk factors. Cardiac rehabilitation programs are a significant component of management and treatment for many cardiac patients. The ability of patients to access and actively participate in such programs can greatly influence the individuals' quality of life. In some cases, lack of access to rehabilitation has been shown to negatively influence patient morbidity and mortality (Sotile, 2005). Several CBT strategies are applicable to the process of cardiac rehabilitation. Some of these are unique to rehabilitation, such as the process of risk factor modification, whereas others are mainstays of health-focused counseling and psychotherapy (Bennett & Carroll, 1994).

OTHER PSYCHOTHERAPEUTIC INTERVENTIONS

Group Therapy

Although individual psychotherapy has long been offered to cardiac patients, there is a paucity of published research on its benefits. On the other hand, studies involving group therapy with cardiac patients, a relatively new area of specialization, have recently been published.

Several clinical trials have demonstrated less morbidity; improved quality of life; and, to some extent, lower mortality for patients who have received psychosocial intervention, generally group therapy, compared with control patients (Allan & Scheidt, 1998). Some clinical techniques for use in a group therapy context have been developed to help cardiac patients increase physical and psychological well-being.

Another study has reported on the use of group therapy for post-MI patients with alexithymia (Beresnevaite, 2000). The premise of this study is that by modifying alexithymic characteristics, such patients will experience decreased morbidity and mortality. This controlled study found that group psychotherapy was able to decrease their alexithymia, a change that was maintained at least 2 years in many patients. It was also found that this group psychotherapy intervention also resulted in fewer cardiac events, that is, reinfarction, sudden cardiac death, or rehospitalization for rhythm disorder or severe angina than in patients whose alexithymia remained unchanged.

EXERCISE AND PHYSICAL THERAPY

Exercise

Exercise has proved beneficial for many cardiac patients and is commonly recommended by cardiologists for physiological reasons, although it also helps modify risk factors such as depression. The contribution of exercise to emotional as well as physical well-being positively affects patients' quality of life (Rozanski et al., 2005; Sin et al., 2004).

Physical Therapy

Some population groups, such as patients with severe physical disability, may require more targeted interventions from rehabilitation professionals to facilitate recovery (Sin et al., 2004). A retrospective study indicated that quality of life for cardiac patients, including patients with depression, is enhanced with a targeted approach to physical therapy (Sin et al., 2004).

MEDICAL TREATMENT

The decision of which medical or surgical treatment modality to use with cardiac disease is based on a number of factors: diagnosis, severity, age, and overall health of the patient. There are four primary modalities.

- *Lifestyle change.* Lifestyle change is aimed at reducing risk factors such as cigarette smoking, alcohol consumption, obesity, elevated blood pressure and cholesterol levels, elevated blood glucose levels, high stress levels, and so on.
- *Medication.* Drugs such as diuretics, angiotensin-converting enzyme (ACE) inhibitors, calcium channel blockers, statins, and beta-blockers all work in different ways to improve cardiovascular functioning.
- *Angioplasty and stent placement.* Angioplasty is a nonsurgical procedure that can be performed to open blocked arteries. A *stent* is a small stainless steel mesh tube that acts as a scaffold to provide support inside the coronary artery.
- *Bypass surgery.* When blood vessels of the heart are severely blocked or damaged, a graft taken from a vessel in the leg is used to create a new route for blood flow to the heart.

MEDICATION

Hundreds of medications are used in the treatment of cardiac disease. The following six classes of medication are commonly prescribed.

- *Diuretics*: These are a class of drugs that work by reducing fluid build-up in the body. As a result, they lower blood pressure, reduce the workload of the heart, and reduce its need for blood and oxygen. There are several diuretics, such as Bumex, Lasix, hydrochlorothiazide, and spironolactone.
- *Beta blockers*: These medications are used in the treatment of angina, high blood pressure, and arrhythmias. They block the response of the heart and blood vessels to nerve stimulation, thereby slowing the heart rate and lowering blood pressure. They include Tenormin, Atenolol, Lopressor, metoprolol, Inderal, and Corgard.
- *Calcium channel blockers*: These medications are used for the prevention of angina and lowering blood pressure by blocking or slowing calcium flow, which results in vasodilation and greater oxygen delivery to the heart muscle. Examples of these are diltiazem, nifedipine, and verapamil. Verapamil is also used to correct certain arrhythmias.
- *ACE inhibitors*: These medications are used to treat high blood pressure or heart failure by decreasing blood pressure and increasing the pumping function of the heart. Examples of these drugs include Vasotec, enalapril, Zestril, Prinivil, Captopril, Monopril, and Lotensin.
- *Statins:* This is a class of drugs that lowers the level of cholesterol in the blood by blocking the enzyme—HMG-CoA reductase—in the liver that is responsible for making cholesterol. Lipitor and Crestor are the most potent, and Lescol is the least potent.
- *Psychotropics:* Psychotropic medication can play an important role in treatment protocol of cardiac patients with psychiatric comorbidities. For example, use of antidepressants for depressed cardiac patients has become the standard of care (Whooley, 2006). Case control studies indicate that the selective serotonin reuptake inhibitors (SSRIs) with a high serotonin transporter affinity may be the preferred pharmacologic treatment for depressed patients with CAD. Of interest, these SSRIs also have an antiplatelet effect that could provide further physiological benefit (Rozanski et al., 2005). The SSRI sertraline is most frequently prescribed (Rozanski et al., 2005; Whooley, 2006). Suls and Bunde (2005) indicated that a combination of anxiolytics and SSRIs was efficacious in treating patients with both anger and depression. Whooley (2006) also recommended bupropion for patients who cannot tolerate the side effects of sertraline or who wish to quit smoking, which is a behavior of particular concern in cardiac patients.

COMBINED TREATMENT

Combined treatment that includes psychosocial interventions is increasingly recommended as beneficial to patients (Sotile, 2005). Evidence supports the view that tailored interventions such as exercise therapy and psychosocial treatments, in addition to medications, do improve treatment outcomes for patients with cardiac disease (Rozanski et al., 2005; Sears et al., 2004; Sin et al., 2004; Suls & Bunde, 2005).

Cardiac patients require multiple levels of treatment, and patients appear to benefit from access to a variety of clinical professionals, including cardiologists, psychologists, physical therapists, and nurses. The biopsychosocial approach to cardiac rehabilitation has been studied extensively, and convincing evidence exists that incorporating multidisciplinary care would prove beneficial for both patients and physicians (Sotile, 2005).

Integrative Treatment Protocol: Cardiac Disease

	1. Key Background Information
Pathology	*Cardiac disease*, also called *cardiovascular disease* (CVD), refers to diseases and conditions affecting the heart and its vessels. CVD can have widespread effects on patient health.
Epidemiology	Coronary artery disease (CAD) is the most common type, affecting one in three adults; it is the leading cause of death for men and women.
Types	Some of the more common cardiac diseases and conditions are CAD, myocardial infarction or heart attack, heart failure, arrhythmias, coronary heart disease, atherosclerosis, hypertension, and stroke
Gender, age, and ethnicity	• Gender: Women's symptoms of CAD differ from those of men, as do referrals for cardiac rehabilitation. • Age: The risks for CAD increase with age. • Ethnicity: African Americans have the highest rates; 25% of Mexican Americans have CVD; CVD is the leading cause of death for Native Americans.
Comorbidities—medical	Diabetes, obesity, and stroke are most common.
Comorbidities—psychiatric	Stress, anxiety, depression, and anger are common and have been shown to negatively influence recovery from heart disease. Psychosocial risk factors of hostility, social isolation, and chronic marital and family conflict can adversely affect patient adherence to treatment.
Prognosis	More than 50% of those who died of cardiac disease had no angina or other symptoms. About 30% of fatal attacks and most surgeries could be avoided with lifestyle changes and by treatment compliance.

	2. Biopsychosocial Assessment
Patient profile	From interview and observation and Illness Perception Questionnaire (IPQ; Weinman, Petrie, Moss-Morris, & Horne, 1996):

(continues)

	• consider illness perception, explanations, treatment expectations; • phase and severity of symptoms and functional impact; • capacity, previous change efforts, and readiness for change; and • personality style or disorder and family and cultural factors.
Illness profile	Identify higher risk cardiac patients: • those who are older and women; • those with implanted cardioverter defibrillators (ICDs); • those who are alone or have low social support; • those with symptoms of anxiety, depression, or other affective disorder; and • those with diabetes, insulin resistance, high cholesterol, and smoking.

3. Intervention Planning

Incorporate key illness profile considerations	Self-efficacy, participation in a cardiac rehabilitation program and return to work, and treatment compliance predict the course of cardiac illness; identify these representations and plan treatment accordingly. Consider higher risks, comorbidities, and key markers such as self-efficacy.

4. Intervention Implementation

Psychoeducational interventions	Educate patients on the nature of cardiac disease, types of rehabilitation, medications for anxiety and depression, exercise therapy, and cardiac technologies such as ICD. Discuss importance of adhering to guidelines for resumption of activities, responding meaningfully to cardiac symptoms, and the value of positive social support.
Cognitive–behavioral therapy (CBT)	Focus on modifying problematic illness representations with cognitive restructuring and/or positive reattribution, treatment-interfering thoughts or behaviors, and interpersonal conflicts and support issues. Refer to specific CBT protocols for arrhythmias, angina, noncardiac chest pain, and cardiac rehabilitation.
Other psychotherapeutic interventions	Individual psychotherapy has long been offered to cardiac patients, but there are no definitive studies on its benefits. Some group clinical techniques have been developed, and there is some evidence that group therapy reduces both morbidity and mortality.
Exercise and physical therapy	Exercise is beneficial for many cardiac patients' emotional and physical well-being. Targeted physical therapy can increase these as well as quality of life, especially for those with depression.
Medical treatment	Decisions about the use of specific medical modalities are based on diagnosis, severity, age, and overall patient health. Key modalities include lifestyle change, medication, angioplasty and stent placement, and bypass surgery.

Medication	Drugs such as diuretics, angiotensin-converting enzyme inhibitors, calcium channel blockers, statins, and beta-blockers all work in different ways to improve cardiovascular functioning.
Combined treatment	Combining tailored interventions such as exercise therapy and psychosocial treatments with medical treatments improves treatment outcomes.

5. Intervention Monitoring

- Review patient's diary of symptoms and functional impairment.
- Track session-to-session progress with regard to compliance, symptom reduction, and functionality.

CASE OF FRED J.

Fred J. is a 56-year-old married Caucasian man, manager of a sporting goods store. He recently sustained a myocardial infarction while playing league softball on his store's team. After an uneventful recovery, his hospital discharge plan was for him to continue in the medical center's highly regarded outpatient cardiac rehabilitation program. The program's professional staff consisted of three cardiologists and two master's level psychologists. Fred had jokingly mentioned to the psychologist conducting his evaluation interview for the outpatient program that he didn't really believe much in psychology but would listen to any professional advice "about getting my sexual side safely back to full power." When queried about this, Fred indicated that he had heard "through the grapevine that many guys were impotent or could die if they started having sex too soon." Because all participants and their spouses in the outpatient program take the Revised Illness Perception Questionnaire prior to their evaluation interview, the psychologist was able to query Fred further about his illness representations. Because of Fred's beliefs that his heart disease would not easily be cured or controlled and that it would be a long time before he could probably return to work, it seemed likely there could be compliance issues with attendance, lifestyle modification, and medication use. Ethel, Fred's wife, had similar beliefs about Fred's curability and return to work. The results of 10 years of clinic data indicated that couples work was indicated when patients and spouses showed this pattern. Accordingly, twice-weekly couples sessions were incorporated into Fred's program schedule.

During these conjoint sessions with Fred and Ethel, the psychologist used CBT to review and modify their treatment-hindering illness beliefs. During the course of these sessions, issues pertaining to symptom control, return to work, compliance with medication, and lifestyle changes as well as sexual performance and activity were discussed. Fred's attendance was above average as was his participation in exercise, meditation-based stress management, and other program modalities. He reported no problems with sexual performance, moods, or energy level. Accordingly, he was able to return to work in 7 weeks rather than in the 6 months he had originally predicted it would take.

11

CHRONIC PAIN

Pain is the sensory and emotional experience of discomfort associated with actual or threatened tissue damage or irritation. Everyone experiences pain sometime throughout the course of life. Pain can be experienced as acute or chronic. *Chronic pain* is pain that persists. In contrast to *acute pain*, wherein pain signals for a short time, in chronic pain, pain signals keep firing for considerably longer—for weeks, months, or even years. Although there is often an initial injury, such as a sprained back, or an ongoing source of pain, such as cancer or arthritis, some individuals will experience chronic pain in the absence of any past injury or body damage. Common chronic pain complaints include headache, musculoskeletal pain, cancer pain, arthritis pain, and psychogenic pain. Anxiety, depression, and anger are common psychological manifestations of the consequences of living with chronic pain. The pain's widespread effects on quality of life can prove devastating for a patient. Developing adequate social support mechanisms and specifically addressing the emotional component of chronic pain is essential for patients' quality of life (Kerns, Rosenburg, & Otis, 2002).

The following sections present basic background on chronic pain as a disease and illness followed by a detailed discussion of various psychological and biopsychosocial treatment intervention options. This discussion includes both clinical and research findings. The chapter concludes with an integrative treatment protocol and a case example illustrating the protocol.

EPIDEMIOLOGY

It is estimated that 15% to 33% of the U.S. population—which translates to about 70 million Americans—is affected by chronic pain. It disables more people than cancer or heart disease. According to the American Pain Foundation (2008), chronic pain costs the U.S. economy more than both combined, about $100 billion a year in medical costs, lost working days, and workman's compensation. These figures are problematic because of the considerable variability in prevalence rates, ranging from 2% to 50% of the population-based prevalence studies. This variability reflects loosely defined criteria for what constitutes chronic pain (Verhaak, Kerssen, Dekker, Sorbi, & Bensing, 1998). When more stringent criteria were used, that is, the *Diagnostic and Statistical Manual of Mental Disorders* (4th ed.; *DSM–IV*; American Psychiatric Association, 1994) criteria for pain disorder, the 12-month prevalence rate of chronic pain was 8.1% compared with 28% (women: 34.2%; men: 22.4%) who reported at least one chronic pain symptom without meeting *DSM–IV* criteria (Frohlich, Jacobi, & Wittchen, 2006). Nevertheless, however loose or stringent the diagnostic criteria used, chronic pain remains the most pervasive symptom in medical practice, the most frequently stated "cause" of disability, and the single most compelling force underlying a person's decision to seek medical care (Fishbain, Rosomoff, Cutler, & Steele-Rosomoff, 2000).

TYPES

The most prevalent chronic pain types are headache (12.7% of all pain sufferers), back pain (8.5% of all pain sufferers), abdominal pain (8.3% of all pain sufferers), and joint pain (7.2% of all pain sufferers; Frohlich et al., 2006). Of the various categories of pain, considerable research exists on two: musculoskeletal pain and pelvic pain.

Musculoskeletal Pain

The findings of a controlled study by Flor, Furst, and Birbaumer (1999) confirm and clarify other studies illustrating a deficient tension perception and a concurrent overestimation of symptoms in patients with chronic musculoskeletal pain. Of interest is the fact that chronic back pain patients also underestimated high muscle tension independent from the patients' main site of pain (Flor et al., 1999).

Pelvic Pain

A controlled study of women and men with pelvic pain, using women and men with low back pain as additional comparison groups, was recently reported. It is one of a few studies that have compared chronic pelvic pain patients with other pain patients (Heinberg, Fisher, Wesselmann, Reed, & Haythornthwaite, 2004). Although women are more frequently affected by chronic pelvic pain, the current body of literature indicates that the sequelae of chronic pain may be more intense for women compared with men when the pain is located in the urogenital region (Heinberg et al., 2004).

SEVERITY

Pain that is considered severe and impairing or dysfunctional involves the experience of high levels of pain, compromised life activities, reduced sense of control, high emotional distress, and low perceived support from significant others (Jamison, Rudy, Penzien, & Mosley, 1994). This contrasts with the experience of low levels of pain, little or no impairment or functional limitations, little or no emotional distress, and the capacity to cope relatively well despite long-standing pain. As the severity of the experience of pain increases, patients may begin to catastrophize their pain experience (Michael & Burns, 2004). Catastrophizing pain is a common but harmful psychological adaptation to pain, and it influences the patients' perception of the consequences of the pain.

CAUSAL FACTORS

There are differing theories about the cause of chronic pain. The biopsychosocial view of the cause of chronic pain is that some form of physical change or pathology—in the muscles, joints, or nerves—travels to and is registered by the brain. Pain perception involves the interpretation of the painful stimuli, whereas appraisal involves the meaning attributed to the pain. These appraisals are influenced by the patient's beliefs and schemas. On the basis of these beliefs and the appraisal process, the patient can choose to ignore the pain and continue his or her previous activity or can choose to stop or diminish the activity and assume the sick role (Engel, 1959). Subsequently, the interpersonal role of pain is shaped by how significant others respond (Turk & Okifuji, 2002). The gate control theory of pain provides a somewhat biopsychosocial view of pain, but it appears to have fallen out of favor.

The biomedical and neurobiological view of chronic pain is that it is "caused" or preceded by various diseases or injuries. Although its exact mechanisms are still unclear, there is growing consensus on how this phenomenon of chronic pain develops and sustains itself. Persistent activation of nociceptive transmission to the dorsal horn appears to activate a process that induces pathological changes that lower the threshold for pain signals to be transmitted. In addition, it appears to generate non-nociceptive nerve fibers to respond to, generate, and transmit pain signals. In chronic pain, this process becomes difficult to reverse or eradicate once it is established (Vadivelu & Sinatra, 2005).

Subsequently, the brain adapts to chronic pain exposure (Flor, 2002). In a controlled trial, pain and pain memories were found to contribute to hyperalgesic states in patients without peripheral nociceptive stimulus. Such pain memories can be influenced by psychological processes such as classical conditioning, which may establish widespread implicit pain memories and enhance the existing memories (Flor, 2002). Flor (2002) analyzed the somatotropic organization of primary somatosensory cortex that is related to chronic pain. The study results indicate that chronic pain leads to an expansion of the cortical zone related to nociceptive input. In addition, the length of chronic pain was positively correlated with the cortical reorganization (Flor, 2002).

GENDER AND ETHNICITY

Gender

Women are more likely than men to report experiencing a variety of recurrent pains (Frohlich et al., 2006). Many women have reported moderate or severe pains from menstruation, pregnancy, and childbirth. In most studies, they have reported more severe levels of pain, more frequent pain, and pain of longer duration than men. They may be at greater risk for pain-related disability than men, but women also respond more aggressively to pain through health-related activities. Furthermore, health care providers are more likely to make unwarranted psychogenic attributions for women's pain than for men's pain (Unruh, 1996). Whereas women show a higher prevalence of headaches, it has been suggested that men report more episodic and chronic cluster headaches as well as testicular pain following infection or trauma (Unruh, 1996). In Western cultures, gender roles for men suggest that men do not ask for help or show tears and that they must endure pain (Castillo, 1997). It is interesting that no gender effects were found on measurements of pain, pain-related disability, or symptoms of depression. Instead, the pain severity or pain site explained the variant adaptation to pain (Heinberg et al., 2004).

Ethnicity

It is essential for clinicians to understand the influence of ethnic, cultural, and language differences and bring specialized skills to interventions with chronic pain patients, particularly because there is such variability in the way in which different ethnic and cultural groups respond to pain. How clients perceive pain, both within themselves or others, and how they communicate their pain to health care providers is often dependent on cultural factors like race, ethnicity, age, gender, sexual orientation, disability, and social class (Chaplin, 1997). For example, Jewish clients may show pain more openly than Asian clients. This may be due to the difference that Asians "in general are taught self-restraint and may be more reluctant to express pain" (Castillo, 1997, p. 196). The communication of pain often depends on whether a client is from a culture in which restraint, stoicism, and fortitude are valued and hence reserve is exhibited in the face of suffering; whether help-seeking or self-caretaking is valued; whether pain is viewed as normal or abnormal; or whether pain is viewed as a type of divine punishment that must be experienced (Castillo, 1997). Finally, religion and spirituality are key cultural factors, and research supports both assessing and integrating into treatment the chronic pain patient's religiosity and religious coping mechanisms as a stress management strategy (Bush et al., 1999).

PSYCHIATRIC COMORBIDITIES

Individuals with chronic pain often develop comorbidities such as depression, anxiety disorders, personality disorders, and substance use disorders and have high prevalence rates (Michael & Burns, 2004). In fact, 56% of those meeting criteria for *DSM–IV* pain disorder met the criteria for at least one other *DSM* disorder. Of these, 53% met the criteria for one of the *DSM* anxiety disorders or mood disorders (Frohlich et al., 2006). In addition, anger appears to be more prevalent among chronic pain patients than among healthy populations (Burns, Bruehl, & Caceres, 2004).

Pain Disorder

Chronic pain is variously defined by expert panels and different medical and mental health organizations. For that reason, some have advocated using the *DSM–IV* definition and criteria for pain disorder (Frohlich et al., 2006). *DSM–IV* requires that specific criteria be met to make the diagnosis of pain disorder. These criteria include the following: The pain is present in one or more anatomical sites, is the predominant focus of the clinical presentation, and is of sufficient severity to warrant clinical attention. The pain must also cause clinically significant distress or impairment, and it must be demonstrated that psychological factors have an important role in the onset, severity, exacerbation, or maintenance of the pain. Subtypes include pain disorder with psychological features—the most common diagnosis—or with psychological and a general medical condition. Further specification is that the pain is acute if the duration is less than 6 months, or chronic if more than 6 months (American Psychiatric Association, 1994).

Anxiety

Chronic pain can lead to anxiety and anxiety disorders such as panic, generalized anxiety, hypochondriasis, and posttraumatic stress disorder (Winterowd, Beck, & Gruener, 2003). It is not surprising that chronic pain patients have many negative events and stressors to deal with apart from their pain, such as job loss, financial hardship, and relational and family conflicts. Prevalence data indicate that of those meeting DSM–IV criteria for pain disorder, 35% also met criteria for an anxiety disorder (Frohlich et al., 2006).

Depression

Depression is also common among pain patients. Of those meeting the DSM–IV criteria for pain disorder, 30% also met criteria for a depressive disorder (Frohlich et al., 2006). Consistent with other research, pain was found to be "the primary condition in 75% of pain cases comorbid with depression, supporting the hypothesis of depression being a consequence of pain" (Frohlich et al., 2006, p. 193). Frohlich et al. (2006) also noted that a predisposition to depression can increase the likelihood of some chronic pain patients developing a full-blown depression. Tennen, Affleck, and Zautra (2006) used pain diaries to measure such behaviors as catastrophizing, perceived control, coping strategies, and effectiveness of coping and found that pain coping and its appraisal was correlated with daily measures of pain and response to pain and that having a previous history of depression and current distress predicted pain intensity.

Substance Use Disorders

It is commonly assumed that chronic pain patients self-medicate with alcohol and other substances. However, whether the use of substances is excessive enough to meet DSM criteria is another matter. Recent data from Frohlich et al. (2006) show that substance use disorders are more frequent in those with DSM–IV pain disorder. Among men, substance use disorder was 9.9%, and among women it was 3.1%. For chronic pain patients not meeting criteria for the pain disorder, the prevalence of meeting criteria for substance use disorders was 6.4% for men and 1.7% for women.

Personality Disorders

Although no single pain-prone personality exists, personality attributes such as introversion, pessimism, low perceived locus of control, negative affect, and personality disorders negatively impact a patient's ability to cope with pain (Gatchel & Weisberg, 2000). Other personality traits that can complicate the treatment process include anger, perfectionism (shown by a deeply felt sense of duty and responsibility and demanding a great deal from self and others), rigidity and inflexible standards or morals, a high need to please others, and viewing physical disability as a solution. Commonly observed personality disorders in chronic pain patients are avoidant, obsessive–compulsive, and histrionic personality disorders.

Anger

Two styles of anger management are anger expression and anger suppression. The *expressive* style is characterized by the direct verbal or physical expression of anger toward family and health care providers and can result in decreased social support, which can contribute to decreased physical and emotional well-being. The *suppressive* style is characterized by "stuffing" anger and hostility, and it affects how well patients adjust to chronic pain. Both styles have been associated with increased chronic and acute pain sensitivity (Burns et al., 2004). In a double-blind controlled study, Bruehl, Yong Chung, Burns, and Biridepalli (2003) found that patients with an expressive anger management style experienced both greater pain sensitivity and cardiovascular stress reactivity.

PROGNOSIS

Because cure and total and sustained relief of pain are the exception, pain management is a realistic outcome for many patients with moderate and even severe chronic pain. They can be helped if they understand and appreciate the range of biological, psychological, and socioenvironmental factors that cause, trigger, and exacerbate pain and the many and varied steps that can be taken to undo what chronic pain has done.

TREATMENT CONSIDERATIONS AND INTERVENTIONS

Treating chronic pain patients is a challenge. Important considerations that can foster treatment success include illness representations, tailoring treatment, biopsychosocial perspective, pain assessment, pain diary, goal and sequencing of multimodal interventions, readiness for change, and pain catastrophizing. Each of these considerations is discussed in this section.

Illness Representations

Beliefs by an individual about the meaning of symptoms, cause of pain, ability to control pain, and the impact of pain on his or her life have been shown to play a central role in chronic pain. Such beliefs have been found to be associated with psychological functioning, physical functioning, coping efforts, and response to treatment (Turk & Okifuji, 2002). An individual's constellation of perceptions and beliefs about a particular disease— understanding of it and its symptoms, cause, duration, impact or consequences, curability, and their ability to control it—is referred to as *illness representation*. There is growing evidence about the clinical value of understanding an individual's illness representations and perceptions regarding chronic pain and particularly in tailoring treatment. Furthermore, treatment-interfering illness representations can be targeted for change with cognitive–behavioral therapy (CBT).

Research on attribution of pain also has clinical relevance. For example, the belief that activity might aggravate the initial injury often results in fear of engaging in rehabilitative efforts and leads to preoccupation with bodily symptoms and to physical deconditioning, which, in turn, can exacerbate pain and maintain disability. Individuals who attribute the cause of their pain to an injury are more likely to view any physical sensation as harmful, which increases anxiety levels. Consequently, these changes can lower pain thresholds and tolerance, which further increases activity avoidance and functional limitations and fosters physical deconditioning (Turk & Okifuji, 2002).

Hobro, Weinman, and Hankins (2004) reported a study using the Revised Illness Perception Questionnaire (Moss-Morris et al., 2002) and other measures to categorize chronic pain patients on the basis of their illness representations. Cluster analysis revealed two categories. Cluster 1, the "adaptors" group, had lower timeline beliefs, fewer pain-related consequences, stronger beliefs in personal and treatment control over pain, better understanding of their pain (i.e., *coherence*), and less emotional distress relating to pain than did Cluster 2, the "nonadaptors" group (Hobro et al., 2004). Identifying such pain groups provides a basis for developing tailored treatment interventions for chronic pain patients. For example, nonadaptors (i.e., those with longer timeline beliefs, more pain-related consequences, weaker beliefs in personal and treatment control over pain, less understanding of their pain, and more emotional distress regarding their pain) will need more intensive and focused treatment.

Tailoring Treatment

Treatment is tailored on the basis of a number of factors unique to a patient. Patients with work-related injuries are likely to be concerned about the financial impact of the injury on themselves and their families. Women are more likely than men to experience chronic pain (Johnson, 2008), which influences their ability to adapt and is a critical consideration in intervention planning. It is important to note that urogenital pain and dental pain may be more intense than pain in other bodily locations and therefore should also factor into treatment development. A positive predictor for treatment outcome is strong spiritual belief. Patients with such beliefs may have better access to supportive social groups than other patients (Koenig, Larson, & Larson, 2001). Results of a study by Heinberg et al. (2004) suggest that tailored psychological interventions may be necessary to address site-specific pain concerns.

Biopsychosocial Perspective

A tailored approach should incorporate the biopsychosocial perspective. Unlike the biomedical model, the biopsychosocial model focuses on the dynamic and reciprocal interaction between biological, psychological, and sociocultural variables that shapes the person's response to pain (Turk & Okifuji, 2002). It is interesting that Arena (2002) found that many patients consider their pain to be primarily biological but expect a clinician to attribute their pain as primarily psychological. Accordingly, patients may be resistant to treatment regimens that they view as largely psychologically focused. With such patients, clinicians would do well to acknowledge the physical component of the pain while addressing the psychological component (Arena, 2002). Thus, framing treatment in a biopsychosocial perspective is essential in order to engage that patient in a collaborative treatment relationship.

Pain Assessment

Both formal and informal rating methods have been used to assess the chronic pain patient. Two formal inventories can be particularly useful. The Pain Stages of Change Questionnaire (Kerns, Rosenberg, Jamison, Caudill, & Haythornthwaite, 1997; see also Jensen, Nielson, Roman, Hill, & Turner, 2000) can be used to assess readiness for change, particularly regarding willingness to adopt a self-management approach to treatment. The Multidimensional Pain Inventory (Greco, Rudy, & Manzi, 2003) classifies pain sufferers in three subgroups: *dysfunctional* represents people with severe pain, compromised life activities, reduced sense of control, and high emotional distress; *interpersonally distressed* represents people with relatively high pain, affective distress, and low perceived support from significant others; and *adaptive copers* represents people with low pain, functional limitations, and emotional distress but who cope relatively well despite long-standing pain. Research on this inventory suggests that it can predict treatment outcomes (Jamison et al., 1994).

A more informal approach is the use of self-rating scales. Three types of self-rating scales to measure pain intensity are commonly used. The first is a visual analog scale, which is a 10-centimeter line with endpoints of *no pain* and *worst pain ever*, and the client marks a point on the line that describes the pain's intensity at a given moment. The second is a variant of the visual analog scale on which the patient rates pain on a 1-to-10 scale where 1 is *no pain*, 5 is *moderate*, and 10 is *the worst imaginable pain*. The third category-rating scale also uses a line, but it is divided into sections with designations such as *no pain, mild pain, discomforting pain, distressing pain, horrible pain*, and *excruciating pain*. The client checks the sections that correspond to the pain experience (Karoly & Jensen, 1987).

Pain Diary

Because these self-rating scales are quick and easy to use, patients are asked to rate their pain frequently, usually on an hourly basis, and record it in their pain diary. Diaries are essential for rating and tracking the antecedents, intervening factors, and consequences of pain. The diary may contain patients' rating of pain with regard to time—when it occurred and its duration—as well as the activity being engaged in at the time, pain severity (0–10), irritability (0–10), and coping behavior or effectiveness (0–10).

Goals and Sequencing of Multimodal Treatment

Because achieving absolute and sustained relief of pain is the exception, the main treatment goals for most chronic pain patients are pain management and increased functioning, such as improved sleep; effective coping and stress reduction skills; and job retraining, if indicated. These goals can be accomplished with several modalities but are more likely achieved with a multimodal and multidisciplinary strategy. In this regard, comprehensive pain programs have been demonstrated to provide both efficacious and cost-effective treatment for the chronic pain patient when compared with several widely used conventional medical treatment modalities (Stanos & Houle, 2006). Furthermore, Morley and Williams (2006) found in their evaluation of randomized controlled trials (RCTs) that any of the treatments offered to patients in studies were too complex, were too brief to offer long-term results, were conducted prematurely, and were not well sequenced (Morley & Williams, 2006). The implication is that an effective, tailored treatment plan will have realistic goals, be multimodal, and will use interventions that are well timed and reasonably sequenced.

Readiness for Change

A patient's readiness to accept and adopt a self-management approach to their pain can significantly influence treatment outcome. The Pain Stages of Change Questionnaire is useful in assessing an individual's readiness to adopt a self-management approach to chronic pain. A high level of commitment to a self-management approach has been found to predict successful treatment (Kerns et al., 2002). In addition, assessing readiness for treatment is important in identifying individuals at risk of prematurely terminating their treatment (Kerns et al., 2002).

Pain Catastrophizing

Pain catastrophizing is a common but harmful cognitive factor among patients with chronic pain. An RCT examining the effects of depression and pain catastrophizing on patients found that catastrophizing increases a patient's sensitivity to pain differently from those whose pain was attributed to underlying depression (Michael & Burns, 2004). Another study found that patients with low back pain were more likely to report catastrophizing than urogenital pain patients. In contrast with previous study findings and expectations, women did not report more catastrophizing than men (Heinberg et al., 2004). Accordingly, clinicians would do well to identify and target pain catastrophizing as a treatment focus and to use CBT and psychoeducation to reduce it.

PSYCHOEDUCATIONAL INTERVENTIONS

Chronic pain patients may have difficulty asserting themselves to meet their needs directly. Instead, they may rely on illness behaviors to control or avoid situations and to solicit attention and care from others. Assertiveness training, problem-solving training, and role-playing are methods used to help such patients express their needs more directly. Other social skills may be lacking in communication, vocational, or sexual areas that are also amenable to specific social skills training. Such psychoeducational interventions can be delivered in both individual and group formats.

Patient Education

Patients often find it difficult to understand the phenomenon of chronic pain. For this reason, it can be beneficial to provide them with a biopsychosocial perspective from which they can make better sense of how psychological and social factors influence and are influenced by basic neurophysiological and neurochemical processes. Clinicians do well to describe the manner in which the deficient endogenous opioid functioning and the adaptation of the brain to long-term nociceptive input influence the perception of pain.

Relaxation Training

Relaxation treatments have been shown to be beneficial to some patients with chronic pain by teaching them how to reduce tension levels in muscles (Arena, 2002). However, in certain individuals, a deficiency in the patients' ability to discern actual muscle tension levels may preclude the patients' ability to lower tension levels in these muscles (Flor et al., 1999).

Social Support

Certain types of social support are not always beneficial for chronic pain patients. For example, in one study, spouses who reinforced the patients' experience of pain enhanced the nociceptive stimulus in those patients (Flor, 2002). McCracken and Yang (2006) measured a variety of personal values in chronic pain patients and found that patients with chronic pain have differential abilities to live according to these values. Patients were, in general, better able to have success in maintaining family values than in maintaining good health (McCracken & Yang, 2006). Furthermore, training the spouses of pain patients to provide pain-relevant support can be a useful aspect of pain management (Kerns et al., 2002).

COGNITIVE–BEHAVIORAL THERAPY

CBT now has an integral and core role in most chronic pain management programs (R. R. Taylor, 2006; Winterowd et al., 2003). Addressing and effectively modifying negative thinking patterns and pessimism in chronic pain patients is where CBT excels as a treatment intervention (Arena, 2002; Michael & Burns, 2004; Winterowd et al., 2003). Another main treatment target for CBT is modifying treatment-interfering illness representations. In addition, CBT strategies are prescribed for instilling hope and increasing motivation and readiness for treatment in chronic pain patients (R. R. Taylor, 2006). Finally, addressing the matter of relapse prevention is essential in the effective treatment of these patients (Winterowd et al., 2003).

Kerns et al.'s (2002) multiple-regression analysis found that patients with self-appraised poor problem-solving skills were more likely to experience both higher levels of pain and functional disability. These patients were also more likely to report symptoms of depression. The study also indicated that pain-relevant support was significantly related to pain and disability but not to patient symptoms of depression. Finally, this study investigated the relationship between problem-solving skills and the patient experience of pain. The application of CBT for the treatment of chronic pain is also supported by the study (Kerns et al., 2002).

Assessment of Illness Representations

White (2001) contended that illness representations are central to CBT treatment. He noted that their assessment is particularly important when chronic pain arises as a result of disorders which have or are perceived by the patient to have an uncertain cause: "It is in these circumstances that patients are most likely to rely upon elements of their illness representation to understand their experience" (White, 2001, p. 130). Specific questions—"What do you think causes your pain?"; "What do suppose will happen to the pain in the future?"; "How do explain it when your pain gets better (or worse)?"—are useful in assessment of pain representations.

Promotion of Pain Reconceptualization

This is essentially a process of reframing the patient's understanding of pain, that is, illness representation. Often this means helping the patient move from a biological model of their pain to a biopsychosocial one (White, 2001). It also involves the use of guided discovery and cognitive restructuring to modify problematic illness representations, particularly about causality.

Reduction of Catastrophizing

Catastrophizers are likely to benefit form self-instruction and from interventions that focus on verbal reattribution. Thus, reduction of catastrophizing involves helping patients to recognize catastrophic cognitions—for example, "This is awful. I can't stand another minute of it"—and how they undermine healthy adjustment and coping. This intervention is likely to be effective when the clinician enables patients to think about the consequences of this way of thinking on their emotions, behavior, and ability to tolerate pain (White, 2001). It is important to note that attention modification strategies, such as distraction and attention control training, are better suited to noncatastrophizers. Furthermore, in a study by Michael and Burns (2004), interventions that emphasized positive coping skills, such as focusing on the pain as benign, had no effects on the thinking patterns of catastrophizing patients.

OTHER PSYCHOTHERAPEUTIC INTERVENTIONS

Hypnotherapy

Hypnotic suggestion appears to be an effective intervention for pain reduction in chronic pain patients who are receptive to suggestion. Nonhypnotic imaginative suggestion may be as effective in reducing pain as hypnotic suggestion, indicated by controlled clinical trial (Milling, Kirsch, Allen, & Reutenauer, 2005). Patient response expectancies seem to be an important mechanism for the placebo and the resulting suggested pain reduction (Milling et al., 2005).

Psychodynamic Psychotherapy

As part of a multimodal strategy, dynamically oriented psychotherapy may be indicated when medical, surgical, or other pain management efforts have failed to relieve chronic pain. Such therapy focuses on dynamic conflicts. When viewed from the perspective of ego functioning, previously intractable pain can be ameliorated (Lakoff, 1983). Dynamically oriented interventions may be particularly beneficial for patients in whom perfectionistic and need-to-please personality traits are prominent. Tumlin (2001) noted some common pain management issues psychotherapists face in working with chronic pain patients, including biological and psychosocial influences; psychopathology in reaction to the pain; and financial, medical, and legal circumstances.

PHYSICAL THERAPY AND OCCUPATIONAL THERAPY

Physical therapy includes massage; stretching; strengthening activities; and low-impact exercise such as walking, swimming, or biking. Occupational therapy involves activities that teach patients to pace themselves and perform activities of daily living and other tasks differently without pain. An analysis of review articles and RCTs for temporomandibular disorders and similar chronic musculoskeletal pain disorders found strong evidence that symptoms improve during the course of treatment with most forms of physical therapy and related treatments (Feine & Lund, 1997).

MEDICAL TREATMENTS

In addition to medications (see below), some of the medical treatments for chronic pain are drug detoxification, acupuncture, local electrical stimulation, brain stimulation, and surgery. Because chronic pain patients can and do use addicting substances to the extent of being physiologically dependent, they may need to be weaned from these medications by a tapered withdrawal over a 10- to 14-day period. When there is also psychological dependence, which is often the case with drugs such as Valium, self-regulated reduction is negotiated with the patient, who may be asked to set goals, keep records, and give positive reinforcement for abstinence.

MEDICATION

Milder forms of pain may be relieved by nonprescription nonsteroidal anti-inflammatory drugs such as aspirin, acetaminophen, and Aleve. More potent pain medications include muscle relaxants; antianxiety drugs such as Valium; antidepressants; prescription nonsteroidal anti-inflammatory drugs such as Celebrex; or a short course of narcotics such as codeine, Fentanyl, Percocet, or Vicodin. Steroid injections at the site of a joint problem or trigger point can reduce swelling and inflammation. With patient-controlled analgesics, people control pain by pushing a button on a computerized pump to self-administer a premeasured dose of pain medicine. Nerve blocks are often a last resort prior to surgery.

COMBINED TREATMENT

A combined or multimodal approach of psychological and medical interventions is indicated for most patients, particularly those with moderate and severe levels of pain. When an analgesic or narcotic medication needs to be reduced or discontinued, the clinician working in collaboration with the prescribing physician can plan a schedule of analgesic reduction, monitor response, provide reassurance, and use selected CBT techniques as the gradual reduction of pain medications occurs.

Integrative Treatment Protocol: Chronic Pain

1. Key Background Information	
Pathology	The sensory and emotional experience of discomfort associated with actual or threatened tissue damage or irritation that persists over an extended period of time— typically more than 6 months.
Epidemiology	The 12-month prevalence rate was 8.1% using *Diagnostic and Statistical Manual of Mental Disorders* (4th ed.; *DSM–IV*; American Psychiatric Association, 1994) criteria of pain disorder; 28% reported chronic pain but did not meet *DSM–IV* criteria (Frohlich et al., 2006).
Types	Most prevalent: headache (12.7%), back pain (8.5%), abdominal pain (8.3%), and joint pain (7.2%).
Causal factors	Biopsychosocial view: painful physical stimuli are registered in the brain, and appraisal and interpretation of the painful stimuli are influenced by the patient's beliefs and schemas.
Severity	Severely distressing and impairing pain involves high levels of pain, compromised life activities, reduced sense of control, high emotional distress, and low perceived support from significant others. Catastophizing is related to severity.
Gender and ethnicity	Women are more likely than men to experience a variety of recurrent pains. Perception, response, and communication to health providers are dependent on race, ethnicity, age, gender, sexual orientation, disability, and social class.
Personality factors	Personality attributes such as introversion, pessimism, low perceived locus of control, negative affect, anger, perfectionism, rigidity, a high need to please others, and belief that disability is a solution and personality disorders such as avoidant, obsessive–compulsive, and histrionic negatively impact a patient's ability to cope with pain.

(continues)

Psychiatric comorbidities	56% of those with *DSM–IV* pain disorder met the criteria for at least one other *DSM* disorder, most commonly an anxiety or depressive disorder, and then personality disorders and substance use disorders.
Prognosis	Many patients with moderate and even severe chronic pain can achieve effective pain management with a biopsychosocial perspective and treatment focus.

2. Biopsychosocial Assessment

Patient profile	From interview and observation and Revised Illness Perception Questionnaire (IPQ-R; Moss-Morris et al., 2002) assessment:
	• IPQ-R factors, especially illness perceptions, explanations, and treatment expectations;
	• severity of symptoms and functional impact;
	• capacity, previous change efforts, and readiness for change; and
	• personality style or disorder and family and cultural factors.
Illness profile	Identify higher risk chronic pain patients:
	• those who catastrophize about pain or with poor coping skills;
	• those with injuries preventing them from engaging in work as a valued role;
	• those with low levels of social support that reinforce negative thinking;
	• women with chronic pelvic pain; and
	• those with pain disorder as defined by the *DSM*, depression, anxiety, anger, or substance use disorders.
Style assessment	• Anger management style: expressive style is related to increased pain sensitivity.
	• Personality style: those with perfectionism, high need to please others, tendency to catastrophize, and who believe they are entitled to be taken care of (disability) appear to be more challenging than those without these factors.
	• Multidimensional Pain Inventory (MPI; Greco et al., 2003). Identifies three subtypes of pain: *dysfunctional* (severe pain, compromised life activities, reduced sense of control and high emotional distress); *interpersonally distressed* (relatively high pain, affective distress, and low perceived support from significant others); *adaptive copers* (low pain, functional limitations, and emotional distress but cope relatively well despite pain).
	• Pain Stages of Change Questionnaire (Kerns et al., 1997). Assesses patient's readiness to adopt a self-management approach. Identifies those at risk for premature termination versus successful responders.
	• Pain diary. Essential for rating and tracking the antecedents, intervening factors, responses, and consequences of pain.
	• Collateral information. Reports from partner, supervisor, and others about antecedents, intervening factors, responses, consequences, reinforcers, and so on.

3. Intervention Planning

Patient and illness profiles	• Illness representations: Nonadaptors, those with longer timeline beliefs, more pain-related consequences, weaker beliefs in personal and treatment control over pain, less understanding of their pain, and more emotional distress regarding their pain, will need more intensive and focused treatment.
	• Pain type: On the basis of the MPI, single focused interventions may be sufficient for adaptive copers; multifactorial interventions are indicated for the dysfunctional type; focus on relational issues is useful with the interpersonally distressed type.
	• Style: Plan intervention strategies on the basis of relevant personality styles, anger management style, religious coping style, and problem-solving style factors.

4. Intervention Implementation

Treatment goals	Main goal is pain management; others include increasing functionality by improving sleep; increasing coping and stress reduction skills; and, when indicated, by job retraining.
Psychoeducational interventions	• Assertiveness training, problem-solving training, and role-playing.
	• Social skills training when there are problems in communication, vocational, or sexual areas. With uncontrolled anger and deficits in problem-solving skills, consider anger management and problem-solving skills training.
	• Relaxation training when indicated can be beneficial in teaching patients how to reduce tension levels in muscles provided the patient can discern actual muscle tension.
Cognitive–behavioral therapy (CBT)	• Cognitive restructuring is useful for modifying problematic illness representations and promoting pain reconceptualization. Positive reattribution is beneficial in countering catastrophizing and negative thinking patterns in pain patients. CBT is often combined with other psychological or medical treatments.
Other psychotherapeutic interventions	• Hypnotherapy: Either hypnotic and nonhypnotic imaginative suggestion appear equally effective for those receptive to suggestion.
	• Dynamic psychotherapy: For patients with prominent perfectionist and need-to-please personality traits.
Medication	Nonprescription nonsteroidal anti-inflammatory drugs (NSAIDs; e.g., aspirin, acetaminophen, Aleve), muscle relaxants, anxiolytic drugs (e.g., Valium), antidepressants, prescription NSAIDs (e.g., Celebrex), narcotics (e.g., codeine, Fentanyl, Percocet, Vicodin); and steroid injections.

(continues)

Integrative Treatment Protocol: Chronic Pain (Continued)

Combined treatment	A multimodal approach of psychological and medical interventions is indicated for most patients with moderate and severe levels of pain.

5. Intervention Monitoring

- Pain diary. Review patient's rating of pain involving time, activity, pain severity (0–10), irritability (0–10); and coping behavior and effectiveness (0–10).
- If treatment involves cognitive restructuring or reattribution interventions, monitor changes in negative thinking and catastrophizing.
- Track session-to-session progress with regard to compliance, symptom reduction, and functionality.

CASE OF JACKIE S.

Jackie S. is a 31-year-old married woman with a 5-month history of neck and lower back pain following an accident in which she was the passenger in a car driven by a coworker. She has been on workman's compensation since the accident and doubts she will ever be able to return to her job as a line inspector at a small manufacturing company. She has been followed by an orthopedic surgeon since the accident. Because her pain complaints seemed to be increasing, he referred her to a psychologist, Phil Brogan, for evaluation and pain management. As part of a comprehensive evaluation, the psychologist administered the Minnesota Multiphasic Personality Inventory—2 (MMPI–2; Butcher, Dahlstrom, Graham, Tellegen, & Kaemmer, 1989), the IPQ-R, and the MPI. Jackie's illness representations were further elaborated in Brogan's interview with her. It is noteworthy that in terms of timeline, Jackie believes that she may never recover and return to work, that she can have little control over her pain, that she will suffer more negative illness consequences, and that she expects more emotional distress associated with her pain. On the MPI she is assessed as a dysfunctional type, meaning she experiences severe pain, high emotional distress, compromised life activities, and a reduced sense of control over her pain and life circumstances. A 2-6-8 profile is noted on the MMPI–2. Histrionic and narcissistic traits are also noted. From past experience Brogan is inclined to think that Jackie may need the kind of intensive and focused treatment that is more likely to be available in a comprehensive pain management program than he is able to provide in his outpatient practice. Accordingly, he works with the referring physician to facilitate her admission into the comprehensive pain management program at the regional academic medical center, the only such center within a 150-mile radius.

Brogan is aware that there is a waiting list for that program and that some HMO and insurance carriers will either not authorize treatment or will pay for only some program components. Even though workman's compensation typically covers such program expenses, it may be a moot point because the program may not be able or willing to accept Jackie for treatment. If the comprehensive pain management program is out of the question, Brogan can provide some services and arrange, if indicated, for other services to be provided by other professionals in the community. On his part, Brogan envisions beginning with individual CBT focused on the treatment-hindering illness representations noted earlier. He would monitor her pain diary and he would work with her in the pain management group in his practice. The group combines pain reduction and symptom control strategies, meditation, assertive communication, problem-solving training, and role-playing. Mindful of her histrionic and narcissistic personality style, he will tailor the CBT and the group process accordingly. He would likely involve a physical therapist and consider referring her for hypnotherapy with a colleague who has been reasonably successful with complex chronic pain patients.

12

DIABETES

Diabetes mellitus, commonly referred to as *diabetes*, is a syndrome characterized by *hyperglycemia*, that is, high levels of glucose or sugar in the blood, that results in varying degrees of impairment in insulin secretion or insulin action or both. Diabetes constitutes one of the largest health-care issues in the United States, and its prevalence is on the rise in part because of obesity and sedentary lifestyles among Americans (Gonder-Frederick, Cox, & Ritterband, 2002). There are three types of diabetes: Type 1, Type 2, and gestational. All tend to be diagnosed in asymptomatic individuals during a routine medical exam with screening blood and urine tests.

Because of the serious medical and psychiatric comorbidities and because of the limitations of the medical management approach, psychological interventions have become a standard of care in the United States and in other Western countries (Gonder-Frederick et al., 2002). Hemoglobin A_{1C} (HbA_{1C}) is a protein in the blood that serves as a useful marker of glycemic control. Accordingly, checking HbA_{1C} blood levels is a routine method for monitoring treatment compliance as well as the outcome of treatment.

The following sections present basic background on diabetes as a disease and illness followed by a detailed discussion of various psychological and biopsychosocial treatment intervention options. This discussion includes both clinical and research findings. The chapter concludes with an integrative treatment protocol and a case example illustrating the protocol.

EPIDEMIOLOGY

There are some 20.8 million children and adults in the United States who have diabetes. This represents 7% of the population. Although 14.6 million have been diagnosed, an estimated 6.2 million people—nearly one third—are unaware that they have the disease (American Diabetes Association, 2007). Approximately 90% of those who have been diagnosed have Type 2 diabetes, which has been associated with obesity in adults and, more recently, with obesity even in adolescents and children. About 1,700 new cases are diagnosed every day in the United States. Diabetes is the seventh leading cause of death among Americans. It is the leading cause of new cases of blindness, kidney failure, and lower extremity amputation. It also greatly increases a person's risk for heart attack or stroke. Diabetes accounts for more than $98 billion in direct and indirect medical costs and lost productivity each year. It could be prevented with early detection, improved delivery of care, and psychosocial interventions (American Diabetes Association, 2007).

TYPES

Three types of the diabetes have been identified, of which the first two types are most prevalent.

Type 1 Diabetes

Previously, this type was called *juvenile diabetes* or *insulin-dependent diabetes*. Typically, it is diagnosed in children, teenagers, and young adults. In Type 1, the beta cells of the pancreas no longer make insulin because the body's immune system has attacked and destroyed them. Individuals with this type can develop *diabetic ketoacidosis*, that is, an accumulation of ketones in the blood, which can result in diabetic coma and death if not aggressively treated.

Type 2 Diabetes

Previously called *adult-onset diabetes* or *noninsulin-dependent diabetes*, Type 2 is the most common form of diabetes. It can develop at any age, even during childhood, but is more likely later in life. It typically begins with *insulin resistance*, a condition in which fat, muscle, and liver cells are unable to use insulin properly. Initially, the pancreas keeps up with the added demand by producing more insulin. Later, the pancreas loses the ability to secrete enough insulin in response to meals. Unfortunately, obesity and inactivity increase the chances of developing this type. Individuals with this type can experience a nonketotic type of coma. About 80% of people with Type 2 diabetes are obese (Gonder-Frederick et al., 2002).

Gestational Diabetes

This type develops in some women during the late stages of pregnancy. Although it usually recedes after childbirth, nearly 40% of the women who experience gestational diabetes during their pregnancy go on to develop Type 2 diabetes later, usually within 5 to 10 years of giving birth. Origins are unclear, but it is believed that gestational diabetes is caused by the hormones of pregnancy creating a shortage of insulin. Because this type is less common, it is beyond the scope of this chapter.

SEVERITY

Generally speaking, Type 1 diabetes tends to be more severe than Type 2. Because the onset of Type 1 diabetes is usually in early life, long term noncompliance with diet and insulin control can result in serious consequences, such as retinopathy, nephropathy, neuropathy, and cardiovascular disease. Diabetes is the leading cause of blindness, nontraumatic lower limb amputation, physiological erectile dysfunction, and end-stage renal disease (Gonder-Frederick et al., 2002). Noncompliance with a Type 2 treatment regimen can also lead to end organ damage but may be less severe if the onset of the disease is later in life.

CAUSAL FACTORS

Diabetes is a disease in which blood glucose levels are elevated. Glucose comes from one's diet, and insulin is the hormone that facilitates glucose transfer into cells to provide energy. In Type 1 diabetes, the pancreas is unable to produce sufficient quantities of insulin. In Type 2 diabetes, cells are unable to adequately utilize insulin, a condition called *insulin resistance*. Without sufficient insulin, glucose is unable to enter cells and remains in the bloodstream. Over time, the accumulation of glucose can damage the eyes, kidneys, and nerves. Severe complications can develop in both types. These include coronary artery disease, blindness, kidney failure, and peripheral neuropathy. The onset of both types is influenced by genetic and environmental factors (Gonder-Frederick et al., 2002).

GENDER, AGE, AND ETHNICITY

Gender

Although the prevalence of diabetes is about the same in males and females, there appear to be differences in their health beliefs and behaviors (Rubin & Peyrot, 1998). Rubin and Peyrot (1998) reported that compared with females, males have higher total diabetes self-efficacy scores and have reported receiving more support from their partners. Moreover, wives of male patients have reported fewer hassles over medication and testing blood glucose levels than have spouses of female patients. Males also have reported that they felt more support and less hassle from wives about diabetes management. Furthermore, they have reported higher quality of life and were less likely to report significant levels of depression and anxiety. Finally, males with diabetes had lower HbA_{1c} levels and fewer medical complications than females with diabetes (Rubin & Peyrot, 1998).

Age

The elderly, many of whom are obese, have the highest prevalence of Type 2 diabetes. The increase in overweight minors has led to an alarming rapid increase in diabetes in that population. Being an adolescent appears to complicate diabetes treatment because adolescents tend to have more difficulty with self-management and personal adjustment than adults with diabetes. Adolescents seem to lack the cognitive ability to manipulate the various aspects of a diabetes self-management program (Schilling, Grey, & Knafl, 2002).

Ethnicity

Those of African, Latin American, Asian, or Aboriginal ethnic ancestry have an increased risk of developing Type 2 diabetes. Risk levels for these groups are between 2 and 6 times higher than for Whites. As a group, non-Whites have a much higher risk for Type 2 and Type 1 than Whites. African Americans are 1.7 times more likely to have diabetes than Whites and twice as likely to experience diabetes-related blindness, amputation, and kidney disease. Hispanic Americans have 2 to 4 times the incidence of Type 2 diabetes of non-Hispanic Whites (Feifer & Tansman, 1999). Furthermore, African American youth have poorer glycemic control than White youth. Finally, lower socioeconomic status is also associated with poor metabolic control and recurrent hospitalization (Gonder-Frederick et al., 2002).

PSYCHIATRIC COMORBIDITIES

Anxiety and depression are the most common comorbidities among adult diabetics, whereas depression, eating disorders, and family conflicts are common among adolescent diabetics (Snoek & Skinner, 2002). Each will be briefly discussed in this section.

Anxiety

Anxiety disorders are reported to be more prevalent in people with diabetes who have poor insulin control. Anxiety also interferes with adequate self-management of diabetes (Redman, 2004).

Depression

Diabetes is a significant risk factor for depression in all age groups (Gonder-Frederick et al., 2002) and appears to precede the development of diabetes (Williams, Clouse, & Lustman, 2006). Depression is more prevalent and severe in diabetics than in the general population (Golden et al., 2006; Snoek & Skinner, 2002), clinical depression having been noted in 15% to 20% of diabetic individuals. It is correlated with negative health behaviors such as smoking, alcohol and other drug abuse, and dysregulation in appetite and eating (Williams et al., 2006). Additionally, depression is associated with poor self-management and metabolic control, high relapse rates, increased complications, and decreased quality of life (Gonder-Frederick et al., 2002). Therefore, depression should be considered a major risk factor for patients with diabetes (Williams et al., 2006).

Eating Disorders

Irregular and disordered eating is pervasive among adolescents with Type 1 diabetes (Daneman, Olmstead, & Rydell, 1998). The prevalence of eating disorders is 62% among adolescents with diabetes, whereas it is only 22% among nondiabetic adolescents (Rydall, Rodin, Olmstead, Devenyi, & Daneman, 1997). Female adolescents with Type 1 may attempt to control their weight by adjusting their insulin levels, as do male adolescent wrestlers with Type 1 (R. P. Hoffman, 2001). Such insulin adjustment is dangerous and can result in long-term diabetic complications (R. P. Hoffman, 2001). Because both weight loss and weight gain can affect glycemic control, close monitoring of glucose levels, disordered eating, and depression are essential.

Smoking and Alcohol Abuse

The pancreas releases insulin, which regulates blood glucose. Alcohol is particularly toxic to the pancreas, and thus heavy alcohol use can cause chronic pancreatitis, which impairs insulin secretion and further complicates diabetes. Smoking not only increases the risk of pancreatic cancer but can also increase blood sugar levels and reduce the body's capacity to properly utilize insulin. Furthermore, chemicals in tobacco can damage blood vessels, muscles, and organs, which may increase risk of diabetes, further complicating it. Pregnant women who smoke have an increased risk of gestational diabetes. A prospective study (Rimm, Chan, Stampfer, Colditz, & Willett, 1995) examined the association between smoking, alcohol consumption, and the incidence of Type I diabetes in middle-aged and older men. It found that cigarette smoking doubled the risk of diabetes among a healthy population of men. Also found was that moderate alcohol consumption among healthy people may be associated with increased insulin sensitivity and a reduced risk of diabetes. Thus, it was concluded that smoking and alcohol may alter the risk of diabetes through long-term effects on insulin secretion and insulin resistance. In short, smoking and alcohol consumption significantly disrupt glycemic control and should be avoided.

Family Dynamics

Family dynamics can play a significant role in the onset, course, and treatment of diabetes. For example, adolescent diabetics from families with high conflict are likely to have had their diabetes triggered by it and tend to have lower glycemic control, whereas those from families with low conflict and high cohesion tend to have better glycemic control. In families with less cohesion and greater conflict, children and adolescents are more likely to experience recurrent episodes of ketoacidosis and severe hypoglycemia. Family conflict can also trigger or exacerbate disordered eating behavior in adolescents (Gonder-Frederick et al., 2002). Often this is due to insulin omission, which has been associated with recurrent diabetic ketoacidosis (Howells et al., 2002). Family dynamics can also foster or hinder an adolescent's sense of self-efficacy. Self-efficacy predicts treatment compliance, autonomy, and life satisfaction. In a randomized controlled trial (RCT) involving routine management or routine management with negotiated telephone support, participants in the two intervention groups showed significant improvement in self-efficacy but no difference in glycemic control (Howells et al., 2002).

PROGNOSIS

Because diabetes is currently considered incurable, disease management wherein glycemic levels are tightly controlled is the goal of treatment. The presumption is that such control will limit the expression of end organ damage such as blindness, kidney failure, and so on. In the past decade, increased awareness and research funding has been directed to primary and secondary diabetes prevention. The specific focus is on insulin resistance and obesity as risk factors for prediabetes. Norris et al. (2005) found nine RCTs focused on this group and concluded that diet modification, physical activity, and behavioral interventions are effective for inducing and maintaining weight loss in prediabetic adults.

TREATMENT CONSIDERATIONS AND INTERVENTIONS

Diabetes appears to be among the most difficult chronic diseases to manage. Understanding the nature of diabetes, the importance of appropriate food intake, and glycemic control is essential to effective self-management. However, achieving and maintaining adequate glycemic control can be most challenging. The benefits of conscientious, daily efforts to control food intake and blood glucose levels often remain invisible in the short term. There is no immediate positive feedback, other than the clinician's stated reassurance that strict glycemic control today will reduce diabetic complications in the future. Such lack of immediate, direct feedback can jeopardize the diabetic's commitment to self-management. It is not surprising that many find it difficult to comply consistently with the treatment regimen.

Illness representations and glycemic control are critical clinical considerations. Such representations can predict glycemic control, and glycemic control provides a key marker of treatment compliance and outcome.

Illness Representations

Research on health beliefs and self-efficacy have shown that the illness representations of people with diabetes are strongly associated with their self-management efforts. Specifically, their beliefs concerning the seriousness of their illness and their beliefs about the effectiveness of their treatment are most predictive of their blood sugar control and diet control (Redman, 2004). In a study of health beliefs about diabetes, males were found to express more confidence about managing their diabetes than females. They were less likely to believe that their health outcomes were a result of fate or some external force. Males reported that they were in control of their disease and had control of any medical complications, long or short term. They also reported fewer episodes of hyperglycemia and lower levels of self-reported depression and anxiety. Spousal reports tended to confirm that males felt more confident and competent in their own ability to manage diabetes (Rubin & Peyrot, 1998).

The behavioral changes necessary for optimal diabetes self-management seem to be largely determined by the illness representations and related beliefs that individuals have about their diabetes, its treatment, and themselves. Those with diabetes need to believe that the outcome of treatment, that is, acceptable glycemic control leading to a lower risk of developing diabetic complications, is worthwhile. They have to be confident that they are capable of achieving this outcome and that their efforts will benefit them (van der Ven, Weinger, & Snoek, 2002). It is interesting that self-efficacy, which reflects confidence, has been found to be a predictor of treatment compliance in diabetes. Furthermore, autonomy was found to predict life satisfaction among those with well-controlled diabetes (Gonder-Frederick et al., 2002). It is arguable that effective self- management requires a high level of self-efficacy and autonomy.

Glycemic Control

Controlling blood glucose levels is an essential strategy in the management of diabetes (Ismail, Winkley, & Rabe-Hesketh, 2004). Various factors seem to influence glycemic control, as noted in a meta-analysis of 25 RCTs (Maharaj, Rodin, & Olmstead, 1998). Results showed that psychological treatments did improve long-term glycemic control and psychological distress but did not improve weight control or blood glucose concentration in Type 2 diabetics. Glycemic control is also influenced by family dynamics. Children whose families have less conflict and greater cohesion experience better glycemic control (Gonder-Frederick et al., 2002). Accordingly, clinicians need to understand and tailor treatment on the basis of the unique factors that are likely to influence glycemic control for particular diabetes patients.

PSYCHOEDUCATIONAL INTERVENTIONS

Self-management is the heart of the treatment of diabetes, and self-management programs for diabetes are more well developed than for any other chronic disease (Redmond, 2004). However, having such programs available is no guarantee of success. Rather, the mark of successful self-management is the degree to which people with diabetes assume responsibility for self-management (Gonder-Frederick et al., 2002). Needless to say, psychoeducational interventions are essential in helping patients assume this responsibility. These interventions include patient education, relaxation training, blood glucose awareness training, and smoking cessation.

Patient Education

Patient education is a critical component of diabetes management. Together with diet and exercise, it is essential in maintaining effective glucose control. Educational efforts are essential in engaging the diabetic in a self-management program that typically requires patients to monitor their glucose levels and food intake (Ellis et al., 2004). A meta-analysis by Ellis et al. (2004) revealed that interventions that included face-to-face delivery, cognitive reframing teaching methods, and exercise content were more likely to improve glycemic control.

Relaxation Training

Relaxation training appears to reduce hyperglycemia and improve glucose tolerance (Gonder-Frederick et al., 2002), particularly important for patients with high anxiety.

Blood Glucose Awareness Training

Blood glucose awareness training is a psychoeducational intervention that incorporates both behavioral and cognitive strategies to improve self-management and decision making in adult Type 1 diabetic patients. It was specifically designed to improve the accuracy of patients' detection and interpretation of relevant blood glucose symptoms and other cues. Blood glucose awareness training both improves accuracy of recognition of current glucose level and improves detection of both hypoglycemia and hyperglycemia. It has been demonstrated to be most effective with patients who are the least accurate in detecting glucose levels. In comparison with dietary patient education, patients receiving blood glucose awareness training have better awareness of blood glucose and better glycemic control (D. Cox et al., 1995). This training is particularly beneficial to patients who are undergoing intensive insulin therapy, are bothered with frequent diabetic ketoacidosis, have had severe hypoglycemia, or who experience wide fluctuations in glucose levels or impaired hypoglycemia awareness (D. Cox et al., 2001).

The long-term benefits of this training are impressive. In a repeated baseline design study (D. Cox et al., 2001), Type 1 diabetic patients received blood glucose awareness training and then completed diaries in which they recorded occurrences of diabetic ketoacidosis, severe hypoglycemia, and motor vehicle violations. From baseline to follow-up, blood glucose awareness training led to improved detection of hypoglycemia and hyperglycemia; improved judgment regarding when to lower high glucose and raise low glucose levels and about not driving while hypoglycemic; reduction in occurrence of diabetic ketoacidosis, severe hypoglycemia, and motor vehicle violations; and improvement in terms of worry about hypoglycemia, quality of life, and diabetes knowledge (D. Cox et al., 2001).

Smoking Cessation

Because tobacco, nicotine, and cigarette smoking can be lethal when combined with diabetes, smoking cessation is essential to self-management. Accordingly, smoking cessation should be part of the tailored treatment plan for every diabetic who smokes or otherwise uses tobacco.

COGNITIVE–BEHAVIORAL THERAPY

Unfortunately, failure in self-management efforts is common among diabetics. This often leads to negative thoughts and feelings such as, "It doesn't matter what I do, there's absolutely no point in trying," or "'I messed up again, I'm such a failure." These negative thoughts, resulting from multiple experiences of failure, foster a pessimistic attitude toward diabetes and one-self, leading to a tendency to "let it all go" instead of renewing efforts. This reinforces a negative cycle of events that can further reinforce poor self-management and control, resulting in even more negative feelings. Fortunately, cognitive–behavioral therapy (CBT) can be effective in breaking this cycle of negative thoughts and feelings.

Relatively few studies of CBT and diabetes have been published. An RCT reported by Lustman, Griffith, Freedland, Kissel, and Clouse (1998) found that the combination of CBT and supportive diabetes patient education was an effective treatment for major depression in patients with Type 2 diabetes. It also improved glycemic control. Two other RCTs reported on the effects of group CBT. In both Snoek et al. (2001) and Weinger et al. (2002), CBT was compared with a patient education intervention that served as the control group. Positive changes were found on self-care behavior and emotional well-being, with modest improvements in glycemic control. Snoek and Skinner (2002) reviewed 11 RCTs and found that CBT is effective in treating depression among patients with Type 2 diabetes as well as lowering HbA_{1C}.

COGNITIVE–BEHAVIORAL GROUP TRAINING

Cognitive–behavioral group training was developed by Snoek, van der Ven, and Lubach (1999) in collaboration with the Joslin Diabetes Clinic. It is a brief intervention combining CBT with psychoeducation for small groups (6 to 8 patients) and is facilitated by a psychologist and diabetes nurse specialist or diabetes educator. Adult patients with Type 1 diabetes in persistent poor glycemic control with no serious medical or psychiatric comorbidity are targets for this group. The goal of cognitive–behavioral group training is to help the patients improve their self-care behaviors, including glycemic control, and to enhance psychological well-being. The intervention consists of four weekly sessions in which one of the following four topics is discussed at each session: CBT–rational emotive therapy and diabetes; stress and diabetes; complications of diabetes and future outlook; and interpersonal relationships, social support, and diabetes. Throughout the sessions, participants work on exploring, challenging, and restructuring their cognitive distortions, with specific focus on the four topics. To facilitate this, participants read assigned information before the session and complete homework assignments that are discussed in the group session. Patients are instructed to fill out an "ABC" worksheet—describing the Activating event, the specific Beliefs that gave rise to these emotions and behaviors, and the unwanted Consequences—in between sessions with regard to situations where they felt distressed or discouraged by their diabetes. To help patients better manage their stress, a progressive muscle relaxation technique is introduced (Snoek et al., 1999).

OTHER PSYCHOTHERAPEUTIC INTERVENTIONS

An RCT compared the effect of cognitive analytic therapy (CAT), a focused time-limited psychotherapy, with patient education provided by a nurse specialist. Patients received either 16 sessions of CAT or 14 to 18 sessions of patient education. Pre- and posttreatment blood glucose control (HbA_{1C}), interpersonal difficulties, and diabetes knowledge were measured before and up to 9 months after treatment was completed. Although patient education initially improved glycemic control, it was not sustained. However, glycemic control and interpersonal difficulties both improved after CAT. The study demonstrated that when psychological difficulties underlying problems with self-care in Type I diabetes were addressed, improvements in diabetes control are likely to continue (Fosbury, Bosley, Ryle, Sonksen, & Judd, 1997).

MEDICAL TREATMENT

Type 1 Diabetes

Medical management of Type 1 diabetes usually includes insulin, diet, and patient education. Because hyperglycemia is responsible for most of the long-term complications of diabetes and because insulin can effectively control blood glucose levels, insulin has been the primary medical treatment. Diet is also useful in maintaining acceptable glucose levels. For patients with nonadherence issues, the use of subcutaneous continuous insulin infusion can be instituted.

Type 2 Diabetes

The medical treatment of Type 2 involves patient education, weight-loss diet, exercise, and self-management. Because Type 2 is highly associated with obesity and weight gain, weight loss and weight management are constant concerns for these patients. A high degree of self-management is required of diabetic patients including self-monitoring of blood glucose concentration, foot care, and administration of medication.

Diet plans generally involve low-fat diets that are tailored to the individual's lifestyle, ethnicity, and culture. The goal is to achieve weight reduction in overweight individuals with Type 2 diabetes. Unfortunately, only about 10% of those with Type 2 have been able to control their diabetes with diet and exercise alone. For most of the rest, insulin injections may be needed to achieve acceptable blood sugar control.

Studies have provided strong evidence that intensive treatment regimens that maintain tighter glucose control delay or prevent development of some of these complications (Gonder-Frederick et al., 2002). Because of the intensive efforts required of patients, adherence is a constant concern. In 1993, the American Diabetes Association created new guidelines for diabetes management (see American Diabetes Association, 2007), and large numbers of patients were suddenly expected to follow intensive and demanding treatment protocols previously recommended only for the most motivated patients. Increasingly, medical management is emphasizing control of hypertension and hyperlipidemia because research has demonstrated that aggressive control significantly reduces diabetes-related deaths, strokes, microvascular incidents, and visual loss (Gonder-Frederick et al., 2002).

MEDICATION

Insulin is the main injectable diabetes medication used primarily for Type I and secondarily for Type II when oral diabetes medications fail. There are five classes of oral diabetes medication, all of which can be beneficial in lowering blood glucose levels. Sulfonylureas stimulate the pancreas to make more insulin. The second- and third-generation ones are the best. Biguanides shut off the liver's excess glucose production.

In this class is metformin—trade name is Glucophage—which appears to be one of the most effective, least expensive, and subsequently one of the most commonly prescribed medications. Alpha-glucosidase inhibitors slow absorption of carbohydrates in the intestine. Thiazolidinediones increase the body's sensitivity to insulin. Meglitinides stimulate the pancreas to make more insulin. These different classes of diabetes medications can be used in combination or with insulin to control blood sugar.

In the treatment of comorbid clinical depression, the selective serotonin reuptake inhibitors bupropion, mirtazapine, and venlafaxine are considered first-line pharmacologic interventions for depression in diabetic patients (Williams et al., 2006).

COMBINED TREATMENT

Combined or combination treatments are becoming the common practice in diabetes. Typically, diet modification and other lifestyle changes are combined with one or more medications. More recently, various psychological interventions have been effectively combined with lifestyle change and diabetic medications.

Integrative Treatment Protocol: Diabetes

1. Key Background Information	
Pathology	Syndrome characterized by hyperglycemia resulting in impairment in insulin secretion or insulin action or both.
Epidemiology	Around 14.6 million Americans have been diagnosed, but an estimated 6.2 million who have the disease have not. Approximately 90% of those who have been diagnosed have Type 2 diabetes.
Types	• Type 1: Previously called *juvenile-onset diabetes*. Requires insulin from the onset. Leading cause of blindness, lower limb amputation, end-stage renal failure, and physiological erectile dysfunction. • Type 2: Previously called *adult-onset diabetes* but increasingly common in adolescents and adults. Insulin not usually required until later stages. More common than Type 1. • Gestational: pregnancy related.
Severity	Type 1 more severe than Type 2. Poor glycemic control can result in blindness, heart attacks, stroke, limb amputation, and erectile dysfunction.
Causal factors	In Type 1, there is insufficient insulin, whereas in Type 2, cells are unable to adequately utilize insulin, resulting in symptoms and organ damage.
Gender and culture	Male:female ratio = 1:1; African American:White = 1.7:1; Hispanic:non-Hispanic White = 3:1. Lower socioeconomic status is associated with poor glycemic control and recurrent hospitalization.
Comorbidities	• Depression: linked to smoking, eating, alcohol and drug problems, and poor glycemic control. • Eating disorders: common in Type 1, particularly adolescent females who use insulin omission to lose weight. • Smoking and alcohol use: Smoking can be lethal in both types; alcohol disrupts glycemic control. • Family dynamics and conflict: Family conflict can trigger diabetes and significantly impact control of blood sugar and may exacerbate disordered eating behavior in adolescents.
Prognosis	Diabetes is currently considered an incurable, progressive disease. Tight control of glycemic levels is the goal of treatment.
2. Biopsychosocial Assessment	
Patient profile	From interview and observation and Revised Illness Perception Questionnaire (IPQ-R; Moss-Morris et al., 2002) assessment: • IPQ-R factors, especially illness perceptions, explanations, and treatment expectations;

(continues)

	• severity of symptoms and functional impact; • capacity, previous change efforts, and readiness for change; and • personality style or disorder and family and cultural factors.
Illness profile	Identify higher risk diabetes patients: • those with anxiety, depression, smoking, substance use, and disordered eating; • those with poor glycemic control, especially adolescents; • those with early signs of diabetes complications; • African American and low socioeconomic status patients; • children or adolescents in families with high levels of conflict; and • those who fail to accept diagnosis.
Glycemic control history	Inquire about patient's efforts to monitor and record glucose levels and how these impact their diet, insulin or medication usage, exercise, stress control, and so on. Seek collateral information from family members, medical records, and other possible sources.
Family functioning and comorbid psychiatric conditions	Carefully rule out depression, eating disorders, anxiety, self-destructive behavior, and interpersonal and family conflict because each can exacerbate the illness and complicate treatment.
Smoking and alcohol history	Assess for past and current usage because continued use will negatively impact treatment.
Self-efficacy	Assess because it is an important predictor of treatment compliance.
HbA_{1c} levels	Medical personnel have primary responsibility for monitoring this blood level, but the clinician should know how to interpret readings because it is an effective biomarker of long-term glucose control as well as alcohol use.

3. Intervention Planning

Patient profile	• Illness representation: Identify problematic representations for modification. • Glycemic control: Plan to monitor HbA_{1c} levels.
Illness and disease type	• Type 1: Basic treatment goal is glycemic control and prevention of diabetes mellitis (DM) complications. • Type 2: Basic treatment goal is glycemic control and weight loss; secondary goal is prevention of DM complications.
Acceptance of illness and acceptance of patient's control over it	Two critical intervention targets early in course of treatment.

4. Intervention Implementation

Psychoeducational interventions	• Combined medical and behavioral health interventions are the norm for both types of DM, irrespective of level of severity.

	• Patient education is the cornerstone of treatment of DM. Includes self-management (i.e., knowledge of the disease process, self-testing and monitoring of blood glucose concentration, administration of insulin and/or other medications, foot care, and regular healthy eating), weight management protocol, relaxation, and stress management.
Blood glucose awareness training	Skill training that incorporates cognitive–behavioral therapy (CBT) strategies to increase self-awareness and decision making, which are reflected in better glycemic control.
Smoking cessation intervention	Essential for smokers.
Cognitive–behavioral therapy	• Individual: Focus can be on modifying problematic illness representations with cognitive restructuring and/or positive reattribution, treatment-interfering thoughts or behaviors, and interpersonal conflicts and support issues. • Group: Improvement of self-care behaviors and glycemic control and to enhance psychological well-being. Structured topics: CBT and diabetes, stress, diabetes complications, and interpersonal relationships and social support.
Other psychotherapeutic interventions	Cognitive analytic therapy has been shown to improve both glycemic control and interpersonal difficulties.
Medical management	• Type 1: Usually consists of insulin, diet and nutritional counseling, glucose monitoring, and patient education. For those with significant noncompliance, use of subcutaneous continuous insulin infusion (pump). • Type 2: Usually consists of diet and nutritional counseling, exercise, patient education, glucose monitoring, and self-management.
Medication	Insulin is the main injectable medication. Five classes of oral antiglycemics are used alone, in combination, or with insulin. Insulin is most common for Type 1, and Glucophage (metformin) is the most common for Type 2.
Combined treatment	Diet modification and other lifestyle changes are combined with one or more medications and/or psychological interventions.

5. Intervention Monitoring

- Review patient's log glucose readings and glycemic control efforts.
- Track session-to-session progress with regard to compliance, glycemic control, comorbid conditions, and overall symptom reduction and functionality.

CASE OF JAN R.

Jan R. is a 34-year-old married African American woman who was referred by her primary care physician to Julie Singleton for consultation. Singleton is a medical psychologist who practices in an internal medicine clinic of a university medical school and consults with clinic patients who are not responding adequately to their treatment. Jan is a financial analyst who has been married for 11 years, and she and her husband Tom have two children. She was diagnosed with Type 2 diabetes mellitus 1 year ago and was begun on a treatment regimen to control her blood sugar and lose weight. The expectation was that with regular monthly medical monitoring and participation in a weekly weight control support group she could lose 30 pounds and maintain a target weight of 132 pounds. Achieving and maintaining both diet and weight could significantly reduce the likelihood that she would need insulin and would slow the progression of the disease. Over the past 8 months, Jan had lost some weight but gained most of it back. Of more concern to her physician was that Jan's blood sugar levels continued to rise even though Glucophage, an oral antiglycemic, had been started 4 months ago. This prompted the psychological consultation.

Jan's responses on the Brief IPQ (Broadbent, Petrie, Main, & Weinman, 2006) prompted follow-up by Singleton, particularly items about Jan's concern about her illness, control over it, and its cause. Jan appeared to be only minimally concerned with her diabetes and did not believe she had much control over it. She believed it was inevitable because "all the women in my family get it. It's this 'fat gene' that we've been cursed with . . . so I just live with it." Singleton further explored Jan's illness representations and continued to do so in three subsequent CBT-focused sessions. The focus was to examine and modify her fatalistic view of her illness. Jan also became involved in one of the clinic's blood glucose awareness training groups to increase her self-awareness and decision making regarding her glycemic control. She also continued in the weight control support group and was beginning to see noticeable progress in weight loss.

13

EPILEPSY

Epilepsy is a neurological condition in which clusters of nerve cells, or *neurons*, in the brain fire abnormally, causing abnormal bursts of electrical discharge in the brain. When this occurs, the result is strange sensations, emotions, and behaviors, or sometimes convulsions, muscle spasms, and loss of consciousness. Symptoms vary depending on the brain area that is affected. During a seizure, neurons may fire as many as 500 times per second, much faster than the normal rate of about 80 times per second. In some individuals, this happens only occasionally, whereas for others, it may happen up to hundreds of times a day.

The following sections present basic background on epilepsy as a disease and illness followed by a detailed discussion of various psychological and biopsychosocial treatment intervention options. This discussion includes both clinical and research findings. Because nonepileptic seizures are a relatively common presentation in medical settings, they are also discussed. The chapter concludes with an integrative treatment protocol and a case example illustrating the protocol.

EPIDEMIOLOGY

About 3 million people in the United States, which is about 1% of the population, have experienced an unprovoked seizure or been diagnosed with epilepsy. For about 80% of those diagnosed with epilepsy, seizures can be controlled with medication or surgery. However, about 20% of people with epilepsy will continue to experience seizures, that is, intractable epilepsy, even with the best available treatment.

TYPES

Seizures are identified by the symptoms and the brain area affected (Koyama, 2005). More than 30 different types of seizures have been identified, but they can be divided into four major categories: focal seizures, generalized seizures, temporal lobe epilepsy (TLE), and nonepileptic seizures.

Focal Seizures

Focal seizures, also called *partial seizures*, occur in just one part of the brain. About 60% of people with epilepsy have focal seizures. These seizures are frequently described by the area of the brain in which they originate. The symptoms of focal seizures can easily be confused with other disorders. For instance, the dreamlike perceptions associated with a complex focal seizure may be misdiagnosed as migraine headaches, which also may cause a dreamlike state. The strange behavior and sensations caused by focal seizures also can be mistaken for symptoms of narcolepsy, fainting, or even mental illness. It may require extensive testing and careful monitoring by a specialist to differentiate between epilepsy and other disorders.

Generalized Seizures

Generalized seizures, also called *tonic-clonic seizures*, are a result of abnormal neuronal activity on both sides of the brain. They may cause loss of consciousness, falls, or massive muscle spasms. There are many kinds of generalized seizures. In *absence seizures*, also called *petit mal seizures*, the individual may appear to be staring into space and/or have jerking or twitching muscles. Tonic seizures cause stiffening of muscles of the body, generally those in the back, legs, and arms. Clonic seizures cause repeated jerking movements of muscles on both sides of the body. *Myoclonic seizures* cause jerks or twitches of the upper body, arms, or legs. *Atonic seizures* cause a loss of normal muscle tone. The affected person will fall down or may drop his or her head involuntarily. Tonic-clonic seizures cause a mixture of symptoms, including stiffening of the body and repeated jerks of the arms and/or legs as well as loss of consciousness. Tonic-clonic seizures are sometimes referred to by an older term: *grand mal seizures.*

Not all seizures can be easily defined as either focal or generalized. Some people have seizures that begin as focal seizures but then spread to the entire brain. Others may have both types of seizures but with no clear pattern. Two other types commonly noted in behavioral health settings are TLE and *nonepileptic seizures*.

Temporal Lobe Epilepsy

TLE is the most common epilepsy syndrome with focal seizures. These seizures are often associated with auras and typically begin in childhood. Research has shown that repeated temporal lobe seizures can cause the hippocampus, important for memory and learning, to shrink over time. Although it may take years of temporal lobe seizures for measurable hippocampal damage to occur, this finding underlines the need to treat TLE early and as effectively as possible.

Nonepileptic Seizures

Similar to but different from epileptic seizures, *nonepileptic seizures* are behavioral events that resemble epileptic seizures but are not caused by electrical disruptions of the brain. Needless to say, nonepileptic seizures present both diagnostic and treatment challenges to clinicians. Once referred to as *psychogenic seizures* and *pseudoseizures*, they are not usually classified as an epilepsy, although they can occur in both individuals who have and those who do not have epilepsy. Persons of all ages may experience nonepileptic seizures, and they occur 3 times more frequently in females than in males. They may arise from various psychological factors, such as from suggestion, from a desire to be excused from work, from the motive of collecting financial compensation, or to escape an intolerable social situation, and they are triggered by a conscious or unconscious desire for increased care and attention, by anxiety, or by pain. It is notable that they seldom occur in the presence of others.

Nonepileptic seizures start with rapid breathing, which leads to a buildup of carbon dioxide and thus can cause symptoms remarkably similar to epileptic seizures, that is, prickling in the face, hands, and feet; stiffening; trembling; writhing and thrashing movements; quivering; screaming or talking sounds; and falling to the floor. These attacks differ from epileptic seizures in that out-of-phase movements of the upper and lower extremities, pelvic thrusting, and side-to-side head movements are evident. However, they vary from one occurrence to another and are not readily stereotyped. Indicators like pupillary dilation, depressed corneal reflexes, the presence of Babinski reflex, autonomic cardiorespiratory changes, tongue biting, and urinary or fecal incontinence are more likely to be seen in epilepsy but are seldom manifested in psychogenic seizures. These attacks may last a few minutes or hours and end as abruptly as they began. Anxiety may be experienced prior to an attack, followed by relief and relaxation afterward, leading some to speculate that psychogenic seizures may occur as a direct response to stress in order to relieve tension. Afterward, patients usually have a vague recollection of the seizure without the usual postseizure symptoms of drowsiness and depression found in epileptic seizures.

SEVERITY

The seizures that occur in epilepsy are often a chronic condition that can significantly impact the affected individual's quality of life, so *status epilepticus* can be a life-threatening condition. Seizures sometimes do cause brain damage, particularly if they are severe, yet most seizures do not seem to have a detrimental effect on the brain.

GENDER AND ETHNICITY

Seizures affect individuals of both genders and all ethnic and cultural backgrounds.

Gender

Some 3 million Americans experience epilepsy, and of these 40% are women of childbearing age. Women with epilepsy cannot safely stop antiepileptic drug treatment because hormones can exacerbate seizures. Pregnant women are at increased risk for seizures, and seizures increase the risk of miscarriage, epilepsy, malformations. and developmental delay in their children. Few minority women seek care for epilepsy, probably because of the negative perceptions about epilepsy in minority communities as well as financial barriers.

Ethnicity

Rates of epilepsy are reported as 1.3 to 2.2 times greater for non-White than for White males and 1.4 to 1.7 times greater for non-White than for White females. Although there is little evidence of racial–ethnic differences in the rates of childhood epilepsy or in the incidence of epilepsy when all ages are considered, prevalence rates are considerably higher in African Americans than in either non-Hispanic Whites or Hispanics for those aged 20 to 59. Native Americans and some Hispanic groups, particularly elderly Hispanic men, also are reported to have a higher prevalence of epilepsy than their non-Hispanic White or non-Hispanic counterparts. Noteworthy is that rates among Native Americans are more than double that for the United States as a whole. In addition, non-White individuals have a higher incidence of *status epilepticus* across all age groups, and they have higher rates of the well-known risk factors for epilepsy such as diabetes, stroke, and depression. Socioeconomic factors, and not biological or genetic differences, appear to be mostly responsible for the racial–ethnic disparities in the occurrence of epilepsy (Szaflarski, Szaflarski, Privitera, Ficker, & Horner, 2006).

CAUSAL FACTORS

Epilepsy is a disorder with many possible causes, and anything that disturbs the normal pattern of neuron activity, from illness to brain damage to abnormal brain development, can lead to seizures. Usually, there is an abnormality in brain wiring, an imbalance in neurotransmitters, or some combination of both these factors. Abnormalities in brain wiring that occur during brain development may disturb neuronal activity and lead to epilepsy. Some epileptics have an abnormally high level of excitatory neurotransmitters that increase neuronal activity, whereas others have an abnormally low level of inhibitory neurotransmitters that decrease neuronal activity. In some cases, the brain's attempts to repair itself after a head injury, stroke, or other problem may inadvertently generate abnormal nerve connections that lead to epilepsy. About 50% of all seizures have no known cause. However, in other cases, the seizures are clearly linked to infection, poisoning, head injury, or other identifiable problems. Ovulation and other hormones can also trigger seizure activity (Maguire, Stell, Rafizadeh, & Mody, 2005).

Finally, trauma appears to be a causal factor in more than 80% of a sample of patients with nonepileptic seizures (Bowman, 1993). Accidents with minor head injuries, surgeries, falls with injuries, and sexual experiences such as rape or the beginning or ending of a sexual relationship were commonly associated with the onset of nonepileptic seizures (Miller, 1994).

PSYCHIATRIC COMORBIDITY

Patients with epilepsy are at increased risk of comorbid psychiatric disorders (Gaitatzis, Trimble, & Sander, 2004). Both anxiety and depression are more common among people with epilepsy than in the general population. Gaitatzis et al. (2004) performed a nonsystematic review of the literature and found that although 6% of patients with epilepsy experience a psychiatric disorder, the rate is 10% to 20% in patients with temporal lobe epilepsy and/or refractory epilepsy. They found that mood disorders were the most prevalent diagnosis, particularly depression, with anxiety coming in a strong second.

Anxiety

Anxiety disorders can have a significant effect on the quality of life of epilepsy patients. Patients with these disorders often overestimate the risk associated with the disease and underestimate their own ability to function with the disease (Beyenburg, Mitchell, Schmidt, Elger, & Reuber, 2005). Anxiety among people with epilepsy is frequently associated with postictal depression or dysphoria, and these states may last for days postseizure (Beyenburg et al., 2005).

Panic Attacks

Patients with epilepsy have panic attacks up to 6 times more frequently than the general population, according to Beyenburg et al. (2005). In addition, panic is the most likely anxiety disorder to be directly generated by a seizure. Epileptic activity in some areas of the brain, particularly the amygdala, can directly cause panic attacks in patients with temporal lobe epilepsy (Beyenburg et al., 2005).

Depression

Depression is relatively common in epilepsy patients, and approximately one third of those hospitalized report mild to moderate symptoms of depression (Mensah, Beavis, Thapar, & Kerr, 2006). It is interesting that men with epilepsy are more at risk for developing depression than women, even though the prevalence rate for depression for women in the general population is significantly higher than for men (Gaitatzis et al., 2004; Mensah et al., 2006).

The etiology of depression in epilepsy is related to disease site, medication, medication side effects, nutritional deficiencies, and perceived lack of control (Beyenburg et al., 2005). In terms of disease site, patients with left temporal lobe epilepsy have a higher likelihood for experiencing depression than other types of epilepsy (Koyama, 2005). With regard to medication, phenobarbital has been associated with depression (Nilsson, Ahlbom, Farahmand, Asberg, & Tomson, 2002), or depression can be an iatrogenic side effect of antiepileptic medications. It can also be due to folate deficiency, which results from long-term use of certain antiepileptic medications (Gaitatzis et al., 2004; Koyama, 2005; Nilsson et al., 2002). Finally, perceived lack of control over seizure occurrence felt by patients can significantly contribute to the development of anxiety and depression (Goldstein, Holland, Soteriou, & Mellers, 2005).

Suicide

Patients with epilepsy appear to have a higher risk of mortality related to suicide (Gaitatzis et al., 2004; Nilsson et al., 2002). These authors reported a suicide rate of 5% to 7% among patients with epilepsy compared with a 1.4% death rate from suicide in the general population in the United States. Nilsson et al. (2002) performed a case-control study and compared epilepsy patients who committed suicide with 171 controls, living epilepsy patients. They found the risk of suicide seemed to increase with high seizure frequency and antiepileptic drug polytherapy. However, the strongest association was with patients diagnosed in early adolescence rather than with disease severity. Other significant associations include comorbid psychiatric illness and inadequate neurologic follow-up (Nilsson et al., 2002).

PROGNOSIS

Although epilepsy cannot currently be cured, for some people it does eventually go away (Giovagnoli, Meneses, & da Silva, 2006). The odds of becoming seizure free are not as good for adults or for children with severe epilepsy syndromes, but it is nonetheless possible that seizures may decrease or even stop over time. This is more likely if the epilepsy has been well controlled by medication or if the person has had epilepsy surgery. Currently available treatments can control seizures at least some of the time in about 80% of people with epilepsy. However, another 20%—about 600,000 people with epilepsy in the United States—have intractable seizures, and another 400,000 believe they receive only partial relief from available treatments (Chapell, Reston, & Snyder, 2003).

TREATMENT CONSIDERATIONS AND INTERVENTIONS

Although seizure disorders represent a chronic medical condition that can be life threatening, a number of medical, surgical, and psychological treatment interventions are available. The recommended treatment strategy for patients with epilepsy or symptoms of epilepsy includes diagnosing new patients, referring patients to specialists, monitoring seizures, helping to improve seizure control by adjusting medications or referring the patient to hospital, minimizing side effects of medications, facilitating structured withdrawal from medications where appropriate, introducing psychological interventions, and psychoeducation to improve quality of life (Scottish Intercollegiate Guidelines Network, 2003).

Although this section summarizes some medical and surgical interventions, it emphasizes the importance of psychological interventions in the effective treatment of epilepsy. A review of the literature indicates that such psychological interventions as psychoeducation, cognitive–behavioral therapy (CBT), psychotherapy, and relaxation methods are effective in treating patients with epilepsy (Scicutella & Ettinger, 2002). A tailored approach to treatment is viewed as essential as well as most effective (Couldridge, Kendall, & March, 2001). Two key treatment considerations in planning and implementating treatment are illness representations and diagnostic considerations.

Illness Representations

The Illness Perception Questionnaire (IPQ; Weinman, Petrie, Moss-Morris, & Horne, 1996) has been shown to be an effective measure for assessing illness representation of individuals with chronic epilepsy (Goldstein et al., 2005). In fact, one IPQ factor, *illness identity*, that is, the symptoms the patient associates with their illness, has been shown to accurately predict their level of anxiety (Goldstein et al., 2005). This confirms the results of a previous study, which found that illness identity was a significant predictor of psychosocial distress (Kemp, Morley, & Anderson, 1999). That study showed that epilepsy patients who presented with adjustment difficulties were characterized by high seizure frequency, avoidance, doubt about their diagnostic label, the belief of minimal control of their illness, and the belief in a poorer outcome. On the other hand, those with better adjustment were characterized by acceptance of their illness, positive coping behaviors, and beliefs that they had some control over their illness and that they would have a better outcome. Besides predicting psychosocial adjustment to epilepsy, the researchers concluded that the illness representations paradigm could be useful in identifying treatment factors for increasing patients' adaptation to their illness (Kemp et al., 1999).

Diagnostic Considerations

Experiencing a seizure does not necessarily mean that a person has epilepsy, because two or more witnessed seizures are required for the diagnosis of epilepsy. A number of different tests are used to diagnose this chronic disease. These include electroencephalogram monitoring; brain scans; various blood tests; and developmental, neurological, and behavioral tests. Accurate diagnosis of the type of epilepsy a person has is crucial for finding an effective treatment.

Differentiating nonepileptic seizures from epileptic seizures is difficult and challenging. Research indicates that in 20% to 30% of cases, physicians who specialize in the diagnosis and treatment of epilepsy are incorrect in distinguishing one from the other. Epileptic seizures are caused by a change in how the brain cells send electrical signals to each other, whereas nonepileptic seizures are triggered by a conscious or unconscious desire for more care and attention. Thus, measuring brain activity with an electroencephalogram and video telemetry are important diagnostic tools. Also, patients exhibiting nonepileptic seizures often lack the exhaustion, confusion, and nausea that is associated with epileptic seizure activity. It is important to remember that nonepileptic seizures can occur in individuals who also experience epileptic seizures. Measuring serum prolactin levels can be diagnostic in patients suspected of having nonepileptic seizures. It has been found that serum levels of prolactin are often elevated just following an epileptic seizure and begin returning to normal within 15 minutes (Wyllie, Luders, & Macmillan, 1984).

PSYCHOEDUCATIONAL INTERVENTIONS

Psychoeducational interventions that foster self-management are a mainstay of epilepsy treatment. Generally speaking, these interventions appear to increase self-efficacy and reduce anxiety and depressive symptoms but are unlikely to reduce seizure activity in patients with well-controlled epilepsy (Engelberts, Klein, Kasteleijn-Nolst Trenité, Heimans, & van der Ploeg, 2002). When psychoeducational interventions are combined with CBT, they can reduce seizure activity (Scicutella & Ettinger, 2002). When used in combination with psychotherapy, psychoeducational interventions are beneficial for nonepileptic seizures (LaFrance & Devinsky, 2004).

Support Groups

Another important component of self-management is epilepsy support groups, which provide individuals and family members a venue in which to process their fears and frustrations and to learn new coping skills. Patients who required surgical interventions were found to benefit from psychological support, including support groups, for the individual and the family. This support assisted patients in acquiring independence and personal autonomy (S. J. Wilson, Bladin, Saling, & Pattison, 2005). After experiencing freedom from seizures, epilepsy patients may require adjustment to living without seizures. Support can be provided to aid patients during this period. Regaining employment or job training, as appropriate, can be very beneficial for these patients in preventing depression (S. J. Wilson et al., 2005).

Diet Modification

Diet modification can be helpful in reducing seizure activity. Maintaining a diet rich in fats and low in carbohydrates, called the *ketogenic diet*, causes the body to break down fats instead of carbohydrates, resulting in a condition called *ketosis*, which has been associated with reduced seizure activity.

COGNITIVE–BEHAVIORAL THERAPY

CBT has also been beneficial in addressing physical and psychological conditions associated with epilepsy. It is interesting to note that a few studies have reported that CBT has been found helpful in reducing the frequency of seizures in some patients (Scicutella & Ettinger, 2002). Patients with epilepsy have been shown to benefit from psychological treatment techniques, such as self-control using cognitive therapy (Pedroso de Souza & Barioni Salgado, 2006). A retrospective study conducted by Beyenburg et al. (2005) found that both physical and psychological conditions benefit from CBT, including a reduction in the frequency of seizures.

OTHER PSYCHOTHERAPEUTIC INTERVENTIONS

Individuals with epilepsy, especially children, can develop behavioral and emotional problems and have an increased risk of poor self-esteem, depression, and suicide. Individual therapy and family therapy can be valuable in increasing coping capacity and resolving conflicts. Seizures can have a deeper meaning for the patient. The treatment of seizures as a symptom of psychodynamics is directed toward understanding the relationship between seizures and their intrapsychic functioning. Emphasis is placed on analysis of defenses and on restructuring the personality in an effort to promote ways of reducing tension and nonseizure ways of coping with life events. Therapy should also identify seizure antecedents, such as emotional, thematic, and symbolic triggers, that reflect unresolved conflicts. It is likely that psychodynamic psychotherapy works at many different levels wherein healthier life adjustment leads to an overall lessening of stress and tension, which in turn may lead to a reduction in seizure activity (Miller, 1994).

Psychodynamic Psychotherapy

Although referral for psychodynamic psychotherapy is not uncommon, particularly for those with nonepileptic seizures, there are relatively few publications in this area. Typical is one by Taube and Calman (1992), which described the use of psychotherapy with epilepsy patients and presented case studies. However, no outcome data were provided. At this time, there are no reported randomized controlled trials on psychotherapy with epilepsy.

Family Therapy

The family context in which epileptic patients find themselves can foster or hinder their treatment. Thus, it is important to the success of treatment that the patient's family accepts the patient's diagnosis and collaborates with the treatment regimen. The family's support may help patients to overcome their own hesitation about accepting the diagnosis. On the other hand, the family's rejection of the diagnosis can undermine the patient's own acceptance of their condition. Family sessions should help families make the necessary changes in their concept of the patient's condition; avoid blaming the patient for the illness; and, it is to be hoped, achieve a new family homeostasis. To encourage collaboration, families should be involved in the treatment from the outset and should participate in most decisions, especially concerning medication (Taube & Calman, 1992).

Psychotherapy for Nonepileptic Seizures

Treatment for nonepileptic seizures begins with calming the person and using controlled breathing to achieve a normal rate. Investigating the cognitive and emotional factors that led to the nonepileptic seizure is essential. Because medications tend to be ineffective in the treatment of nonepileptic seizures, referral for psychotherapy is essential. Because the vast majority of psychogenic seizures involve intrapsychic and interpersonal dynamics—including early trauma—as well as behavioral manifestations, focused psychotherapy, including behavioral interventions, is usually indicated (Miller, 1994).

Numerous case reports have demonstrated various psychotherapeutic approaches with this disorder. Unfortunately, in their extensive literature review of psychotherapy interventions with nonepileptic seizures, LaFrance and Devinsky (2004) found no randomized controlled trials and only one prospective, uncontrolled study of a therapeutic program for nonepileptic seizures patients. That program consisted of supportive psychotherapy and some additional modalities. After an average of 12 weeks of treatment, one half of the patients experienced a cessation of nonepileptic seizures at the end of treatment.

MEDICAL TREATMENT

Among the medical modalities used in the treatment of epilepsy are medication and surgery. Common medications used with seizure are noted in the "Medication" section to follow. Issues involving surgery and surgical referral are described here.

When seizures cannot be adequately controlled by medications, surgery may be recommended. Surgery is used to remove the *seizure focus* (i.e., the small area of the brain where seizures originate) or to treat underlying conditions (i.e., when seizures are caused by a brain tumor, hydrocephalus, or other conditions). Once the underlying condition is successfully treated, seizures may *remit*, that is, disappear. When seizures originate in part of the brain that cannot be removed, surgeons may implant a vagus nerve stimulator or use magnetic cranial stimulation, in which a strong magnet is held outside the head to influence brain activity in hopes of reducing seizure activity.

The Scottish Intercollegiate Guidelines Network (2003) recommended that physicians consider surgical referral if the patients' epilepsy proves to be drug resistant. Garcia (2006) also considered surgery an appropriate option with medically refractory epilepsy. Beyenburg et al. (2005) found that successful epilepsy surgery usually improves the patient's quality of life and also improves mood disorders. Furthermore, Garcia suggested that most patients with mood disorders experience improvement after surgery and that new psychiatric symptoms are rare afterward.

S. J. Wilson et al. (2005), in an alternative approach to outcome research, recommended a tailored approach for treating epilepsy patients following surgery. Both the patient and the caregivers were found to be underprepared for the changes that occur after surgery. The study further suggested a complex relationship between positive psychosocial adjustment in people with epilepsy and freedom from seizures (S. J. Wilson et al., 2005).

MEDICATION

The most common approach to treating epilepsy is to prescribe antiepileptic drugs. More than 20 different antiepileptic drugs are used, the choice depending on factors such as the type and frequency of seizures, the person's lifestyle and age, and the person's overall health. Most seizures can be controlled with one drug at the optimal dosage, but a combination of drugs is used if monotherapy fails to effectively control a patient's seizures (Gilliam & Santos, 2005).

Antiepileptic Drugs

Several new antiseizure or anticonvulsant drugs have been developed. These include gabapentin (Neurontin), lamotrigine (Lamictal), pregabalin (Lyrica), tiagabine (Gabitril), and topiramate (Topamax). Gabapentin has the fewest side effects, so it typically is the first one tried. Older antiseizure drugs such as carbamazepine (Tegretol), phenytoin (Dilantin), and valproic acid (Depakene) generally have more side effects than do the newer drugs. Accordingly, they are used only when the newer medications prove ineffective.

The Scottish Intercollegiate Guidelines Network (2003) recommended that the initial antiepileptic drug treatment decision should be made by a specialist. Antiepileptic drugs should be offered after the first tonic-clonic seizure if the patient had previous myoclonic, absence, or partial seizures. They may also be offered if the patient has a congenital neurologic deficit or considers the risk of seizure recurrence unacceptable (Scottish Intercollegiate Guidelines Network, 2003).

Alvarez-Silva, Alvarez-Rodriguez, Perez-Echeverria, and Alvarez-Silva (2006) conducted a literature review and found that medications used to treat panic attacks, such as benzodiazepines, may be helpful in treating simple partial seizures with a psychic content. In addition, some research suggests that serotoninergic medications have a reinforcing effect on GABAergic transmission, potentially sharing a therapeutic mechanism with antiepileptic drugs (Alvarez-Silva et al., 2006).

Psychotropic Drugs

Beyenburg et al. (2005) found that antidepressants are essential treatments for patients with epilepsy and mood disorders. The selective serotonin reuptake inhibitors were found to be beneficial and did not appear to affect the seizure threshold in patients (Beyenburg et al., 2005).

COMBINED TREATMENT

Mood disorders in patients with epilepsy are prevalent. Tailored multidisciplinary treatment from neurologists, psychologists, psychiatrists, and neuropsychiatry is of benefit to patients (Beyenburg et al., 2005). Depending on the individual symptoms and needs of a patient, there are several therapeutic modalities for the clinician to consider. For patients with mood disorders, benzodiazepines, antidepressants, psychoeducation, and CBT have been found beneficial.

Integrative Treatment Protocol: Epilepsy

1. Key Background Information	
Pathology	A neurological condition in which nerve cells in the brain fire abnormally, causing strange sensations, emotions, and behavior, or sometimes convulsions, muscle spasms, and loss of consciousness. Two or more witnessed seizures are required for the diagnosis of epilepsy.
Epidemiology	2.3 million Americans have experienced an unprovoked seizure or been diagnosed with epilepsy.
Types of seizures	Four categories: focal seizures, generalized seizures, temporal lobe epilepsy, and nonepileptic seizures.
Gender and ethnicity	40% of people with epilepsy are women of childbearing age. About twice as prevalent among non-Whites. Highest rates for Native Americans and older Hispanic men.
Severity	Often a chronic condition that significantly impacts quality of life and sometimes is life threatening.
Causal factors	Illness, an abnormality in brain wiring, an imbalance in neurotransmitters, or some combination in epileptic seizures. Early trauma is implicated in nonepileptic seizures.
Psychiatric comorbidities	2 to 3 times higher than in people without epilepsy. Mood disorders are the most prevalent diagnosis, particularly depression, with anxiety a strong second, particularly panic attacks. Suicide rate is 4 times higher than in people without epilepsy, especially for young adolescents and those with high seizure frequency and multiple-drug regimens.

(continues)

Prognosis	80% of epilepsy cases can be well controlled with medication or surgery, whereas 20% of cases are intractable, even with the best available treatment.

2. Biopsychosocial Assessment

Patient profile	From interview and observation and the Revised Illness Perception Questionnaire (IPQ-R; Moss-Morris et al., 2002) assess: • IPQ-R factors, especially illness perceptions, explanations, and treatment expectations; • severity of symptoms and functional impact; • capacity, previous change efforts, and readiness for change; and • personality style or disorder and family and cultural factors.
Illness profile	Identify higher risk epilepsy patients, using the following guidelines: • any indication of suicidal ideation, especially young adolescents or those with severe epilepsy on multiple antiepileptics; • female patients with seizures related to the menstrual cycle; • those exhibiting symptoms of depression, anxiety, or panic attacks; and • those who are unemployed, and/or who have low social support or negative support systems.
Diagnosis	Two or more witnessed seizures are required to make the diagnosis. Common tests include electroencephalogram (EEG) monitoring; brain scans; blood tests; and developmental, neurological, and behavioral tests.
Lab test	Serum prolactin levels can rule out nonepileptic seizures if suspected.

3. Intervention Planning

Illness profile	Illness representations, particularly illness identity, predict level of anxiety and psychosocial distress among epilepsy patients. If indicated, plan to modify such representations.
Type and severity	Match specific medications and specific psychotherapeutic focus for different types and levels of severity.

4. Intervention Implementation

Psychoeducational interventions	Particularly valuable because psychoeducation increases treatment compliance and successful adaptation and reduces fear of seizures. When paired with individual counseling, especially cognitive–behavioral therapy (CBT), psychoeducation reduces anxiety, depression, and even seizure activity. Group therapy is as effective as individual psychoeducation. Emphasizing regaining employment can help prevent depression. Those who require surgical intervention benefit from psychological support for the individual and the family to regain independence and personal autonomy.

Support groups	Especially helpful for epileptic children with behavioral and emotional problems, poor self-esteem, depression, or suicidal ideation. Family counseling and support groups help coping capacity and resolving conflicts.
Diet modification	Ketogenic diet—high fat and low carbohydrate—can reduce seizure activity.
Spirituality	Can increase self-efficacy and reinforce development of positive coping skills if incorporated into psychoeducational or self-management programs.
Cognitive–behavioral therapy	CBT is helpful in increasing self-control and reducing the frequency of seizures in some patients. Focus can be on modifying problematic illness representations with cognitive restructuring and/or positive reattribution, reducing treatment-interfering thoughts or behaviors, and working on interpersonal conflicts and support issues.
Other psychotherapeutic interventions	• Psychodynamic psychotherapy: Although there are no randomized controlled trials, referral for this intervention is not uncommon. It focuses on the link between seizures and their intrapsychic functioning and identifies seizure antecedents and symbolic triggers. • Psychotherapy for nonepileptic seizures: Because this type involves intrapsychic and interpersonal dynamics and often trauma, focal psychotherapy may be indicated. • Family therapy: Because the family can be a potent ally in treatment, family sessions can foster the patient's acceptance of his or her diagnosis and commitment to treatment regimen.
Medication	Antiepileptics: These are the most common medical treatment wherein the drug choice is based on type and frequency of seizures as well as the patient's lifestyle and age. Psychotropics: With comorbid depression, selective serotonin reuptake inhibitors are beneficial and do not lower the seizure threshold. With comorbid anxiety or panic attacks, benzodiazepines or selective serotonin reuptake inhibitors may be helpful in treating simple partial seizures with a psychic content.
Surgery	Consider surgical referral if the epilepsy proves to be drug resistant or is otherwise medically refractory.
Combined treatment	Depending on type, symptoms, severity, and patient needs, therapeutic modalities and interventions may be combined and tailored. Collaboration with neurologists, psychologists, and psychiatrists can be helpful and may be essential for effective care. It is not uncommon for antiepileptics, benzodiazepines, antidepressants, psychoeducation, and CBT to be combined and provided simultaneously or sequentially.

5. Intervention Monitoring

- Review patient's diary of symptoms and functional impairment.
- Track session-to-session progress with regard to compliance, symptom reduction, and functionality.

CASE OF LESLIE S.

Leslie S. is a 27-year-old single Caucasian woman who was referred by her family physician to Jon Cole, a neurologist with a specialty practice in epilepsy. Cole works in a group practice with four other neurologists and two psychologists.

Leslie reports a history of tonic-clonic seizures since the age of 16. The first of these seizure episodes was witnessed and treated at a major academic medical center in another city. One year ago, Leslie moved and began reporting increased seizure activity to her new family physician. Although he acceded to her request for a prescription for Dilantin, he was uncomfortable with her request for a disability evaluation, particularly when she began to scream at him for not immediately agreeing with the request. This prompted the referral to Cole. Prior to the initial evaluation, Cole had received and reviewed a copy of Leslie's medical records from the academic medical center, which documented a single episode of a witnessed tonic-clonic seizure at age 16 but no other observed seizures since then. It was noted that at ages 19 and 21 Leslie had been admitted for treatment of "recurring" seizures, although neither episode was witnessed. This led Cole to wonder if Leslie might now be presenting with nonepileptic seizures. Because it is not uncommon for a differential diagnosis to include both epileptic and nonepileptic seizures, it is essential that a comprehensive diagnostic evaluation be completed to arrive at the most likely diagnosis. During his evaluation of Leslie, Cole placed her in a room outfitted with strobe lighting, which he indicated to her typically provoked seizures in epilepsy patients. Leslie had a "seizure" within 10 minutes—that is, she engaged in seizurelike behavior, but continuous EEG monitoring showed no seizure activity. Blood work was immediately drawn, including prolactin levels, then and 15 minutes later.

In addition to a nonconfirmatory EEG study, prolactin levels showed no change. Such results are consistent with a diagnosis of nonepileptic seizures. Gerald Vann, one of the group's psychologists, completed the remainder of the comprehensive biopsychosocial evaluation. Prior to this, Leslie took the IPQ-R and the Minnesota Multiphasic Personality Inventory—2 (MMPI–2; Butcher, Dahlstrom, Graham, Tellegen, & Kaemmer, 1989). In their meeting, Vann reviewed her responses on the IPQ-R and elicited additional information on her illness representations. It was notable that she believed her seizures were somewhat controllable but would be lifelong and were incurable. It was also her belief that all her seizures were real, even if many of them had not been witnessed. She displayed histrionic and borderline traits during the evaluation and tearfully reported early childhood sexual abuse by her alcoholic stepfather while her mother stood by watching. Somatization was a prominent finding on the MMPI–2. On the basis of this comprehensive biopsychosocial evaluation, the diagnosis of nonepileptic seizure was made.

Like other individuals with a documented history of an epileptic seizure and a subsequent diagnosis of a nonepileptic seizure, Leslie was a candidate for psychoeducation and psychotherapy rather than for antiepileptic medication. Leslie had no previous experience with psychotherapy but was willing to contract for 12 sessions of brief dynamic psychotherapy with Vann. She found it helpful to "have someone really listen to me" and contracted to continue after the 12th session. She reported no further seizures, and she decided against pursuing her disability claim.

14

HYPERTENSION

Hypertension, which is also called *high blood pressure*, is a medical condition in which one's blood pressure is persistently elevated. Persistent hypertension is one of the risk factors for strokes, myocardial infarction or heart attacks, heart failure, and arterial aneurysm, and it is a major cause of chronic renal failure. Because uncontrolled hypertension increases the risk of stroke and other cardiovascular disease and results in nearly 1 million deaths in the United States each year, it is essential that hypertension be diagnosed and effectively treated (Hajjar & Kotchen, 2003). What is normal and what is elevated blood pressure? In the past what constituted "normal" blood pressure was higher than what expert panels consider healthy or normal today. Currently, some experts consider the "gold standard" to be below 120/80 millimeters of mercury (mm Hg), whereas others set it at 115/75 mm Hg (Chobanian et al., 2003).

The following sections present basic background on hypertension as a disease and illness followed by a detailed discussion of various psychological and biopsychosocial treatment intervention options. This discussion includes both clinical and research findings. The chapter concludes with an integrative treatment protocol and a case example illustrating the protocol.

EPIDEMIOLOGY

Currently, two thirds of Americans over the age of 60 have elevated blood pressures. More than 43 million individuals in the United States have hypertension, but fewer than one third of that number achieve adequate level of blood pressure control (Chobanian et al., 2003). Hypertension is a causative factor in stroke and cardiovascular disease, which are the leading causes of death among both men and women and across all racial and ethnic groups.

TYPES

The conventional classification of hypertension is as either *essential hypertension* or *primary hypertension* and *secondary hypertension*. In essential hypertension, no specific medical cause can be found. In secondary hypertension, high blood pressure is a result of or is caused by another medical condition such as kidney disease or a tumor of the adrenal gland. By far, essential hypertension is the more common of these two types.

Another classification of hypertension has been proposed: *nonneurogenic essential hypertension* and *neurogenic hypertension* (Mann, 2003). This distinction is based on Mann's clinical observation and published research (Mann & Gerber, 2001a, 2001b; Mann & James, 1998).

Nonneurogenic Hypertension

Nonneurogenic hypertension is the same as essential or primary hypertension but is largely mediated by the pathophysiologic mechanisms of volume and the renin-angiotensin system. Both genetic and lifestyle factors contribute to this type of hypertension, and it tends to respond to a diuretic, an angiotensin-converting enzyme inhibitor, or a calcium channel blocker medication.

Neurogenic Hypertension

Neurogenic hypertension differs significantly from essential hypertension. This type of hypertension is partly mediated by the sympathoadrenal system and therefore is not responsive to medications useful for nonneurogenic hypertension. It also appears to be mediated by psychological factors, particularly repressed emotions. In contrast to felt emotions, repressed emotions, defensiveness (Jorgenson, Johnson, Kolodziej, & Schreer, 1996), and repressive coping styles are major factors in neurogenic hypertension (Mann, 2003). Repressed emotion, genetic predisposition, and overweight have been shown to be additive risk factors leading to hypertension (Mann & James, 1998). It appears that severe life stressors, such as trauma, are triggers for neurogenic hypertension in those who are genetically predisposed and repressors.

SEVERITY

Severity of hypertension has been classified by stage by the Joint National Committee on Prevention, Detection, Evaluation, and Treatment of High Blood Pressure (Chobanian et al., 2003). Two formal stages of hypertension were given, although there are actually four:

1. Normal: <120/<80 mm Hg.
2. Prehypertension: 120–139/80–90 mm Hg.
3. Stage 1 hypertension: 140–159/90–99 mm Hg.
4. Stage 2 hypertension: >160/>100 mm Hg.

CAUSAL FACTORS

Research indicates that approximately 40% of hypertension cases are determined by biological and genetic factors, 30% to 40% by lifestyle factors, and the remaining 20% to 25% by psychological factors (Mann, 2006). An important biological factor that is impacted by psychological factors is *sympathetic tone* (the basal level of the sympathetic nervous system). Factors that contribute to increased sympathetic tone in hypertension are angiotensin II; insulin resistance; dietary salt sensitivity; hypersensitivity to stress; impaired baroreceptor reflexes; genetic factors; vascular compression of the medulla; and psychological factors, such as repressed emotions (Mann, 2003). Lifestyle factors influencing hypertension include excessive dietary sodium, obesity related to increased caloric intake and physical inactivity, excessive alcohol intake, and excess psychological stress (Kaplan & Opie, 2006). Among all cases of hypertension, including severe hypertension, a specific identifiable cause is found only 10% of the time (Mann, 2003).

GENDER AND ETHNICITY

Highest rates of hypertension were found among women, non-Hispanic Blacks, and older individuals in the National Health and Nutrition Examination Survey (Hajjar & Kotchen, 2003; see also the survey Web site: http://www.cdc.gov/nchs/nhanes.htm).

Gender

Hypertension is more common in men than women. However, during their lifetimes, one in four women in the United States will be diagnosed with hypertension, and the incidence has risen 30% in just the past decade. Although women's risk of developing hypertension is much lower than that of men the same age, the incidence of hypertension in women is similar to that of men when women reach menopause. It is believed this increased incidence is due to loss of estrogen, which is known to protect against hypertension, after menopause (Farag & Mills, 2004).

Ethnicity and Socioeconomic Status

African Americans present with almost twice the rate of hypertension of White Americans (Farag & Mills, 2004). Within the non-White population, unexplained differences in symptomatic expression have been noted. For example, African Americans exhibited the greatest decrease in interbeat interval and increase in preejection measures, whereas Caribbean Americans had the largest decrease in cardiac output and least stress-related blood pressure increases (Farag & Mills, 2004).

Differences in socioeconomic status (SES) and hypertension have been noted. For instance, it was found that stress had a persistent and significant impact on quality of life among all low-SES hypertension patients compared with higher SES hypertension patients (Ames, Jones, Howe, & Brantley, 2001).

PSYCHIATRIC COMORBIDITIES

Comorbidity studies are somewhat limited. Data presented in this section involve anger, other repressed emotions, and trauma.

Suls, Wan, and Costa (1995) reviewed a series of meta-analyses to evaluate the relationship between anger and hypertension but found only inconsistent support for the connection between anger and chronically elevated blood pressure. Mann (2000) evaluated the research with regard to a relationship between anger and hypertension but also concluded no clear link exists. He found the same lack of association for anxiety and depression.

Mann (2000) reported an association between emotional defensiveness and hypertension in persons with a history of trauma. In fact, he found in most of these patients that a combination of antihypertensive treatment with alpha and beta blockade with antidepressants and anxiolytics is effective, and in 3 of these patients, psychological intervention alone was sufficient to resolve the hypertension. Therefore, he recommended screening hypertension patients for defensiveness and a history of trauma. He also reported that anger and childhood trauma reduced response to angiotensin-converting enzyme (ACE) inhibitor and diuretic monotherapy (Mann & Gerber, 2001a, 2001b).

Mann (2003) explored the relationship between psychological characteristics and antihypertensive drug therapy and found that response to the alpha–beta combination was not correlated with psychological characteristics. However, he confirmed a distinction in response of patients with childhood trauma (25%) and those without (79%), suggesting a history of trauma as a moderating variable to treatment effectiveness. He also reported resistant hypertension in patients who lacked close attachment to others and experienced inhibited anger expression. Combined alpha–beta blockade is recommended for these patients over ACE inhibitors or diuretics (Mann, 2003).

PROGNOSIS

Currently, no cure exists for hypertension. Hypertension is a major risk factor for cardiovascular morbidity and mortality, such as stroke and heart failure (Kaplan & Opie, 2006). Therefore, controlling blood pressure with conventional treatment, that is, a combination of lifestyle changes and antihypertensive medicines, is indicated. However, even in patients with well-controlled hypertension, fewer than a third are protected from stroke or heart attack (Fauvel, 2003). Accordingly, primary and secondary prevention are essential with hypertension and center on recognizing, avoiding, or eliminating known risk factors for hypertension. Even those at risk because of age, race, or sex or those who have an inherited risk can lower their chance of developing hypertension. Three health behaviors—cigarette smoking, lack of physical activity, and poor nutrition—are major risk factors for cardiovascular diseases.

TREATMENT CONSIDERATIONS AND INTERVENTIONS

The Seventh Report of the Joint National Committee on Prevention, Detection, Evaluation, and Treatment of High Blood Pressure not only updated the stages of hypertension but also set the standard for treatment at each of the four stages (Chobanian et al., 2003). It is noteworthy that the committee emphasized the role of psychological interventions, including lifestyle change, as a significant component of combined or integrated hypertension treatment and prevention. Currently, hypertensive self-management programs usually focus on home blood pressure monitoring with a protocol in which individuals adjust their own drug therapy if readings consistently exceed their established limits. Exercise, relaxation exercises, and diet modification are standard elements of these protocols. Noteworthy is the articulation of neurogenic hypertension (Mann, 2003) and its psychological basis. Furthermore, new medications have recently become available that when combined with psychological treatments offer a new measure of hope for the treatment of this disease and illness.

Key treatment considerations for hypertension include specific indications for psychological interventions, illness representations, diagnosis, and the perplexing matter of treatment compliance. In a disease that is silent of symptoms for the majority of patients, treatment compliance is a major problem. Compliance is both a problem and a critical marker of treatment adherence and clinical progress. Clinicians would do well to focus on illness representations because they have been shown to be key predictors of treatment compliance.

Indications for Psychological Interventions

Linden and Moseley (2006) recommended that psychological interventions be initiated as first-line treatments under the following circumstances: (a) when medication side effects are severe; (b) when lifestyle changes alone are insufficient in achieving normotensive blood pressure, and the patient needs psychological support to implement changes; (c) when the patient prefers nondrug treatment, has an interest in self-regulation, and is realistic; (d) when the patient has a family history of hypertension and cardiac disease and wants preventative measures; and (e) when the patient reports a stressful lifestyle, and blood pressure has increased over time. It is probably advisable to add problematic illness representation to this list.

Illness Representations

An individual's constellation of perceptions and beliefs about a particular disease—understanding of it and its symptoms, cause, duration, impact or consequences, curability, and ability to control it—is referred to as *illness representation*. S. Ross, Walker, and MacLeod (2004) studied such representations among hypertensive patients. They found that patients who believed in the necessity of their medication and believed they had the ability to control their illness were more likely to be compliant with treatment than those who did not share these beliefs. They also found that beliefs about the value of specific medications and their understanding of the disease predicted treatment compliance. Accordingly, clinicians are encouraged to explore patients' understanding of their illness and beliefs about the value of medication and their ability to control it.

Because illness representations are influenced by ethnic and cultural values, it is not surprising that there are cultural differences in such representations. In research that studied the cause and control of hypertension with medication, there were significant differences among respondents based on culture. Both Europeans and those born in West Indies were queried about the cause and control of hypertension with medication. Nearly one half of the respondents identified stress or worry as a cause of their hypertension. However, although all were aware of the importance of controlling their blood pressure with medication, less than half of the West Indians were classified as medication compliers and preferred the use of traditional herbal remedies instead. This contrasted with high levels of compliance among the Europeans (Morgan & Watkins, 1988).

Diagnosis

Office blood pressure measurement by a physician with a mercury sphygmomanometer remains the standard because its relationship with cardiovascular prognosis has been demonstrated. Although blood pressure units available for home measurement may not be as accurate as office blood pressure measurement, it is more important that patients do daily monitoring of their blood pressure, particularly if it is in the high range. Clinicians need to recognize that blood pressure is extremely variable over time and is influenced by physical activity as well as mental stress. One such stressor is that of having a physician or other clinician measure one's blood pressure, often resulting in artificially high readings, which is referred to as the *white coat effect*. Accordingly, serial readings are reported, both at home and in the clinic, to establish an accurate base rate.

Treatment Compliance

Compliance is a major issue for patients with hypertension given that few, if any, symptoms are experienced, and many have the disease long before it is diagnosed. Hence, hypertension is called the "silent killer" and is strongly associated with poorly controlled hypertension (Johnell, Råstam, Lithman, Sundquist, & Merlo, 2005). Reportedly, 55.8% of patients are noncompliant with their medication regimen (Hassan et al., 2006). A basic reason for noncompliance is poor communication, a lack of understanding of the disease (Hassan et al., 2006), and lack of family support (D. K. Wilson & Ampey-Thornhill, 2001). Hassan et al. (2006) also found that patient dissatisfaction and medication barriers were associated with noncompliance. Illness representations are a key predictor of treatment compliance, particularly beliefs about the necessity of medication and the personal ability to control illness (S. Ross et al., 2004). Finally, younger patients and those with low social participation are more likely to be noncompliant (Hassan et al., 2006).

PSYCHOEDUCATIONAL INTERVENTIONS

The literature on psychoeducation in hypertension is almost nonexistent. Given that hypertension is a silent disease—overt symptoms are rarely experienced compared with other chronic diseases—self-management is quite important in hypertension. If one considers the paucity of published reports, it may seem that self-management of blood pressure control is not being widely practiced. The reality is that some clinics do incorporate patient education, relaxation, meditation, diet modification, and exercise as part of hypertensive treatment.

COGNITIVE–BEHAVIORAL THERAPY

So far, cognitive–behavioral therapy (CBT) appears to have had limited application to the treatment of hypertension. Some consider stress management, meditation, breathing techniques, and biofeedback to be CBT or cognitive–behavioral interventions in the treatment of hypertension. Blumenthal, Sherwood, LaCaille, Georgiades, and Goyal (2005), in their review of the literature, found only one study that showed significant reduction in blood pressure using the above interventions, whereas other studies and reviews of meta-analyses showed unimpressive results. There is also one comparison study (Spurgeon, Hicks, Barwell, Walton, & Spurgeon, 2005) in which CBT was used with medical patients with diabetes, asthma, and hypertension in a general medical setting in England. In this study, which emphasized developing personal responsibility, CBT was provided in eight 90-minute sessions over 2 months to patients diagnosed with diabetes, asthma, and hypertension. Results at the end of treatment and 6 months later showed significant improvement in psychological well-being. However, only the hypertension patients showed significantly less medical service utilization in the 12-month period following CBT. It was hypothesized that hypertensive patients did better than the other patients because of the significant psychological component of that disease. It was not indicated whether blood pressure readings moved toward the normotensive range. In addition to this comparative study, there has been considerable research published on both cognitive and behavioral interventions with hypertension.

Cognitive Interventions

In 1993, Eisenberg et al. reviewed the available randomized controlled trials (RCTs) and concluded that cognitive interventions for patients with essential hypertension was superior to no therapy at all but not to "credible sham techniques" or self-monitoring. They also reported that cognitive–behavioral interventions prescribed without behavioral or psychoeducational interventions, such as weight loss, control of salt and alcohol, and regular exercise, were not as effective as standard antihypertensive medications.

Behavioral Interventions

Linden and Moseley (2006) reviewed more than 100 RCTs of behavioral treatments for control of blood pressure. Most notable was the finding that for all patients except the most severely hypertensive, drug treatments resulted in increased mortality rather than decreased. They also found that the amount of change in blood pressure was positively correlated with reduction in psychological stress and change in anger coping styles, leading to the conclusion that successful stress reduction and changes in anger coping styles were the most promising for psychological interventions related to hypertension. One of these studies showed that multicomponent nondrug treatment was as effective in controlling blood pressure as standard antihypertensive medications; the nondrug approach also resulted in desirable reductions in body weight (Linden & Moseley, 2006).

OTHER PSYCHOTHERAPEUTIC INTERVENTIONS

When repressed emotion is considered a causative factor in neurogenic hypertension, psychotherapy that focuses on such repression can be a viable treatment intervention (Mann, 2006). This is particularly true when early life physical and sexual trauma are involved; psychotherapy may be the only viable treatment option. Dynamically oriented therapies are a reasonable choice. At this point, little or no clinical research has been reported in this area.

MEDICAL TREATMENT

Conventional medical treatment of mild hypertension today typically begins with lifestyle changes, that is, the patient is advised to lose weight, reduce sodium, and engage in regular exercise. If that is not sufficient to achieve normotensive blood pressure readings, drug treatment is begun. Some (e.g., Moser, 2005) have contended that antihypertensive medications should not be delayed but rather should be the starting point of treatment, along with the usual lifestyle interventions. Moser (2005) proposed continuing this combined regimen and stopping medication after 6 to 9 months to evaluate progress.

MEDICATIONS

Choosing medications for hypertension and then monitoring their therapeutic effects and side effects requires considerable knowledge and skill. Many primary care physicians and even some specialists are not aware of the differential drug response between those with psychologically linked hypertension and those with biologically linked hypertension, the latter comprising the majority of cases of essential hypertension.

Two meta-analyses of RCTs of hypertensive treatments concluded that (a) decreasing blood pressure by means of any drug was more effective than placebo in reducing cardiovascular mortality, (b) all classes of antihypertensive medications reduced cardiovascular mortality equally, and (c) different classes of antihypertensives differentially prevented cardiovascular morbidity (Kaplan & Opie, 2006). However, diuretic-based regimens yielded more new cases of diabetes than other regimens that did not include diuretics (Kaplan & Opie, 2006). Although beta blockers reduced risk of stroke by half, that risk was still 16% higher for those using beta blockers than other drugs (Kaplan & Opie, 2006).

Beta blockers combined with diuretics should be avoided when a risk of diabetes is present (Kaplan & Opie, 2006). Furthermore, for patients with refractory hypertension, it is suggested that both neurogenic and nonneurogenic mechanisms be considered as contributory, given the highly variable individual responses of such patients (Mann, 2003). Finally, for patients with resistant hypertension who lack close attachment to others and experience inhibited anger expression, combined alpha–beta blockade is recommended (Mann, 2000).

Nonneurogenic Hypertension

Research has indicated that diuretics (Diuril, Lasix, Aldactone, etc.), ACE inhibitors (Vasotec, Prinivil, Zestril, etc.), angiotensin receptor blockers, or a combination are the treatment choice with more biologically linked hypertension (Holtzman et al., 1988; Mann & Gerber, 2001a, 2001b).

Neurogenic Hypertension

Research has indicated that a combination of alpha blockers (Cardura, Hytrin, etc.) and beta blockers (Tenormin, Toprol, Kerlone, etc.) is the treatment of choice (Mann & Gerber, 2001a, 2001b).

COMBINED TREATMENT

For some time, combined treatments have been common practice with hypertension. Typically, diet modification and other lifestyle changes are combined with one or more medications. More recently, various psychological interventions have been effectively combined with lifestyle change and medications (Linden & Moseley, 2006).

1. Key Background Information	
Pathology	Medical condition in which blood pressure is persistently elevated.
Epidemiology	Afflicts 43 million Americans, but fewer than one third achieve an adequate level of blood pressure control.
Severity	Rated by stages: normal (<120/<80 mm Hg), prehypertension (120–139/80–90 mm Hg), Stage 1 hypertension (140–159/90–99 mm Hg), and Stage 2 hypertension (>160/>100 mm Hg).
Types	1. Essential hypertension or nonneurogenic (most common type); 2. neurogenic hypertension; and 3. secondary hypertension.
Causal factors	Cause of essential type is unknown, whereas secondary type is related to a medical condition or tumor. Overall, 40% of cases are attributed to biological and genetic factors, 30% to 40% to lifestyle factors, and 20% to 25% to psychological factors.
Gender, age, and ethnicity	After menopause, rates for women are similar to those for men. African American:White American rate is 2:1. Risk increases with ethnicity, low socioeconomic status, obesity, alcohol consumption, and age.
Psychiatric comorbidities	Limited data suggest anger, trauma, and repressed emotions.
Prognosis	No cure for essential hypertension. Because it is a major risk factor for stroke and for kidney and heart failure, the goal is blood pressure control and prevention of complications.

2. Biopsychosocial Assessment	
Patient profile	From interview and observation and Revised Illness Perception Questionnaire (IPQ-R; Moss-Morris et al., 2002) assess: • IPQ-R factors especially illness perceptions, explanations, treatment expectations; • severity of symptoms and functional impact; • capacity, previous change efforts, and readiness for change; and • personality style or disorder and family and cultural factors.
Illness profile	Identify higher risk hypertensive patients: • adolescents with elevated blood pressure and obesity; • elderly patients; • African American patients and low-income patients; • obese patients, particularly if sleep apnea is present; • patients with excessive alcohol consumption; • patients with a history of tachycardia or renal insufficiency; • patients with a history of childhood trauma; • patients who lack close attachment to others; and • patients with inhibited anger expression and/or defensiveness.

(continues)

Type	Distinguish nonneurogenic or essential hypertension from neurogenic hypertension. Clues to neurogenic hypertension include the following: • repressor coping style, that is, those with a burden of repressed emotions and who present with an even-keeled disposition and deny ever feeling "down"; • history of severe prior trauma or abuse, particularly during childhood; • belief or conviction that severe prior trauma has no lingering effects; • family history of hypertension and obesity; and • defensiveness and emotional illiteracy.
Treatment compliance	Major issue given symptoms are "silent."

3. Intervention Planning

Illness profile	Illness representations: Explore patients' beliefs about the value of medication, their understanding of their illness, and their ability to control it; also consider cultural differences in such representations. If indicated, plan to modify such representations.
Stage and symptom severity	It is important to assess stage because each stage requires unique treatment.

4. Intervention Implementation

Tailor standard self-management protocol which includes blood pressure monitoring plus exercise, relaxation exercises, diet modification and cognitive–behavioral therapy (CBT), psychotherapy or other psychological interventions. Stage 2 interventions usually involve two or more medications and extensive and intensive lifestyle modifications and psychological interventions compared with Stage 1, which typically involves lifestyle modification and possibly one medication.

Essential (nonneurogenic) hypertension	
Psychoeducational	Various psychoeducational interventions can facilitate lifestyle changes (i.e., modified diet, salt restriction, exercise, weight control, and stress management). Compliance issues are common. Consider individual compliance intervention strategy and/or family compliance counseling strategy.
Psychotherapeutic interventions	• CBT interventions, individual or in groups, can focus on problematic illness representations, high-risk psychosocial factors, barriers to treatment, and compliance problems. Emphasize personal responsibility. • Other psychotherapeutic interventions: When early life physical and sexual trauma are involved, dynamically oriented therapies can be a reasonable choice.
Medication	Alpha blockers (Cardura, Hytrin, etc.) and beta blockers (Tenormin, Toprol, Kerlone, etc.) are the treatment of choice.

Neurogenic hypertension	
Psychoeducational interventions	Identify and discuss neurogenic basis of hypertension. Provide information on repressor coping style and psychotherapy and other treatment options.
Psychotherapeutic interventions	Dynamic psychotherapy is effective in those with histories of early childhood trauma and who exhibit a repressor style (i.e., even-keeled individuals who deny anger and hurt) as well as those with early trauma histories who are perfectionistic and defensive.
Medication	Diuretics (Diuril, Lasix, Aldactone, etc.), angiotensin-converting enzyme inhibitors (Vasotec, Prinivil, Zestril, etc.), and angiotensin receptor blockers, or a combination, are the treatment choice with more biologically linked hypertension.

5. Intervention Monitoring

- Have patient log response to treatment regimen, including lifestyle modification, in a diary.
- Monitor treatment compliance via various markers such as blood pressure readings and other markers.

CASE OF HARLAN G.

Harlan G. is a 43-year-old African American, male realtor who was diagnosed with Stage 1 hypertension by his family physician some 16 months ago. In otherwise good health, Harlan has been under considerable stress in large part because of the housing market slump. Although compliant with a two-drug medication regimen, a salt-substitute diet, and maintaining near ideal weight, Harlan's blood pressure remains in the 145/100 mm Hg range. Frustrated with only minimal progress, his physician referred Harlan to a psychologist who specialized in treating chronic illness.

Before their first session, the psychologist had Harlan complete the Brief Illness Perception Questionnaire (BIPQ; Broadbent, Petrie, Main, & Weinman, 2006), a 9-item screening inventory, that taps into an individual's illness representations. Following up on his BIPQ responses, the psychologist found that Harlan's illness representations did not seem to be incompatible in any way with the planned treatment regimen. Notable was that Harlan's perception of causality—his explanatory model of his hypertension—was decidedly biopsychosocial. He viewed his illness as resulting from hereditary factors (i.e., he reported that his natural father had been hypertensive) as well as from job and interpersonal stress (i.e., he and his wife had been experiencing marital conflict). Harlan's personality style could be characterized by perfectionism and a high need to please others. In addition, his style of dealing with conflict was conflict avoidance and emotional distancing. Further inquiry elicited that Harlan had been placed in foster care by his teenaged mother who was unable to care for him. He lived with four families before being adopted at age 6. His foster and adopted family situations were all characterized by physical abuse, emotional abuse, and neglect. Further inquiry found that Harlan was rejection sensitive and experienced occasional rageful outbursts that "came out of the blue," indicating repressed emotion.

On the basis of Harlan's limited response to medication and salt restriction, his perfectionism and need to please, his early life abuse, and his repressed emotion, the psychologist concluded that Harlan's diagnosis was most likely neurogenic hypertension. Harlan agreed to work on "stress" issues both current and from early life in 12 planned psychotherapy sessions. After 9 of these sessions, the physician reported to the psychologist that Harlan's blood pressure was now normotensive.

15

IRRITABLE BOWEL SYNDROME

Irritable bowel syndrome (IBS) is a disorder that interferes with the normal functions of the large intestine (i.e., colon). It is characterized by the following symptoms: crampy abdominal pain, bloating, constipation, and diarrhea in the absence of "alarm symptoms" such as weight loss, bleeding, anemia, fever, or frequent nocturnal symptoms. IBS does not permanently damage the intestines or lead to cancer or intestinal bleeding, and it is not related to Crohn's disease or ulcerative colitis. Individuals with IBS appear to have colons that are more sensitive and react to things that might not bother other people.

The following sections present basic background on IBS as a disease and an illness followed by a detailed discussion of various psychological and biopsychosocial treatment intervention options. This discussion includes both clinical and research findings. The chapter concludes with an integrative treatment protocol and a case example illustrating the protocol.

EPIDEMIOLOGY

IBS is one of the more common chronic illnesses in the United States: One in five Americans experience it, making it one of the most commonly diagnosed disorders today. It is the second leading cause of absenteeism from work and school after the common cold. It occurs more often in women than in men, and it usually begins around age 20 (Drossman, 1999). In one third of cases, constipation is the defining feature; in another third, the characteristic is diarrhea; and in the final third, there is a combination of the two, usually in an alternating pattern.

TYPES

In IBS, the epithelium appears to work properly, but fast movement of the colon's contents can overcome the absorptive capacity of the colon. The result is too much fluid in the stool. In other individuals, colonic movement is too slow, too much fluid is absorbed, and constipation develops. Thus, two subtypes of IBS can be identified, the *diarrhea-dominant subtype* and the *constipation-dominant subtype*. As is noted below, treatment differs for each subtype.

SEVERITY

Although IBS engenders considerable discomfort and distress, most individuals can control their symptoms with diet, stress management, and medications prescribed by their physician. Nevertheless, for some individuals, IBS can be disabling in that affected individuals may be unable to work, go to social events, or travel even short distances. Approximately 70% of patients experience a form characterized by occasional symptoms. These individuals are able to maintain normal daily activities, exhibit little or no psychosocial difficulties, and their IBS is considered *mild* (Drossman, 1999). About 25% of patients have a *moderate* form. These individuals experience symptoms that may be debilitating at times (Drossman, 1999). The final 5% of patients experience a *severe* form, which is characterized by constant symptoms. These individuals also experience more psychosocial difficulties, seek more health care, and demonstrate more psychiatric diagnoses (Drossman, 1999).

CAUSAL FACTORS

Although the cause of IBS is unknown, theories and some research address the question of causality. It is commonly thought that IBS results from a disturbance in the brain–gut axis, which comprises the neural network that includes both the central nervous system (CNS) and the enteric nervous system (Lackner et al., 2006). Other theories of the underlying mechanisms are visceral hypersensitivity and gut dysmotility (Drossman, 1999).

Research suggests that those with IBS seem to have a heightened colon sensitivity, and reactivity has long been considered a key mechanism in understanding the clinical symptoms and course of IBS (Lucak, 2005). Some evidence indicates that the immune system is also involved. IBS symptoms appear to result from abnormal motility of the colon, that is, the contraction of the colon muscles, the movement of its contents, and the regulation of fluids in and out of the colon. In short, the colon may contract too much or too little or may absorb too much or too little water. It is important to note that though the normal function of the colon is disrupted in IBS, there is no physiopathology to the colon as there is in ulcerative colitis and Crohn's disease.

Functional magnetic resonance imaging shows differences in central processing of visceral stimuli between men and women, with men having greater activation in areas of the brain related to cognitive responses and women's brains activating in areas controlling emotional and autonomic processing (Lucak, 2005). The brains of IBS patients fail to use CNS downregulating mechanisms, which results in intensification of pain perception (Lucak, 2005). The colon responds strongly to factors that tend not to be bothersome for non-IBS individuals. People with IBS seem to be particularly sensitive to stressors, foods, and negative emotions. Specific factors that can negatively affect IBS patients are large meals; spicy and greasy foods; bloating from gas in the colon; medicines; foods containing wheat, rye, barley, chocolate, milk products, or alcohol; drinks with caffeine, such as coffee, tea, or colas; and relational conflict or emotional upsets.

So how do psychological factors trigger and/or exacerbate IBS symptoms? Three pathways have been postulated as likely biopsychosocial mechanisms by which psychological factors influence the expression of IBS. The first pathway is directly through biological systems that mediate gut function and sensation. The second is through the adoption of illness behaviors that are exacerbate IBS symptoms and compromise function. The third pathway is through mediating the risk of IBS onset (Lackner, 2003).

GENDER AND ETHNICITY

Gender

More women than men present with symptoms of IBS, with rates as high as 1.44:1 (Blanchard & Scharff, 2002). Women with IBS report more IBS symptoms during their menstrual periods. Although this may suggest that reproductive hormones can exacerbate IBS problems, research data indicate that menstrual cycle hormonal fluctuations in IBS are unlikely to be a major explanation for changes in symptoms (Heitkemper, Jarrett, Cain, Burr, & Crowell, 2003).

Ethnicity

The prevalence of IBS is similar among African Americans and Whites, but there are sociodemographic differences between the groups. For example, African Americans with IBS and diarrhea are significantly more likely to have lower incomes compared with White patients, who tend to have higher incomes. However, age, sex, and education differences have not been observed (Wigington, Johnson, & Cosman, 2003).

PSYCHIATRIC COMORBIDITIES

IBS patients are particularly vulnerable to psychiatric comorbidity. Recent studies of IBS patients seeking treatment have indicated that 50% to 90% have a lifetime history of or currently have one or more common psychiatric conditions. These include major depressive disorder, generalized anxiety disorder, panic disorder, social phobia, somatization disorder, and posttraumatic stress disorder (Lydiard & Falsetti, 1999).

It is noteworthy that many IBS patients may also have a history of early trauma, which could further complicate treatment (Blanchard & Scharff, 2002). A number of studies have documented a higher level of preadolescent sexual and physical abuse among female patients with functional gastrointestinal (GI) disorders like IBS than comparable female patients with organic GI disorders. These IBS patients also tended to have histories of various psychiatric disorders. Blanchard and Scharff (2002) speculated that such "early abuse may be responsible for frequently reported psychological distress and psychiatric comorbidity seem among IBS patient samples" (p. 727).

PROGNOSIS

IBS is a non-life-threatening chronic condition. It seldom causes intestinal bleeding nor does it lead to cancer or other bowel diseases such as Crohn's disease or ulcerative colitis. However, a Mayo Clinic longitudinal study found that bowel diseases did occur in fewer than 10% of IBS patients monitored (Owens, Nelson, & Talley, 1995). IBS is a lifelong condition for most, although symptoms eventually disappear in approximately 30% of cases. For the others, even though symptoms cannot be eliminated, with appropriate treatment symptoms can be effectively controlled. Nevertheless, treatment requires a long-term commitment, and it may take 6 months or longer before the patient notices substantial improvement. It is interesting that psychological interventions appear to reduce somatic symptoms as much as or even more than psychological symptoms.

TREATMENT CONSIDERATIONS AND INTERVENTIONS

A major difficulty in managing the care of IBS patients is the lack of correlation between clinical symptoms and actual gut physiology. This contrasts markedly with GI diseases such as ulcerative colitis and Crohn's disease, where such a correlation is present (Drossman, 1999). Because of the limited effectiveness of standard medical care, a number of psychological interventions have been used in the treatment of IBS. These include biofeedback, relaxation training, brief psychodynamic therapy, behavioral and cognitive interventions, and various combinations of these treatments. Although some have found that psychological interventions have demonstrated mixed results with regard to which type of therapy is most effective, their value is undisputed. In fact, on the basis of their meta-analysis of 17 studies, Lackner, Morley, Dowzer, Mesmer, and Hamilton (2004) concluded that psychological treatments may be more effective in reducing somatic symptoms of IBS than psychological symptoms. Furthermore, Blanchard and Scharff (2002) reviewed 21 randomized controlled trials and found strong evidence to support the benefit of hypnotherapy, cognitive therapy, and brief psychodynamic therapy.

Key considerations in planning and implementing treatment are illness representations, diagnosis and diagnostic criteria, and treatment decisions based on symptom severity. Each is briefly discussed in this section.

Illness Representations

Patients' beliefs about their IBS illness are important (Lackner et al., 2006) and probably should be assessed and incorporated in treatment planning. A study of the illness representations, using the Illness Perception Questionnaire (Weinman, Petrie, Moss-Morris, & Horne, 1996), queried members of a large support network of IBS patients in the United Kingdom. Those who believed that the consequence or impact of their illness was serious indicated that they experienced a lower quality of life and lower satisfaction with health. They also reported experiencing high levels of anxiety and depression. Those who held the belief that they had little control over their IBS reported lower quality of life, lower satisfaction with health, and higher depression scores. Finally, those who attributed their illness to a psychological cause reported high levels of anxiety. These findings indicate that the illness representations of IBS sufferers may prove useful for treatment (Rutter & Rutter, 2002)

Diagnosis and Diagnostic Criteria

IBS is considered a diagnosis of exclusion because there are no pathophysiological changes in the colon and because there is no specific biological marker for it. Generally speaking, IBS is diagnosed on the basis of a complete medical history that includes a careful description of symptoms and a physical examination (Fass et al., 2001). No particular test is specific for IBS; however, diagnostic tests may be performed to rule out diseases such as Crohn's and ulcerative colitis. These tests may include stool or blood tests, X-rays, or *endoscopy* (viewing the colon through a flexible tube inserted through the anus). If these tests are all negative, a diagnosis of IBS may be based entirely on history and symptoms, that is, the intensity and duration of abdominal pain during the past year, the nature and quality of the pain in relation to bowel function, and bowel frequency and stool consistency. The main diagnostic criterion for this disorder is abdominal pain or discomfort for at least 12 weeks out of the previous 12 months that has two of the following three features: (a) It is relieved by having a bowel movement; (b) when it starts, there is a change in how often the patient has a bowel movement; and (c) when it starts, there is a change in the form of the stool or the way it looks.

Treatment Decisions Based on Symptom Severity

Considering level of severity is essential in making treatment decisions. For example, patients with *mild* symptoms may not require psychological interventions regardless of dominant symptoms. For them, education, a symptom diary, referral to an IBS-knowledgeable dietician, and pharmacological intervention as appropriate should be provided. For patients with *moderate* symptoms, there is likely to be psychiatric comorbidity and greater disruption in their lives. Thus, these patients can benefit from psychological treatment in addition to the conventional medical management. For patients with *severe* symptoms, usually a combination of strategies is needed. This typically will include diet modification, pharmacological intervention, and either cognitive–behavioral therapy (CBT) or brief psychodynamic therapy. These patients can be offered the option of gut-oriented hypnotherapy, particularly if traditional medical treatment has failed to relieve their symptoms.

PSYCHOEDUCATIONAL INTERVENTIONS

Psychoeducational interventions include a variety of methods that range from patient education to relaxation, meditation and mindfulness, exercise, stress management, and social skills training. Patient education is an essential component of psychoeducation for IBS. Because patients can find IBS a puzzling medical condition with regard to causes, diagnosis, and difficulty in treating it, patient education can play a significant part in engaging patients in the treatment process. Because psychosocial factors play such a prominent part of this illness, presenting a biopsychosocial understanding of it to patients is critically important in their being able to collaborate with clinicians and commit to monitoring symptoms and stressors and engaging in relaxation, stress management, and other psychoeducational interventions.

Psychoeducation appears to be a particularly potent intervention in IBS. A major randomized controlled trial study by Blanchard et al. (2007) compared group-based cognitive therapy (CT) with psychoeducational support groups and a treatment that involved intensive symptom and daily stress monitoring. On a composite GI symptom measure derived from daily symptom diaries, both the CT and the psychoeducational support groups were significantly more improved than those in the intensive symptom monitoring condition, but the CT group and psychoeducational support group did not differ from each other (Blanchard et al., 2007)

Relaxation Training

Relaxation training has been an oft-used intervention with IBS patients in individual and group contexts. In one study, it appears that the benefits of relaxation therapy and stress management with IBS patients in psychoeducational support groups were inconclusive (Lucak, 2005).

COGNITIVE–BEHAVIORAL THERAPY

Some of the earliest efforts to use CBT with chronic medical conditions involved clinical research on IBS by Blanchard and colleagues. Work on a CT approach to IBS was developed by Blanchard (2001) and refined by Lackner (2003). In this approach, IBS patients participate in 10 weekly group sessions of CT designed to reduce GI symptoms and related distress by identifying and correcting maladaptive beliefs and information-processing errors. Treatment is provided in small groups of 3 to 6 patients and focuses on four areas: (a) education about IBS and triggers, (b) training on cognitive appraisal and excessive worrying, (c) restructuring core beliefs, and (d) problem-solving training. Weekly homework assignments are given (Lackner et al., 2006). R. R. Taylor (2006) ably described and illustrated cognitive restructuring and other CBT interventions with patients with GI dysfunction.

Several studies have demonstrated the effectiveness of CT in IBS patients in changing symptoms by altering the underlying appraisal and thought patterns that drive excessive emotional or physiological reactions. (Lackner et al., 2004, 2006). These changes confirm other studies with similar findings that CT is efficacious either alone or in a CBT protocol. Although CBT has not been found to be superior to psychoeducational interventions, cognitive therapy alone has produced consistently effective results (Blanchard & Scharff, 2002). In a recent study described in the "Psychoeducational Interventions" section in this chapter, both CT and the psychoeducational support groups were significantly more improved than those in the intensive symptom monitoring condition, but the CT group and psychoeducational support group did not differ (Blanchard et al., 2007).

Particularly noteworthy is that CT appears to foster neurobiological changes. It was recently reported that reduced neural activity was discovered in the amygdala following CT (Lackner et al., 2006). In fact, Lackner et al. (2006) theorized that CT and pharmacotherapy appear to achieve therapeutic results through a common limbic–cortical pathway and that CT serves to functionally "rewire" brain circuitry, thereby reducing IBS symptoms.

OTHER PSYCHOTHERAPEUTIC INTERVENTIONS

Brief Psychodynamic Therapy

Brief dynamically oriented therapy encourages the patient to explore interpersonal conflicts entwined with bowel symptoms that result in pain and distress and has been shown to have some efficacy with IBS patients (Lackner et al., 2004). The treatment was administered over 3 months for 7 to 10 visits. Pain was improved in patients at posttreatment and 12 months later (Blanchard & Scharff, 2002).

Hypnotherapy

Hypnotherapy for IBS consistently produces significant results and improves cardinal symptoms (pain, bowel habits, and bloating) for a majority of patients, has positive effects on noncolonic symptoms, and provides a general sense of well-being. Whitehead (2006) reported that of 11 empirical studies between 1984 and 2002, all demonstrated the effectiveness of hypnotherapy on IBS symptoms even for patients nonresponsive to medical treatments, with positive effects lasting 1 to 2 years after the end of treatment. In one exception, Gonsalkorale, Houghton, and Whorwell (2002) found that males with diarrhea-predominant bowel pattern had a significantly lower average response rate than other IBS patients. The number of hypnosis treatment sessions varied in the empirical research, with the shortest course of treatment (four sessions over 7 weeks) showing the least improvement. Studies seem to indicate that the highest success rates used seven-session protocols (Whitehead, 2006). The highly regarded Manchester model of gut-oriented hypnotherapy uses 12 or more sessions aimed at teaching patients skills to voluntarily self-regulate physiological arousal (Lackner et al., 2004). This model includes an initial hypnotic induction using arm levitation followed by sessions for general relaxation, with attention to increased control of intestinal motility and ego strengthening (Blanchard & Scharff, 2002). The Manchester group's outcome data of their 12-session protocols indicate that this approach is most likely to be successful when integrated into a combined treatment program (Gonsalkorale et al., 2002; Whorwell, 2006). Finally, it should be noted that although this modality can be exceptionally beneficial, it is both labor intensive and not suitable for all patients.

MEDICAL TREATMENT

Conventional medical treatment consists of diet modification and first-line medications such as antispasmodics, antidiarrheals, laxatives, and anti-depressants as appropriate (Whorwell, 2006), alone or in combination. The recent addition of receptor-modifying drugs is now considered first line. However, empirical evidence seems to show that pharmacological approaches are frequently unable to control patients' severe symptoms (Whorwell, 2006). Patients should be encouraged to keep a symptom diary to identify and monitor exacerbating triggers, but clinicians should be alert for patients who obsess over symptoms (Lucak, 2005).

Diet Modification

Often, patients with constipation are told to try high-fiber diets despite compelling evidence that this may exacerbate symptoms in some (Whorwell, 2006). Patients whose symptoms are exacerbated by high-fiber diets are commonly told to exclude cereal fiber for three months. Burden (2001) recommended evaluation by an IBS-knowledgeable dietician and reviewed the limited role of exclusion diets, the move away from high-fiber diets toward manipulation of fiber in the diet, evaluating caffeine in the diet, and identifying individual dietary issues related to symptoms.

Medication

Antispasmodics or smooth muscle relaxants and tricyclic antidepressants (TCAs) have some value in the treatment of diarrhea-dominant IBS patients. TCAs like imipramine have a constipating effect and have long been used to reduce or eliminate abdominal pain and diarrhea in patients with diarrhea-dominant IBS. Poynard, Regimbeau, and Benhamou (2001) performed a meta-analysis of antispasmodics on IBS symptoms and found a 53% improvement compared with 41% with the placebo. This is noticeably lower than the effect of TCAs. TCAs are the most widely studied antidepressants used to treat IBS; they have been used to treat it for 30 years (Lucak, 2005). Lucak (2005) reported that TCAs significantly reduced abdominal pain and other IBS symptoms in patients with diarrhea-dominant IBS but not constipation-dominant IBS (perhaps because, as mentioned, they tend to promote constipation). Recent trials of desipramine and paroxetine showed improvement in quality of life without relief of GI symptoms (Lucak, 2005).

However, with constipation-dominant IBS, serotonergic drugs like desipramine and Paxil are better because they are not constipating. They do improve quality of life but are less effective than TCAs in relieving abdominal symptoms. Serotonin is believed to be a mediating chemical of gut function, including motility and sensitivity (Lucak, 2005). Although 3% to 5% of serotonin is in the CNS, 95% is synthesized and stored in the gut (Lucak, 2005). Antagonism of serotonin receptors results in delayed colonic transit, decreased visceral pain, and decreased gut secretion (Lucak, 2005). One serotoninergic drug, Tegaserod (Zelnorm) has been demonstrated to be effective in women with constipation-dominant IBS (Lucak, 2005).[1] Lotronex is used for patients with diarrhea-dominant IBS.

COMBINED TREATMENT

Because of the limited success of the conventional medical treatment strategy in the treatment of IBS patients with moderate and severe symptoms, combined treatment has assumed a central role. Typically, integrating psychological interventions with medical treatment strategies is the starting point when patients present with moderate and severe symptoms. It has been hypothesized that combined treatment exerts a therapeutic effect through a common limbic–cortical pathway, which results in reduced IBS symptoms (Lackner et al., 2006). These effects include significant reduction in pain, GI symptom severity, and anxiety.

Two or more psychological treatments also can be combined and used without medication in some patients. Whitehead (2006) reported substantial improvement in IBS symptoms with the use of hypnosis and CBT.

Integrative Treatment Protocol: Irritable Bowel Syndrome (IBS)

1. Key Background Information	
Pathology	Disorder that interferes with normal colon functions resulting in crampy abdominal pain, bloating, constipation, and diarrhea in the absence of weight loss, bleeding, anemia, or fever. Does not permanently damage the intestines or lead to cancer or bleeding. Not related to Crohn's disease or ulcerative colitis.
Types	Classified as *diarrhea-dominant* and *constipation-dominant* types. A third type is a combination of the two, usually in an alternating pattern.
Epidemiology	20% of Americans experience IBS symptoms. It is one of the most common diagnoses in medical practice and the second most common reason for work absenteeism.

---

[1]It should be noted that in March 2007, at the request of the Food and Drug Administration, Novartis, the manufacturer of Zelnorm, removed Zelnorm from the market because of serious side effects.

Gender and ethnicity	Occurs more often in women than in men and usually begins around age 20. There are similar rates of prevalence of IBS in African Americans and Whites, but African American patients have reported more diarrhea and lower incomes compared with White patients.
Causal factors	Cause is unknown, but may result from a disturbance in the brain–gut axis, causing heightened colon sensitivity and reactivity such that the colon contracts too much or too little or may absorb too much or too little water.
Psychiatric comorbidities	50% to 90% of patients may have major depressive disorder, generalized anxiety disorder, panic disorder, social phobia, somatization disorder, and posttraumatic stress disorder. Some may also have a history of early trauma.
Prognosis	Not life threatening. In fewer than 10% of cases, leads to other bowel disease. Symptoms disappear in 30% of cases but can be well controlled in others.

2. Biopsychosocial Assessment

Patient profile	From interview and observation and Revised Illness Perception Questionnaire (IPQ-R; Moss-Morris et al., 2002) assess: • IPQ-R factors, especially illness perceptions, explanations, and treatment expectations; • severity of symptoms and functional impact; • capacity, previous change efforts, and readiness for change; and • personality style or disorder and family and cultural factors.
Illness profile Identify higher risk IBS patients	• Those who experience periodic, debilitating symptoms. • Those who experience constant, debilitating symptoms because they have more psychosocial difficulties, seek more health care, and demonstrate more psychiatric comorbidity. • Those with "alarm symptoms" such as weight loss, bleeding, anemia, fever, and frequent nocturnal symptoms.
Type	Identify whether diarrhea or constipation is the dominant symptom pattern.
Nutritional assessment	Evaluation by an IBS-knowledgeable dietician is indicated, especially with moderate and severe symptoms.
Symptom diary	Have patients identify and monitor exacerbating triggers and symptoms; but keep alert for patients who obsess over symptoms (i.e., *symptom amplifiers*).
Psychiatric comorbidities	Identify and plan treatment accordingly.

(continues)

3. Intervention Planning

Patient and illness profiles	
Illness representations	IBS patients' perceptions about their illness—particularly about cause, consequences, and control—are important in planning treatment.
Diagnosis and diagnostic criteria	A diagnosis of exclusion based on a complete medical history and physical exam. No specific biological marker exists, but diagnostic tests may be performed to rule out Crohn's and ulcerative colitis. Diagnostic criteria for this disorder include abdominal pain or discomfort for at least 12 weeks out of the previous 12 months; the pain or discomfort must have two of the following three features: (a) it is relieved by having a bowel movement; (b) when it starts, there is a change in how often the patient has a bowel movement; and (c) when it starts, there is a change in the form of the stool or the way it looks. Severity and type are key intervention targets and provide the basis for tailoring (see below).
Symptom severity	• Mild symptoms: usually do not require psychological interventions. • Moderate symptoms: patients experience greater disruption and/or psychiatric comorbidity; benefit from combined psychological and medical management. • Severe symptoms: require a combination of strategies, including diet, medical management, and various psychological interventions.
Type	Diarrhea-dominant: goal is to reduce or eliminate abdominal pain and diarrhea; diet, medication, and psychological interventions as indicated. Constipation-dominant: goal is to normalize bowel function; medication, and psychological interventions as indicated.

4. Intervention Implementation

Psychoeducational interventions	A wide variety of patient education strategies have been effective in supporting lifestyle change. Interestingly, relaxation therapy and stress-management have had limited benefits compared to other strategies.
Cognitive–behavioral therapy (CBT)	Cognitive therapy (CT) works by altering the underlying appraisal patterns that drive excessive emotional or physiological reactions. CT is efficacious either alone or in a CBT protocol; by itself, CT has produced consistently effective results. CBT is also effective but not superior to psychoeducational interventions or to CT alone.
Other psychotherapeutic interventions	• Brief psychodynamic therapy has been shown effective in helping patient to explore interpersonal conflicts associated with bowel symptoms that result in pain and distress.

	• Hypnotherapy: gut-oriented hypnotherapy (7-session protocol or the 12-session Manchester protocol) has produced significant improvement in pain, bowel habits, and bloating as well as providing a general sense of well-being.
Medical treatment strategy	Standard treatment consists of diet change and first-line medications such as antispasmodics, antidiarrheals, laxatives, and antidepressants.
Medication	Antispasmodics are less effective than tricyclic antidepressants (e.g., imipramine), which are beneficial with diarrhea-dominant IBS, whereas serotonergic drugs (e.g., desipramine and Paxil) are beneficial with constipation-dominant IBS. For women, Lotronex has been shown to work best with diarrhea-dominant IBS.
Combined treatment	Integration of psychological interventions has assumed a key role in treatment of moderate and severe symptoms because the conventional medical treatment strategy has limited value. Combined treatment is the starting point for patients with moderate and severe symptom presentations.

5. Intervention Monitoring

Review patient's symptom diary of symptoms, severity, and triggers.

CASE OF GINI T.

Gini T. is a 29-year-old female account executive diagnosed with IBS some 2 years ago, just after her wedding. In the months before the wedding, she began experiencing abdominal pain and persistent diarrhea and thinking it was just "nerves." She tried several over-the-counter medications without much relief. She said her honeymoon was nearly ruined by her symptoms. On the advice of a friend, she consulted with a gastroenterologist, who made the diagnosis. She also noted that her symptoms interfered with her job performance and her relationship with her husband and that she had been experiencing feelings of increasing isolation and depression. The gastroenterologist who evaluated her referred her to the clinic's IBS program. She met with the program director, a clinical health psychologist, who began by performing a biopsychosocial evaluation. Most notable was that her perceptions of cure and control were pessimistic; she believed she would become unemployed and hopelessly homebound out of fear of having an "accident" in public and painfully embarrassing herself. This was not inconsistent with her obsessive–compulsive personality style, that is, her workaholism and perfectionism. The program director discussed with her the gastroenterologist's characterization of her IBS as the diarrhea-dominant subtype of moderate severity. He indicated that this form of IBS responded best to diet, medication, and psychological interventions. They then discussed how treatment would be tailored to her: She would work with a clinic nutritionist, her gastroenterologist, one of the program's psychologists, and a psychology intern. She would keep a daily symptom diary, participate in a psychoeducational support group run by the psychology intern, and meet with the psychologist for individual sessions involving CBT and hypnotherapy. The individual CBT would focus on her treatment-interfering illness representations and perfectionistic features. In individual sessions, her illness representations became more realistic and she responded well to the gut-oriented hypnotherapy in terms of self-regulation of physiological arousal. The psychoeducational support group provided her with useful information from other members about IBS, its course, and its prognosis. Emotional support and reassurance from other group participants was invaluable to her. Needless to say, her diary tracking of her symptoms was thorough. Although her perfectionistic style seemed to moderate only a bit, she was quite pleased with the decrease in pain and increase in "colon control," her code words for better control of diarrhea symptoms.

16

SYSTEMIC LUPUS ERYTHEMATOSUS

Systemic lupus erythematosus (SLE), sometimes referred to as *lupus*, is an autoimmune disease in which antibodies attack healthy tissue. Patients often experience such symptoms as joint and muscle pain, skin rash, fatigue, mouth ulcers, hair loss, and weight loss (Moses, Wiggers, Nicholas, & Cockburn, 2005). The disease can affect any body system, including the skin, joints, kidney, heart, lungs, nervous system, blood, and other organs or systems (Giffords, 2003). Pain and fatigue are some of the most difficult and dispiriting symptoms that SLE patients endure (Sohng, 2003).

A distinctive feature of this medical condition is that the diagnosis process is often difficult and lengthy. In other words, a formal diagnosis of SLE may not be made for quite some time after symptoms are first brought to a physician—in the past, such a diagnosis might not be made for 5 to 7 years. More recently, the time frame has shortened, largely because of advances in diagnostic assessment. Today, the average time period for a diagnosis of SLE ranges from 1 to 3 years (Giffords, 2003). Needless to say, this delay can be frustrating and distressing for both patients and family members.

The following sections present basic background on SLE as a disease and illness followed by a detailed discussion of various psychological and biopsychosocial treatment intervention options. This discussion includes both clinical and research findings. The chapter concludes with an integrative treatment protocol and a case example illustrating the protocol.

EPIDEMIOLOGY

The Lupus Foundation of America has estimated that approximately 1.5 million Americans have some type of lupus. Of these, more than 70% have SLE. This means that approximately 1 million Americans suffer from SLE (Giffords, 2003).

TYPES

Besides SLE, three other types of lupus are recognized. The first is *discoid lupus erythematosus*, a chronic skin disorder in which a red, raised rash appears on the face, scalp, or elsewhere. The second type is *subacute cutaneous lupus erythematosus*, a milder disease characterized by skin lesions that appear on parts of the body exposed to sun. The third is *drug-induced lupus*, which is caused by medications and presents with symptoms similar to those of SLE. Because the causes, impact, and treatment vary so widely among the four types, this chapter addresses background and treatment issues involving SLE only.

SEVERITY

In addition to being the most common, SLE is the most devastating disease and challenging illness of the four types. It is also a perplexing disease in that the course and symptoms can vary greatly from one patient to another. Symptoms can range from mild to severe and may come and go over time, and for many, SLE is characterized by periods of exacerbation of symptoms, called *flares*, and periods of remission. Nevertheless, for some the experience of SLE is that of mild disease with little variation. For others, it is a more severe disease with little variation. For yet others, it is a progressively worsening disease that waxes and wanes.

Some common symptoms, however, characterize this condition: painful or swollen joints (arthritis), unexplained fever, extreme fatigue, a characteristic red skin rash across the nose and cheeks (i.e., the so-called *butterfly* or *malar* rash), chest pain when deep breathing, unusual loss of hair, pale or purple fingers or toes from cold or stress (i.e., *Raynaud's phenomenon*), sensitivity to the sun, swelling in legs or around eyes, mouth ulcers, and swollen glands. Some experience headaches, dizziness, depression, confusion, and seizures. New symptoms may continue to appear years after the initial diagnosis, and different symptoms can occur at different times.

GENDER AND ETHNICITY

Gender and Age

For reasons not fully understood, 9 out of 10 people with SLE are women. Although SLE can occur at any time throughout the life cycle, its incidence during the childbearing years is 10 to 15 times higher than at other times of life.

Ethnicity

Although lupus may affect White women, it is 2 to 3 times more common in African American, Latina, Asian, and Native American women (Giffords, 2003). Genetic factors may influence the frequency of occurrence, with Asian ethnicities more commonly affected (Ebert, Chapman, & Shoenfeld, 2005). It is interesting to note that SLE can run in families, but the risk is rather low.

CAUSAL FACTORS

SLE is a complex disease, and its cause is unknown. There has been much speculation about causes, triggers, and exacerbants. It is likely that a combination of genetic, environmental, and possibly hormonal factors work together to cause the disease. Although a specific "SLE gene" has yet to be identified, studies have suggested that several genes may be involved in determining an individual's vulnerability and likelihood for developing the disease as well as which tissues and organs will be affected and the severity of disease. Some have suggested that certain toxins may be causal. Cigarette smoke exposes a vulnerable individual to upwards of 400 toxins and, according to one meta-analysis, may be causally linked to SLE (Costenbader et al., 2004). Furthermore, certain factors are believed to trigger SLE. These include stress, sunlight, certain drugs, and viruses. It is likely that a combination of factors is involved in the expression of the disease.

MEDICAL COMORBIDITIES

Premenopausal women with lupus appear to be at increased risk of other diseases, such as diabetes mellitus, familial hypercholesterolemia, and polycystic ovary syndrome (Manzi et al., 1997). Women with lupus may also be at increased risk of myocardial infarction and angina (Manzi et al., 1997). Manzi et al. (1997) found that women with lupus ages 35 to 44 were more than 50 times more likely to have a myocardial infarction than women without lupus. This is likely due to both treatment and disease factors. The significant factors appeared to be older age at lupus diagnosis, longer lupus disease duration, longer corticosteroid use, hypercholesterolemia, and postmenopausal status.

PSYCHIATRIC COMORBIDITIES

Psychological distress is common in SLE patients, and anxiety and depression are common (Moses et al., 2005; Walker et al., 2000). Other comorbidities include lupus psychosis and headache. Half of the SLE patients studied by Segui et al. (2000) experienced emotional problems as a result of SLE, and some 15% to 60% developed depression. Nevertheless, anxiety appears to be a greater concern for SLE patients than depression.

Anxiety

Acute episodes of increased anxiety levels and psychological distress are common in SLE patients (Segui et al., 2000). Disease activity is known to cause anxiety, which can exacerbate SLE; extreme stress may even trigger SLE (Doria et al., 2004). According to Segui et al.'s (2000) recent prospective study, it may also be that the anxiety associated with SLE could be better attributed to the result of living with a debilitating, recurrent, and often painful disease.

Depression

Disturbances of mood such as depression, nervousness, confusion, decreased concentration, and insomnia are common in SLE and can be severe (Moses et al., 2005). The chronic progression of SLE functions as a long-term stressor for patients, which increases their probability of developing depression. In many cases, the worsening quality of life is not necessarily related to the severity, activity, or damage of the disease (Rinaldi et al., 2006). In their multiple regression analysis, Kozora, Ellison, Waxmonsky, Wamboldt, and Patterson (2005) found that increased depressive symptoms in patients appeared to be related to the use of disengaging and expressive emotional coping styles. The results were consistent with those of other studies.

Lupus Psychosis

Some SLE patients experience psychotic features during the illness course, a condition called *lupus psychosis*. It has been speculated that the presence of anti-P antibodies is potentially related to the development of lupus psychosis in SLE patients (Ebert et al., 2005).

Headache

Although patients with SLE may report instances of headache, Mitsikostas, Sfikakis, and Goadsby (2004) found in their meta-analysis that headaches were not associated with the disease itself, and patients were better treated with traditional primary headache methods. However, migraines with aura may be more frequent among SLE patients (Mitsikostas et al., 2004). Mitsikostas et al. suggested that evaluation for mood disorders may be helpful in treating patients with SLE who report symptoms of headache associated with the disease in order to differentiate comorbidity.

PROGNOSIS

At present, there is no cure for SLE. However, it can be effectively treated and managed, and most individuals with the disease can lead active, healthy lives. Most SLE patients (78%) have reported that they are coping well with their illness. Pain (65%), lifestyle changes (61%), and emotional problems associated with the illness (50%) were noted as the most difficult factors for coping with SLE. With appropriate medical care and self-management, 80% to 90% of those with SLE can expect to live a normal life span. Considering the morbidity and mortality of SLE, some patients adapt and manage quite well, considering the lessened quality of life often associated with having a painful and potentially fatal disease (Giffords, 2003).

TREATMENT CONSIDERATIONS AND INTERVENTIONS

Because of the variability—more than any other chronic illness—of its course and severity, SLE requires a tailored treatment approach. Because SLE patients are not a homogeneous group, these patients benefit from targeted strategies that account for their individual psychosocial and behavioral responses to pain. Disease severity appears to be a useful focus for targeting treatment (Moses et al., 2005). Measures that are helpful in planning tailored treatment include psychosocial and behavioral adaptation assessments, which provide data on distress due to pain, relationship difficulties, and limitations on activity (Greco, Rudy, & Manzi, 2003). Treatments to be tailored include coping skills training; cognitive restructuring; increasing self-esteem; breathing and relaxation exercises; social problem solving; communication-skills training; and individual, group, and family therapy (Rinaldi et al., 2006). Specific treatment considerations include illness representations, family dynamics and social support, quality of life, and diagnosis. Each of these is briefly addressed here.

Illness Representations

An individual's constellations of perceptions and beliefs about a particular disease—understanding of it and its symptoms, cause, time or illness duration, impact or consequences, curability, and ability to control it—is referred to as their *illness representation*. Illness representations in SLE tend to be sensitive predictors of treatment compliance, treatment outcomes, and well-being. Recent research has demonstrated three clinically relevant considerations. First, beliefs about ability to control SLE are key to effective treatment compliance. Second, illness representations change over time. Third, clinicians can effectively work with patients to modify their beliefs about control of SLE.

Goodman, Morrissey, Graham, and Bossingham (2005b) identified the illness representations of SLE patients using a semistructured interview informed by the self-regulatory model (Leventhal, Diefenbach, & Leventhal, 1992). A noteworthy finding was that beliefs about ability to control one's SLE are important in treatment compliance and clinical outcomes. Goodman et al. also found that over time, illness representations did in fact change for various reasons. The implication of these findings is that clinicians should be prepared for the likelihood of changes in the illness representations over the course of the patient's illness because this could be helpful in informing interventions for such patients (Goodman et al., 2005b). Another study by Goodman, Morrissey, Graham, and Bossingham (2005a) addressed treatment-interfering illness representations. They particularly focused on beliefs about patients' inability to control their SLE condition and symptoms, and they developed an intervention for changing such beliefs (Goodman et al., 2005a). This is described further in the "Cognitive–Behavioral Therapy" section in this chapter.

Family Dynamics, Social Support, and Employment

Because of the protracted time lag between symptom expression and SLE diagnosis, family dynamics—particularly marital conflict—are commonly associated with this disorder. Karasz and Ouellette (1995) studied women with lupus and reported that disease severity was linked to psychological distress when there was a strain of valued social roles. They suggested that clinicians find ways to help SLE patients maintain their valued roles, especially with regard to family and work.

A retrospective study by Moses et al. (2005) found that the social support needs and occupational concerns of some SLE patients were not being adequately met by family or health services personnel. The employment capacity of SLE patients varies, but the lack of employment or underemployment of SLE patients has financial and emotional ramifications for them (Moses et al., 2005). Segui et al. (2000) found that pain was the most important factor in impairment of general functioning and occupational activity.

Quality of Life

The reasons for decreased quality of life among SLE patients remain a subject of debate (Rinaldi et al., 2006). In many cases, the worsening quality of life is not necessarily related to the severity or damage of the disease. It may be that the frequency of exacerbations of the illness is more related to reduced quality of life (Doria et al., 2004). Two other factors that may negatively impact quality of life are a passive coping attitude and joint pain (Rinaldi et al., 2006).

Diagnosis

Diagnosing SLE is often difficult, and it may take months or even years for a correct diagnosis to be made and confirmed as new symptoms appear. Unfortunately, no single test can confirm the diagnosis. The most useful tests identify certain autoantibodies such as the antinuclear antibody, anti-DNA, anti-Sm, anti-RNP, anti-Ro, and anti-La tests.

The diagnosis and treatment of SLE is typically a collaborative effort between the patient and several types of health care clinicians: family physicians or internists, rheumatologists, clinical immunologists, nephrologists, hematologists, dermatologists, and neurologists as well as nurses, psychologists, mental health counselors, and social workers. The range and effectiveness of treatments for SLE have increased dramatically, giving clinicians more choices in managing the disease. It is important for the patient to work closely with clinicians and take an active role in self-managing the disease.

PSYCHOEDUCATIONAL INTERVENTIONS

Although medication is typically a part of treatment, self-management, including several environmental and psychosocial interventions, is the mainstay of treatment. Because stress is both a trigger and response to SLE, effectively managing stress is a key goal of self-management. Relaxation techniques include deep breathing, mental imagery, progressive muscle relaxation, and biofeedback.

Sohng (2003) conducted a quasi-experimental study in which half the patients were assigned to an experimental group that provided a self-management course on SLE that addressed fatigue, pain, disease activity, coping skills, self-efficacy, and depression. The group participated in six weekly 2-hour sessions for groups of 10 to 15 literate adults of all ages. The remaining patients were in a control group that received no interventions. Patients in the treatment group showed significant improvement in fatigue, coping skills, self-efficacy, and depression but not in pain or disease activity.

Exercise

Although patients with SLE often experience significant fatigue, Tench, McCarthy, McCurdie, White, and D'Cruz (2003) found in a controlled study that graded exercise therapy led to greater improvement than relaxation therapy or no intervention in SLE patients. However, an initial effect on fatigue was not sustained on 3-month follow-up. There was no significant change in aerobic fitness, but participants also did not experience any flare in disease activity or other serious adverse events.

Environmental Interventions

Environmental factors that trigger or exacerbate SLE include ultraviolet light, particularly sunlight; certain foods; and bacterial and viral infections. Interventions usually involve limiting or eliminating exposure to these factors, such as advising patients to avoid strong sunlight (Moses et al., 2005). Accordingly, avoiding exposure to the midday sun is essential to the well-being of most SLE patients (Sperry, 2006b).

Smoking Cessation

Given recent evidence of a link between smoking and SLE, a link between SLE and vascular disease, and the known correlation between smoking and vascular disease, patients who smoke should be advised to quit smoking and may benefit from smoking cessation assistance.

COGNITIVE–BEHAVIORAL THERAPY

Cognitive–behavioral therapy (CBT) is particularly beneficial in addressing the multifactorial issues of living with SLE. One of the most useful applications of CBT is in modifying illness representations that could or do hinder treatment. Goodman et al. (2005a) developed and tested a cognitive and behavioral–based intervention for modifying such treatment-hindering illness representations. The intervention did change patients' treatment control and emotional representations: It enhanced their perceptions that treatment could control their lupus and reduced their perceptions of the emotional impact of their lupus and overall stress.

Other uses include altering maladaptive thoughts and behaviors. In a multiple regression analysis study, cognitive–behavioral interventions aimed at altering maladaptive coping styles and behaviors appeared to be useful treatments for SLE patients (Kozora et al., 2005). Rinaldi et al. (2006) also recommended coping skills training that involves cognitive restructuring, increasing self-efficacy and self-esteem, breathing and relaxation, social problem solving, and communication-skills training.

Pain is a common concern for SLE patients. Greco, Rudy, and Manzi (2004) assessed the effects of a CBT-based stress-reduction program on pain, psychological function, and physical function in SLE patients who were experiencing pain. In this randomized controlled trial, patients received either biofeedback-assisted CBT, a symptom-monitoring support intervention, or usual medical care alone. Results indicated that CBT participants had significantly greater reductions in pain and psychological dysfunction compared with the symptom-monitoring support group and the usual medical care group. At a 9-month follow-up evaluation, CBT continued to exhibit relative benefit compared with usual medical care in psychological functioning (Greco et al., 2004).

CBT can be particularly useful in dealing with denial of the illness as well as changing negative thinking and reducing the excessive use of drugs, avoidance of activity, and dependence on others. CBT can foster and reward the opposites of these thoughts and behaviors, that is, responsibility, independence, activity, and a desire to free oneself from the constraints of SLE rather than be bound by it. CBT can help patients attend to what they think and say about their illness and provide a method of redirecting their thinking in a positive direction. Furthermore, clients can be helped to recognize their self-talk attitudes and identify beliefs that make it more difficult for them to live with this chronic condition (Digeronimo, 2002). As with other chronic illnesses, it is essential to self-management that patients understand the relationship between the way they think about their health and the way they feel as reflected in their energy level, their attitudes, their moods, and their behavior.

OTHER PSYCHOTHERAPEUTIC INTERVENTIONS

Supportive–Expressive Group Psychotherapy

There have been few reported studies of psychotherapy with SLE patients. A randomized clinical trial was conducted to determine if brief supportive–expressive group psychotherapy could reduce the psychological distress and improve the quality of life for patients with SLE (Dobkin et al., 2002). The study found that there was not enough evidence for practitioners to recommend that SLE patients participate in this therapeutic method (Dobkin et al., 2002).

Couples Group Therapy

Like other chronic illnesses, SLE can take a toll on close interpersonal relationships. Marital discord and divorce are not uncommon in SLE. Karlson et al. (2004) reported a randomized trial with 122 SLE patients and their partners. The patients in the treatment group received a 1-hour intervention about self-efficacy, couples communication about lupus, social support, and problem solving followed by monthly phone follow-up for 6 months. The control group received an attention placebo, a 45-minute video about lupus, and monthly phone calls. The treatment group scored higher in couple communication, self-efficacy, and mental health status and had lower fatigue scores. There was no effect on disease activity.

MEDICAL TREATMENT

Once SLE has been diagnosed, the physician will develop a treatment plan tailored to the severity of the disorder as well as the patient's age, sex, health, symptoms, and lifestyle. Because of the variability of SLE and response to interventions, the treatment plan is likely to change over time. Even though there is no standardized medical treatment plan for SLE, there is an overall treatment goal. The basic goal of SLE treatment is to relieve symptoms and protect organs by decreasing inflammation and the level of autoimmune activity in the body. Patients with mild symptoms may need little or no treatment or only intermittent courses of anti-inflammatory medications. Those with more serious presentations, for example, damage to internal organs, may require a rigorous medication regimen to suppress the overactive immune system.

Abnormal levels of prolactin have been reported in SLE patients. An open-label pharmacological study conducted by Walker et al. (2000) examined the effects of prolactin lowering bromocriptine in patients with SLE. Patients were prescribed prolactin for a range of 7 to 12 months, and prolactin was found to positively affect certain mood states. Anxiety, anger–hostility, and overall distress improved during treatment (Walker et al., 2000).

COMPLEMENTARY AND ALTERNATIVE MEDICAL TREATMENTS

Lately, complementary and alternative medical treatments (CAM) have become popular in the treatment of SLE, both because of the cost of conventional medications and their potential for serious side effects. Alternative treatment approaches include massage, chiropractic, special diets, nutritional supplements, herbs, and fish oils. The use of CAM was found to be common in SLE patients. In a survey of 707 SLE patients, 352 (49.8%) reported using CAM at similar rates across Canada, the United States, and the United Kingdom. These users were younger and better educated than nonusers and exhibited poorer levels of self-rated health status and lowered satisfaction with conventional medical care (Moore et al., 2000). Moore et al. (2000) hypothesized that the use of CAM indicates care-seeking behavior for these patients. Compared with other common medical conditions, these rates of CAM use by patients with SLE are considerably higher than for those who reported using CAM to treat diabetes (20%), which is comparable to the use of CAM among the general population (Yeh, Eisenberg, Davis, & Phillips, 2002).

MEDICATION

There are currently several conventional medical treatments for SLE. They are prescribed on the basis of the type and severity of symptoms. For those with joint or chest pain or fever, nonsteroidal anti-inflammatory drugs such as ibuprofen and naproxen may be used alone or in combination with other drugs to control pain, swelling, and fever. Antimalarials, such as hydroxychloroquine (Plaquenil), although originally developed to treat malaria, have been found useful for treating SLE. The mainstay of SLE treatment involves the use of corticosteroid hormones such as prednisone (Deltasone), hydrocortisone, methylprednisolone (Medrol), and dexamethasone (Decadron, Hexadrol). Corticosteroids work by rapidly suppressing inflammation and can be given by mouth, in creams applied to the skin, or by injection. For some individuals whose kidneys or central nervous systems are affected by SLE, an immunosuppressive drug may be used, such as cyclophosphamide (Cytoxan) and mycophenolate mofetil (CellCept). These drugs effectively dampen the overactive immune system by blocking the production of immune cells. In some patients, methotrexate (Folex, Mexate, Rheumatrex), a disease-modifying antirheumatic drug, may be used to help control the disease.

Psychotropics

Because depressed and anxious SLE patients appear to be helped by medication, a psychopharmacology referral may be warranted. Antidepressants are beneficial for depressed patients, and bromocriptine appears to be beneficial for patients with elevated prolactin levels in order to lower anxiety, anger–hostility, and overall feelings of distress.

COMBINED TREATMENT

Because of the great variability of the course and severity of this medical condition, tailored treatment is required. For most patients with moderate and severe SLE, this means combined treatment. Usually, one or more medications or medical treatments will be combined with one or more psychological treatments as indicated by a biopsychosocial assessment.

Integrative Treatment Protocol: Systemic Lupus Erythematosus (SLE)

1. Key Background Information	
Pathology	An autoimmune disease that leads to inflammation and tissue damage. Affects joints, skin, kidneys, heart, lungs, blood vessels, and brain. Has periods of exacerbation of symptoms, called *flares*, and periods of remission.
Epidemiology	Affects 500,000 to 1.5 million Americans.
Severity	Symptoms can range from mild to severe and wax and wane over time. Some cases remain relatively stable, and others progressively worsen.
Types	Four types of lupus include discoid lupus erythematosus, subacute cutaneous lupus erythematosus, drug-induced lupus, and SLE.
Causal factors	Not known; it is speculated that a genetic vulnerability is triggered by hormones, toxins, viruses, bacteria, or other stressors.
Gender, age, and ethnicity	90% of those who have SLE are women; it is 10 to 15 times more frequent during child-bearing years; and it is 2 to 3 times more common in African American, Latina, Asian, and Native American women than in White women.
Comorbidities—medical	Diabetes mellitus, familial hypercholesterolemia, polycystic ovary syndrome, myocardial infarction, and angina.
Comorbidities—psychiatric	Anxiety and disturbances of mood such as depression, nervousness, confusion, decreased concentration, and insomnia are common, as is migraine headache; less common is lupus psychosis.
Prognosis	SLE is not curable, but symptoms and autoimmune activity can be decreased. Enhancing adjustment and avoiding or delaying disability foster well-being.
2. Biopsychosocial Assessment	
Patient profile	From interview and observation and Revised Illness Perception Questionnaire (IPQ-R; Moss-Morris et al., 2002) assessment: • IPQ-R factors, especially illness perceptions, explanations, and treatment expectations; • severity of symptoms and functional impact; • capacity, previous change efforts, and readiness for change; and • personality style or disorder and family and cultural factors.

Illness profile	Identify higher risk SLE patients:
	• those with severe disease, frequent flare-ups, and/or rapidly progressive symptoms;
	• those displaying anxiety, depression, or psychotic symptoms;
	• those with maladaptive coping strategies;
	• those who are unemployed, with relational conflict and/or loss of valued roles; and
	• those who smoke.
Lab test results	Check these markers when there is a change in health status: aNA, anti-DNA, anti-Sm, anti-RNP, anti-Ro, and anti-La.

3. Intervention Planning

Basic and specific illness profiles	
Illness representations	Patient beliefs about ability to control SLE are key to effective treatment; these representations change over time. It is important to modify patient beliefs about control of SLE.
Severity	Consider a multimodal approach for those with a severe level, frequent flare-ups, and/or rapidly progressive course.
Psychiatric comorbidities	Consider treating depressive and other symptoms aggressively and simultaneously with medical and psychological treatment of SLE.

4. Intervention Implementation

Importance of collaboration	Because of the complexity of SLE, it is essential that there be collaborative relations among the patient and all clinicians involved.
Psychoeducational interventions	Because SLE patients are exquisitely sensitive to both external and internal stressors, effective stress management is a key goal of self-management. Relaxation techniques are important stress relievers. They include deep breathing, mental imagery, progressive muscle relaxation, and biofeedback.
Environmental interventions	Avoiding strong sunlight is a standard recommendation.
Exercise therapy	Can be beneficial for both the physical impact of the disease and the psychological disturbances associated with SLE.
Pain management	Would be appropriate for many patients and might be a significant help to some patients in maintaining employment.
Smoking cessation	Because of the link between smoking and vascular disease, advise patients to quit smoking and initiate or refer for smoking cessation.
Cognitive–behavioral therapy (CBT)	Changing treatment-hindering illness representations, especially about treatment "control," is essential. CBT is also effective in dealing with illness denial; changing negative thinking; increasing self-efficacy; and decreasing excessive use of drugs, avoidance of activity,

(continues)

	and dependence on others. Useful techniques are cognitive restructuring, breathing and relaxation, problem solving, and communication skills training. Both individual and group modes of CBT treatment are useful.
Other psychotherapeutic interventions	Supportive–expressive group psychotherapy: There is some, but not convincing, evidence that this group therapy approach can reduce the psychological distress and improve the quality of life for patients with SLE.
	Couples group therapy: When relational discord is noted, group-based interventions with couples that focus on communication about lupus, self-efficacy, social support, and problem solving should be considered. These interventions can increase communication, self-efficacy, and emotional well-being.
Medical treatment	Basic goal is to relieve symptoms and protect organs by decreasing inflammation and the level of autoimmune activity in the body. Those with mild symptoms may need little or no treatment or only intermittent courses of anti-inflammatory medications. Those with more serious presentations, like organ damage, may require a rigorous medication regimen to suppress the overactive immune system.
Alternative and complementary medical treatment	Such approaches include special diets, nutritional supplements, fish oils or omega 3 fatty acids, ointments for pain relief, chiropractic treatment, and homeopathy.
Medication	Commonly used medications: <ul><li>nonsteroidal anti-inflammatory drugs such as ibuprofen and naproxen;</li><li>antimalarials such as hydroxychloroquine (Plaquenil); corticosteroid hormones such as prednisone (Deltasone), hydrocortisone, methylprednisolone (Medrol), and dexamethasone (Decadron, Hexadrol);</li><li>immunosuppressive drugs such as cyclophosphamide (Cytoxan) and mycophenolate mofetil (CellCept); and</li><li>an antirheumatic drug, methotrexate (Folex, Mexate, Rheumatrex).</li></ul>
Psychotropics	Because depressed and anxious SLE patients can be helped by antidepressants, a psychopharmacology referral may be warranted. Bromocriptine has benefited those with elevated prolactin levels and lowers distress, anxiety, and hostility.
Combined treatment	Because of variability of course and severity, tailored combined treatment is required for most patients with moderate and severe SLE.

5. Intervention Monitoring

- Review patient's diary of symptoms and functional impairment with particular attention to distress due to pain, relationship difficulties, and limitations on activity.
- Track session-to-session progress with regard to compliance, symptom reduction, and functionality, including stress, interpersonal relations, pain, and activity level.

CASE OF MICHELLE T.

Michelle T. is a 38-year-old single Caucasian woman and is the producer of a local children's television show. She was diagnosed with SLE 4 years ago, although in looking back she recalls having experienced some mild symptoms since her late 20s. The diagnosis was made by a rheumatologist whom she consulted about her worsening joint pain. He treated her with a conventional medical approach for 3 years, during which time she experienced a number of flares, and she began exhibiting depressive symptoms. Medications, including cortisone injections, helped somewhat, but she reported only a partial response to antidepressants. Because her flares seemed to be associated with work or interpersonal stressors, the rheumatologist suggested a psychiatric referral, which she refused, stating that she could lose her job "if there was any suspicion that I was crazy. You don't know how conservative people are around here." After further discussion, she said she would be willing to see a psychologist for "stress management." The psychologist was Eugene Wallinsky, who practiced clinical health psychology and psychotherapy.

During their first meeting, Wallinsky focused on her illness representations and the impact of the SLE on all aspects of her life. He found that she had only partially accepted her illness and that she seemed to be continually looping between the phases of crisis and stabilization without ever progressing to the phases of resolution and integration. When queried about her depression, she reported some vegetative symptoms such as insomnia and decreased appetite but attributed these to her medications. She denied suicidal ideation, but with some embarrassment, revealed that she never really took the antidepressant because of what she had heard in the media about sexual side effects. She did admit that she pushed herself hard "to stay at the top of my game at work" but was concerned that she couldn't handle stress like she had when she was in her 20s.

She did agree to a course of CBT that would focus on stress and looking at the place of illness in her life. In subsequent meetings, her illness representations, particularly illness denial, were processed. She found Wallinsky's description of the four phases of chronic illness intriguing and easily recognized her looping pattern. She agreed that this pattern was not helpful, and they worked on ways in which she could transition to the resolution phase. She began to report less stress and pain but was still feeling depressed. The introduction of exercise seemed to further ease her pain but did nothing for her depression. They discussed antidepressants with a low sex side effects profile, and Michelle gave permission for Wallinsky to communicate with her rheumatologist about prescribing such a medication. Four weeks later, that medication seemed to be working quite well—that is, she felt more upbeat and was sleeping better, without the dreaded side effects.

REFERENCES

Aalto, A., Heijmans, M., Weinman, J., & Aro, A. (2005). Illness perceptions in coronary heart disease: Sociodemographic, illness-related, and psychosocial correlates. *Journal of Psychosomatic Research, 58*, 393–402.

Abraido-Lanza, A. F. (2004). Social support and psychological adjustment among Latinas with arthritis: A test of a theoretical model. *Annals of Behavioral Medicine, 27*, 162–171.

Affleck, G., Urrows, S., Tennen, H., & Higgins, P. (1992). Daily coping with pain from rheumatoid arthritis. *Pain, 51*, 221–229.

Alexander, F. (1950). *Psychosomatic medicine.* New York: Norton.

Allan, R., & Scheidt, S. (1998). Group psychotherapy for patients with coronary heart disease. *Journal of Group Psychotherapy, 48*, 187–214.

Alvarez-Silva, S., Alvarez-Rodriguez, J., Perez-Echeverria, M. J., & Alvarez-Silva, I. (2006). Panic and epilepsy. *Anxiety Disorders, 20*, 353–362.

American Cancer Society. (2005). *Cancer facts and figures, 2005.* Atlanta, GA: Author.

American Cancer Society. (2007). *Cancer facts and figures: 2007.* Atlanta, GA: Author.

American Diabetes Association. (2007). *Annual review of diabetes.* New York: Author.

American Heart Association. (2006). *Heart disease and stroke statistics: 2006 update.* New York: Author.

American Pain Foundation. (2008). *Talking points on pain.* Baltimore: Author.

American Psychiatric Association. (1980). *Diagnostic and statistical manual of mental disorders* (3rd ed.). Washington, DC: Author.

American Psychiatric Association. (1994). *Diagnostic and statistical manual of mental disorders* (4th ed.). Washington, DC: Author.

Ames, S. C., Jones, G. N., Howe, J. T., & Brantley, P. J. (2001). A prospective study of the impact of stress on quality of life: An investigation of low-income individuals with hypertension. *Annals of Behavioral Medicine, 23*, 112–119.

Antoni, M. H., Lehman, J. M., Kilbourn, K. M., Boyers, A. E., Culver, J. L., Alferi, S. M., et al. (2001). Cognitive–behavioral stress management intervention decreases the prevalence of depression and enhances benefit finding among women under treatment for early-stage breast cancer. *Health Psychology, 20*, 20–32.

Arena, J. G. (2002). Chronic pain: Psychological approaches for the front-line clinician. *Psychotherapy in Practice, 58*, 1385–1396.

Astin, J. A., Beckner, W., Soeken, K., Hochberg, M. C., & Berman, B. (2002). Psychological interventions for rheumatoid arthritis: A meta-analysis of randomized controlled trials. *Arthritis and Rheumatism, 47*, 291–302.

251

Bandura, A. (1986). *Social foundations of thought and action: A social cognitive theory.* Englewood Cliffs, NJ: Prentice-Hall.

Barlow, J. H., Turner, A. P., & Wright, C. C. (1998). Long-term outcomes of an arthritis self-management programme. *British Journal of Rheumatology, 37,* 1315–1319.

Barlow, J., Wright, C., Sheasby, J., Turner, A., & Hainsworth, J. (2002). Self-management approaches for people with chronic conditions: A review. *Patient Education and Counseling, 48,* 177–187.

Barsky, A., & Ahern, D. (2004). Cognitive behavior therapy for hypochondriasis: A randomized controlled trial. *JAMA, 291,* 1464–1470.

Barsky, A., & Borus, J. (1999). Functional somatic syndromes. *Annals of Internal Medicine, 130,* 910–921.

Bass, C., & Mayou, R. (1995). Chest pain and palpitations. In R. Mayou & M. Sharpe (Eds.), *Treatment of functional somatic symptoms* (pp. 328–352). Oxford, England: Oxford University Press.

Becker, L. (1989). Family systems and compliance with medical regimen. In C. Ramsey (Ed.), *Family systems in medicine* (pp. 416–431). New York: Guilford Press.

Bediako, S. M., & Friend, R. (2004). Illness-specific and general perception of social relationships in adjustment to rheumatoid arthritis: The role of interpersonal expectations. *Annals of Behavioral Medicine, 28,* 203–210.

Bennett, P., & Carroll, D. (1994). Cognitive–behavioral interventions in cardiac rehabilitation. *Journal of Psychosomatic Research, 38,* 169–182.

Beresnevaite, M. (2000). Exploring the benefits of group psychotherapy in reducing alexithymia in coronary heart disease patients: A preliminary study. *Psychotherapy and Psychosomatics, 69,* 117–122.

Beyenburg, S., Mitchell, A. J., Schmidt, D., Elger, C. E., & Reuber, M. (2005). Anxiety in patients with epilepsy: Systematic review and suggestions for clinical management. *Epilepsy & Behavior, 7,* 161–171.

Blackwell, B. (Ed.). (1997). *Treatment compliance and the therapeutic alliance.* New York: Taylor & Francis.

Blanchard, E. B. (2001). *Irritable bowel syndrome: Psychosocial assessment and treatment.* Washington, DC: American Psychological Association.

Blanchard, E. B., Lackner, J. M., Sanders, K., Krasner, S., Keefer, L., Payne, A., et al. (2007). A controlled evaluation of group cognitive therapy in the treatment of irritable bowel syndrome. *Behaviour Research and Therapy, 45,* 633–648.

Blanchard, E. B., & Scharff, L. (2002). Psychosocial aspects of assessment and treatment of irritable bowel syndrome in adults and recurrent abdominal pain in children. *Journal of Consulting and Clinical Psychology, 70,* 725–738.

Bloom, B., & Cohen, R. (2007). Summary health statistics for U.S. children: National Health Fitness Survey, 2006. National Center for Health Statistics. *Vital Health Statistics, 10,* 234.

Blumenthal, J., Sherwood, A., LaCaille, L., Georgiades, A., & Goyal, T. (2005). Lifestyle approaches to the treatment of hypertension. In N. A. Cummings,

W. T. O'Donohue, & E. V. Naylor (Eds.), *Psychological approaches to chronic disease management* (pp. 87–115). Reno, NV: Context Press.

Bordin, E. S. (1994). Theory and research on the therapeutic working alliance: New directions. In A. O. Horvath & L. S. Greenberg (Eds.), *The working alliance: Theory, research and practice* (pp. 13–37). Oxford, England: Wiley.

Bowman, E. (1993). Etiology and clinical course of pseudoseizures: Relationship to trauma, depression, and dissociation. *Psychosomatics, 34*, 333–342.

Brennan, J. (2001). Adjustment to cancer—Coping or personal transition? *Psycho-Oncology, 10*, 1–18.

Broadbent, E., Petrie, K. J., Main, J., & Weinman, J. (2006). The Brief Illness Perception Questionnaire (BIPQ). *Journal of Psychosomatic Research, 60*, 631–637.

Bruehl, S., Yong Chung, O., Burns, J. W., & Biridepalli, S. (2003). The association between anger expression and chronic pain intensity: Evidence for partial mediation by endogenous opioid dysfunction. *Pain, 106*, 317–324.

Brummett, B., Babyak, M., Mark, D. B., Clapp-Channing, N., Siegler, I., & Barefoot, J. (2004). Prospective study of perceived stress in cardiac patients. *Annals of Behavioral Medicine, 27*, 22–30.

Burden, S. (2001). Dietary treatment of irritable bowel syndrome: Current evidence and guidelines for future practice. *Journal of Human Nutrition and Dietetics, 14*, 231–243.

Burns, J. W., Bruehl, S., & Caceres, C. (2004). Anger management style, blood pressure reactivity, and acute pain sensitivity: Evidence for "Trait × Situation" models. *Annals of Behavioral Medicine, 27*, 195–204.

Bush, E. G., Rye, M. S., Brant, C. R., Emery, E., Pargament, K. I., & Riessinger, C. A. (1999). Religious coping with chronic pain. *Applied Psychophysiology and Biofeedback, 24*, 249–260.

Butcher, J. N., Dahlstrom, W. G., Graham, J. R., Tellegen, A. M., & Kaemmer, B. (1989). *Minnesota Multiphasic Personality Inventory—2 (MMPI–2): Manual for administration and scaring.* Minneapolis: University of Minnesota Press.

Byer, B., & Myers, L. (2000). Psychological correlates of adherence to medication in asthma. *Psychology, Health & Medicine, 5*, 389–393.

Callahan, L. F., Cordray, D. S., Wells, G., & Pincus, T. (1996). Formal education and five-year mortality in rheumatoid arthritis: Mediation by helplessness scale scores. *Arthritis Care & Research, 9*, 463–472.

Cameron, L., Booth, R., Schlatter, M., Ziginskas, D., Harman, J., & Benson, S. (2005). Cognitive and affective determinants of decisions to attend a group psychosocial support program for women with breast cancer. *Psychosomatic Medicine, 67*, 584–589.

Carlick, A., & Biley, F. C. (2004). Thoughts on the therapeutic use of narrative in the promotion of coping in cancer care. *European Journal of Cancer Care, 13*, 308–317.

Carr, R. E., Lehrer, P. M., & Hochron, S. M. (1995). Predictors of panic-fear in asthma. *Health Psychology, 14*, 421–426.

Carr, R. E., Lehrer, P. M., Hochron, S. M., & Jackson, A. (1996). Effect of psychological stress on airway impedance in individuals with asthma and panic disorder. *Journal of Abnormal Psychology, 105*, 137–141.

Castillo, R. (1997). *Culture and mental illness: A client-centered approach.* Belmont, CA: Brooks/Cole.

Chaney, J. M., Mullins, L. L., Uretsky, D. L., Doppler, M. J., Palmer, W. R., Wees, S. J., et al. (1996). Attributional style and depression in rheumatoid arthritis: The moderating role of perceived illness control. *Rehabilitation Psychology, 41*, 205–223.

Chapell, R., Reston, J., & Snyder, D. (2003, May). *Management of treatment-resistant epilepsy: Evidence Report/Technology Assessment No. 77* (AHRQ Publication No. 03-0028). Rockville, MD: Agency for Healthcare Research and Quality.

Chaplin, S. (1997). Somatization. In W. Tseng & J. Strelzer (Eds.), *Culture and psychopathology: A guide to clinical assessment* (pp. 67–86). Philadelphia: Brunner-Routledge.

Chen, Y. Y., Gilligan, S., Coups, E. J., & Contrada, R. J. (2005). Hostility and perceived social support: Interactive effects on cardiovascular reactivity to laboratory stressors. *Annals of Behavioral Medicine, 29*, 37–43.

Chobanian, A. V., Bakris, G. L., Black, H. R., Cushman, W. C., Green, L. A., Izzo, J. L., Jr., et al. (2003). Seventh report of the Joint National Committee on prevention, detection, evaluation, and treatment of high blood pressure. *Hypertension, 42*, 1206–1252.

Clark, D. M., Salkovskis, P. M., Hackman, A., Wells, A., Fennell, M., Ludgate, J., et al. (1998). Two psychological treatments for hypochondriasis: A randomised controlled trial. *British Journal of Psychiatry, 173*, 218–225.

Coleman, M., & Newton, K. (2005). Supporting self-management in patients with chronic illness. *American Family Physician, 72*, 1503–1510.

Costenbader, K., Kim, D., Peerzada, J., Lockman, S., Nobles-Knight, D., Petri, M., & Karlson, E. (2004). Cigarette smoking and the risk of systemic lupus erythematosus: A meta-analysis. *Arthritis and Rheumatism, 50*, 849–857.

Couldridge, L., Kendall, S., & March, A. (2001). "A systemic overview—A decade of research." The information and counselling needs of people with epilepsy. *Seizure, 10*, 605–614.

Cox, D., Gonder-Frederick, L., Polonsky, W., Schlundt, D., Julian, D., & Clarke, W. (1995). A multicenter evaluation of blood glucose awareness training-II. *Diabetes Care, 18*, 523–528.

Cox, D., Gonder-Frederick, L., Polonsky, W., Schlundt, D., Kovatchev, B., & Clarke, W. (2001). Blood glucose awareness training (BGAT-2): Long-term benefits. *Diabetes Care, 24*, 637–642.

Cox, R. P. (Ed.). (2003). *Health-related counseling with families of diverse cultures: Family, health, and cultural competencies.* Westport, CT: Greenwood Press.

Daneman, D., Olmstead, M., & Rydell, A. (1998). Eating disorders in young women with Type 1 diabetes: Prevalence, problems, and prevention. *Hormone Research, 50*, 79–86.

Danielson, C., Hamel-Bissell, B., & Winstead-Frey, P. (1993). *Families, health, and illness*. St. Louis, MO: Mosby.

Davis, A., Kreutzer, R., Lipsett, L., King, G., & Shaikh, N. (2006). Asthma prevalence in Hispanic and Asian American ethnic subgroups: Results from the California Healthy Kids Survey. *Pediatrics, 118*, 363–370.

De La Cancela, V., Jenkins, Y., & Chin, J. (1998). Psychosocial and cultural impact on health status. In V. De La Cancela, J. Chin, & Y. Jenkins (Eds.), *Community health psychology: Empowerment for diverse communities* (pp. 57–84). New York: Routledge.

Derogatis, L. R., Morrow, G. R., Fetting, J., Penman, D., Piasetsky, S., Schmale, A. M., et al. (1983). The prevalence of psychiatric disorders among cancer patients. *JAMA, 249*, 751–757.

Devine, E. C. (1996). Meta-analysis of the effects of psychoeducational care in adults with asthma. *Research in Nursing & Health, 19*, 367–376.

Digeronimo, T. (2002). *New hope for people with lupus*. New York: Prima.

Dobkin, P. L., DaCosta, D., Joseph, L., Fortin, P. R., Edworthy, S., Barr, S., et al. (2002). Health-related quality of life in Italian patients with systemic lupus erythematosus: II. Role of clinical, immunological and psychological determinants. *Rheumatology, 43*, 1580–1586.

Doherty, W., & Baird, M. (1983). *Family therapy and family medicine: Toward the primary care of families*. New York: Guilford Press.

Doria, A., Rinaldi, S., Ermani, M., Salaffi, F., Iaccarino, A., Ghirardello, A., et al. (2004). Counterbalancing patient demands with evidence: Results from a pan-Canadian randomized clinical trial of brief supportive–expressive group psychotherapy for women with systemic lupus erythematosus. *Annals of Behavioral Medicine, 24*, 88–99.

Driscoll, K. A., Cukrowicz, K. C., Reardon, M. L., & Joiner, T. E., Jr. (2004). *Simple treatments for complex problems: A flexible cognitive behavior analysis approach to psychotherapy*. Mahwah, NJ: Erlbaum.

Drossman, D. A. (1999). Review article: An integrated approach to the irritable bowel syndrome. *Alimentary Pharmacological Therapy, 13*(Suppl. 2), 3–14.

Dunbar, S., & Summerville, J. (1997). Cognitive therapy for ventricular dysrhythmia patients. *Journal of Cardiovascular Nursing, 12*, 33–44.

Duncan, B., Solovey, A., & Rusk, G. (1992). *Changing the rules: A client-directed approach to therapy*. New York: Guilford Press.

Dunlop, D., Manheim, L., Song, J., & Chang, R. (2001). Epidemiology, outcomes, and treatment: Arthritis prevalence and activity limitations in older adults. *Arthritis and Rheumatism, 44*, 212–221.

Ebert, T., Chapman, J., & Shoenfeld, Y. (2005). Anti-ribosomal P-protein and its role in psychiatric manifestations of systemic lupus erythematosus: Myth or reality? *Lupus, 14*, 571–575.

Eisenberg, T., Delbanco, B., Kaptchuk, T., Kupelnick, B., Kuhl, J., & Eisenberg, C. (1993). Cognitive behavioral techniques for hypertension: Are they effective? *Annals of Internal Medicine, 118*, 964–972.

Ellis, S. E., Speroff, T., Dittus, R. S., Brown, A., Pichert, J. W., & Elasy, T. A. (2004). Diabetes patient education: A meta-analysis and meta-regression. *Patient Education and Counseling, 52,* 97–105.

Engel, G. (1959). Psychogenic pain and the pain-prone patient. *American Journal of Medicine, 26,* 899–918.

Engelberts, N. H., Klein, M., Kasteleijn-Nolst Trenité, D. G., Heimans, J. J., & van der Ploeg, H. M. (2002). The effectiveness of psychological interventions for patients with relatively well-controlled epilepsy. *Epilepsy & Behavior, 3,* 420–426.

Eriksson, M., & Lindstrom, B. (2005). Validity of Antonovsky's Sense of Coherence Scale: A systematic review. *Journal of Epidemiological Community Health, 59,* 460–466.

Evers, A. W. M., Kraaimaat, F. W., Geenen, R., & Bijlsma, J. W. J. (1998). Psychosocial predictors of functional change in recently diagnosed rheumatoid arthritis patients. *Behaviour Research and Therapy, 36,* 179–193.

Evers, A., Kraaimaat, F., van Riel, P., & de Jong, A. (2002). Tailored cognitive–behavioral therapy in early rheumatoid arthritis for patients at risk: A randomized controlled trial. *Pain, 100,* 141–153.

Falvo, D. (2005). *Medical and psychosocial aspects of chronic illness and disability* (3rd ed.). Boston: Jones & Bartlett.

Farag, N., & Mills, P. (2004). What's next in behavioral hypertension research? *Annals of Behavioral Medicine, 27,* 1–2.

Fass, R., Longstreth, G. F., Pimentel, M., Fullerton, S., Russak, S. M., Chiou, C. F., et al. (2001). Evidence- and consensus-based practice guidelines for the diagnosis of irritable bowel syndrome. *Internal Medicine, 161,* 2081–2088.

Fauvel, J. (2003). Neither perceived job stress nor individual cardiovascular reactivity predict high blood pressure. *Hypertension, 42,* 1112–1116.

Feifer, C., & Tansman, M. (1999). Promoting psychology in diabetes primary care. *Professional Psychology: Research and Practice, 30,* 14–21.

Feine, J., & Lund, J. (1997). An assessment of the efficacy of physical therapy and physical modalities for the control of chronic musculoskeletal pain. *Pain, 71,* 5–23.

Fennell, P. A. (2003). *Managing chronic illness using the four-phase treatment approach: A mental health professional's guide to helping chronically ill people.* Hoboken, NJ: Wiley.

Fifield, J., McQuillan, J., Tennan, H., Sheehan, T. J., Reisine, S., Hesselbrock V., & Rothfield, N. (2001). History of affective disorder and the temporal trajectory of fatigue in rheumatoid arthritis. *Annals of Behavioral Medicine, 23,* 34–41.

Fishbain, D. A., Rosomoff, H., Cutler, R. B., & Steele-Rosomoff, R. (2000). Chronic pain treatment meta-analyses: A mathematical and qualitative review. *Pain Medicine, 1,* 199.

Flor, H. (2002). The modification of cortical reorganization and chronic pain by sensory feedback. *Applied Psychophysiology and Biofeedback, 27,* 215–227.

Flor, H., Furst, M., & Birbaumer, N. (1999). Deficient discrimination of EMG levels and overestimation of perceived tension in chronic pain patients. *Applied Psychophysiology and Biofeedback, 24,* 55–66.

Fosbury, J., Bosley, C., Ryle, A., Sonksen, P., & Judd, S. (1997). A trial of cognitive analytic therapy in poorly controlled Type I patients. *Diabetes Care, 20,* 959–964.

Fox, O. (2001). Congruence of illness representation between older adult heart failure patients and their spouses or partners and its relationship to adherence behavior. *Dissertation Abstracts International: Section B: The Sciences and Engineering, 62*(6-B), 2664.

Frohlich, C., Jacobi, F., & Wittchen, H. (2006). *DSM–IV* pain disorder in the general population: An exploration of the structure and threshold of medically unexplained pain symptoms. *European Archives of Psychiatry and Clinical Neuroscience, 256,* 187–196.

Gaitatzis, A., Trimble, M. R., & Sander, J. W. (2004). The psychiatric comorbidity of epilepsy. *Acta Neurologica Scandinavica, 110,* 207–220.

Garcia, P. A. (2006). Mood disorders and epilepsy surgery: Lightening the burden in more ways than one? *Epilepsy Currents, 6,* 112–113.

Gatchel, R., & Weisberg, J. (2000). *Personality characteristics of patients with pain.* Washington, DC: American Psychological Association.

Genuis, M. (1995). The use of hypnosis in helping cancer patients control anxiety, pain, and emesis: A review of recent empirical studies. *American Journal of Clinical Hypnosis, 37,* 316–324.

Giffords, E. (2003). Understanding and managing systemic lupus erythematosus (SLE). *Journal of Social Work in Health Care, 37,* 57–72.

Gilliam, F. G., & Santos, J. M. (2005). Review: Adverse psychiatric effects of antiepileptic drugs. *Epilepsy Research, 68,* 67–69.

Giovagnoli, A. R., Meneses, R. F., & da Silva, A. M. (2006). The contribution of spirituality to quality of life in focal epilepsy. *Epilepsy & Behavior, 9,* 133–139.

Golden, S. H., Williams, J. E., Ford, D. E., Yeh, H.-C., Sanford, C. P., Nieto, F. J., & Brancati, F. L. (2006). Anger temperament is modestly associated with the risk of Type 2 diabetes mellitus: The Atherosclerosis Risk in Communities Study. *Psychoneuroendocrinology, 31,* 325–332.

Goldstein, L. H., Holland, L., Soteriou, H., & Mellers, J. D. (2005). Illness representations, coping styles and mood in adults with epilepsy. *Epilepsy Research, 67,* 1–11.

Gonder-Frederick, L. A., Cox, D. J., & Ritterband, L. M. (2002). Diabetes and behavioral medicine. *Journal of Consulting and Clinical Psychology, 70,* 611–625.

Gonsalkorale, W. M., Houghton, L. A., & Whorwell, P. J. (2002). Hypnotherapy in irritable bowel syndrome: A large-scale audit of a clinical service with examination of factors influencing responsiveness. *American Journal of Gastroenterology, 97,* 954–961.

Good, G. E., & Beitman, B. D. (2006). *Counseling and psychotherapy essentials: Integrating theories, skills, and practices.* New York: Norton.

Goodman, D., Morrissey, S., Graham, D., & Bossingham, D. (2005a). The application of cognitive–behaviour therapy in altering illness representations of systemic lupus erythematosus. *Behaviour Change, 22,* 156–171.

Goodman, D., Morrissey, S., Graham, D., & Bossingham, D. (2005b). Illness representations of systemic lupus erythematosus. *Qualitative Health Research, 15,* 606–619.

Greco, C., Rudy, T., & Manzi, S. (2003). Adaptation to chronic pain in systemic lupus erythematosus: Applicability of the Multidimensional Pain Inventory. *Pain, 4,* 39–50.

Greco, C., Rudy, T., & Manzi, S. (2004). Effects of a stress-reduction program on psychological function, pain, and physical function of systemic lupus erythematosus patients: A randomized controlled trial. *Arthritis and Rheumatism, 51,* 625–634.

Griffin, K., Friend, R., Kaell, A. T., & Bennett, R. S. (2001). Distress and disease status among patients with rheumatoid arthritis: Roles of coping styles and perceived responses from support providers. *Annals of Behavioral Medicine, 23,* 133–138.

Griffith, J., & Griffith, M. (2001). *Encountering the sacred in psychotherapy: How to talk with people about their spiritual lives.* New York: Guilford Press.

Gustafsson, P., Kjellman, N., & Cederbald, M. (1986). Family therapy in the treatment of severe childhood asthma. *Journal of Psychosomatic Research, 30,* 369–374.

Hackman, R., Stern, J., & Gershwin, M. (2000). Hypnosis and asthma: A critical review. *Journal of Asthma, 37,* 1–15.

Hajjar, I., & Kotchen, T. (2003). Trends in prevalence, awareness, treatment and control of hypertension in the United States, 1988–2000. *JAMA, 289,* 2560–2572.

Hamilton, N., Zautra, A. J., & Reich, J. (2005). Affect and pain in rheumatoid arthritis: Do individual differences in affective regulation and affective intensity predict emotional recovery from pain? *Annals of Behavioral Medicine, 29,* 216–224.

Harper, R. (2004). *Personality-guided therapy in behavioral medicine.* Washington, DC: American Psychological Association.

Hassan, N. B, Hasanah, C. I., Foong, K., Naing, L., Awang, R., Ismail, S. B., et al. (2006). Identification of psychosocial factors of noncompliance in hypertensive patients. *Journal of Human Hypertension, 20,* 23–29.

Heijmans, M., Foets, M., Rijken, M., Schreurs, K., de Ridder, D., & Bensing, J. (2001). Stress in chronic disease: Do the perceptions of patients and their general practitioners match? *British Journal of Health Psychology, 6,* 229–243.

Heinberg, L. J., Fisher, B. J., Wesselmann, U., Reed, J., & Haythornthwaite, J. A. (2004). Psychological factors in pelvic/urogenital pain: The influence of site of pain versus sex. *Pain, 108,* 88–94.

Heitkemper, M., Jarrett, M., Cain, K., Burr, R., & Crowell, M. (2003) Relationship of bloating to other GI and menstrual symptoms in women with IBS. *American Journal of Gastroenterology, 98*, S264–S266.

Hicks, R. E., & Harris, G. (2001). Identifying patients with asthma whose beliefs and attitudes may place them "at risk": The development and initial validation of the Asthma Navigator. *Journal of Applied Health Behavior, 3*, 1–7.

Hobro, N., Weinman, J., & Hankins, M. (2004). Using the self-regulatory model to cluster chronic pain patients: The first step towards identifying relevant treatments? *Pain, 108*, 276–283.

Hoffman, D. (1993). Arthritis and exercise. *Primary Care, 20*, 895–910.

Hoffman, R. P. (2001). Eating disorders in adolescents with Type 1 diabetes. *Postgraduate Medicine, 109*(4), 67–74.

Holtzman, J. L., Kaihlanen, P. M., Rider, J. A., Lewin, A. J., Spindler, J. S., & Oberlin, J. A. (1988). Concomitant administration of terazosin and atenolol for the treatment of essential hypertension. *Archives of Internal Medicine, 148*, 539–543.

Horne, R., & Weinman, J. (2002). Self-regulation and self-management in asthma: Exploring the role of illness perceptions and treatment beliefs in explaining non-adherence to preventer medication. *Psychology and Health, 17*, 17–32.

Howells, L., Wilson, A. C., Skinner, T. C., Newton, R., Morris, A. D., & Greene, S. A. (2002). A randomized control trial of the effect of negotiated telephone support on glycaemic control in young people with Type 1 diabetes. *Diabetic Medicine, 19*, 643–648.

Hughes, J. W., Tomlinson, A., Blumenthal, J. A., Davidson, J., Sketch, M. H., & Watkins, L. L. (2004). Social support and religiosity as coping strategies for anxiety in hospitalized cardiac patients. *Annals of Behavioral Medicine, 28*, 179–185.

Hunt, L. W. (2001). How to manage difficult asthma cases. *Postgraduate Medicine Online.* Retrieved February 13, 2008, from http://www.postgradmed.com/issues/2001/05_01/hunt.htm

Huntley, A., White, A. R., & Ernst, E. (2002). Relaxation therapies for asthma: A systematic review. *Thorax, 57*, 127–131.

Ismail, K., Winkley, K., & Rabe-Hesketh, S. (2004). Systematic review and meta-analysis of randomized controlled trials of psychological interventions to improve glycaemic control in patients with Type 2 diabetes. *The Lancet, 363*, 1589–1597.

Jamison, R., Rudy, T., Penzien, D., & Mosley, T. (1994). Cognitive behavioral classification of chronic pains: Replication and extension of empirically derived patient profiles. *Pain, 57*, 277–292.

Jarrett, S. R., Ramirez, A. J., Richards, M. A., & Weinman, J. (1992). Measuring coping in breast cancer. *Journal of Psychosomatic Research, 36*, 593–602.

Jensen, M. P., Nielson, W. R., Romano, J. R., Hill, M. L., & Turner, J. A. (2000). Further evaluation of the pain stages of change questionnaire: Is the transtheoretical model of change useful for patients with chronic pain? *Pain*, *86*, 255–264.

Jessop, D., & Rutter, D. (2003). Adherence to asthma medication: The role of illness representations. *Psychology and Health*, *18*, 595–612.

Johnell, K., Råstam, L., Lithman, T., Sundquist, J., & Merlo, J. (2005). Low adherence with antihypertensives in actual practice: The association with social participation—A multilevel analysis. *BMC Public Health*. Retrieved February 13, 2008, from http://www.biomedcentral.com/1471-2458/5/17

Johnson, S. K. (2008). *Medically unexplained illness: Gender and biopsychosocial implications*. Washington, DC: American Psychological Association.

Jorgensen, R., Johnson, B. T., Kolodziej, M. E., & Schreer, G. E. (1996). Elevated blood pressure and personality: A meta-analytic review. *Psychological Bulletin*, *120*, 293–320.

Kaplan, N. M., & Opie, L. H. (2006). Controversies in hypertension. *The Lancet*, *367*, 168–175.

Karasz, A., & Ouellette, S. (1995). Role strain and psychological well-being in women with systemic lupus erythematosus. *Women & Health*, *23*(3), 41–49.

Karlson, E., Liang, M., Eaton, H., Huang, J., Fitzgerald, L., Rogers, M., & Daltroy, L. (2004). A randomized clinical trial of a psychoeducational intervention to improve outcomes in systemic lupus erythematosus. *Arthritis and Rheumatism*, *50*, 1832–1841.

Karoly, P., & Jensen, M. (1987). *Multimethod assessment of chronic pain*. New York: Pergamon Press.

Katz, P. P., & Yelin, E. H. (1993). Prevalence and correlates of depressive symptoms among persons with rheumatoid arthritis. *Journal of Rheumatology*, *20*, 790–796.

Keefe, F. J., Affleck, G., Lefebvre, J., Underwood, L., Caldwell, D. S., & Drew, J. (1997). Living with rheumatoid arthritis: The role of daily spirituality and daily religious and spiritual coping. *Journal of Pain*, *2*, 101–110.

Keefe, F., & Caldwell, D. (1997). Cognitive behavioral control of arthritis pain. *Medical Clinics of North America*, *81*, 277–290.

Keefe, F., Caldwell, D., Baucom, D., Salley, A., Robinson, E., Timmons, K., et al. (1996). Spouse-assisted coping skills training in the management of osteoarthritic knee pain. *Arthritis Care Research*, *9*, 279–291.

Keefe, F. J., Caldwell, D. S., Williams, D. A., Gil, K. M., Mitchell, D., & Robertson, C. (1990). Pain coping skills training in the management of osteoarthritis knee pain: A comparative study. *Behavior Therapy*, *21*, 49–62.

Keefe, F., Smith, S. J., Buffington, A. L. H., Gibson, J., Studts, J. L., & Caldwell, D. S. (2002). Recent advances and future directions in the biopsychosocial assessment and treatment of arthritis. *Journal of Consulting and Clinical Psychology*, *70*, 640–655.

Keller, M., McCullough, J., Jr., Klein, D., Arnow, B., Dunner, D., Gelenberg, A., et al. (2000). A comparison of nefazodone, the cognitive behavioral analysis system of psychotherapy, and their combination for the treatment of chronic depression. *New England Journal of Medicine, 342,* 1462–1470.

Kemp, S., Morley, S., & Anderson, E. (1999). Coping with epilepsy: Do illness representations play a role? *British Journal of Clinical Psychology, 38,* 43–58.

Kerns, R. D., Rosenberg, R., Jamison, R. N., Caudill, M. A., & Haythornthwaite, J. (1997). Readiness to adopt a self-management approach to chronic pain: The Pain Stages of Change Questionnaire (PSOCQ). *Pain, 72,* 227–234.

Kerns, R. D., Rosenburg, R., & Otis, J. D. (2002). Self-appraised problem solving and pain-relevant social support as predictors of the experience of chronic pain. *Annals of Behavioral Medicine, 24,* 100–105.

Klein, D., Santiago, N., Vivian, D., Arnow, B., Blalock, J., Dunner, D., et al. (2004). Cognitive Behavioral Analysis System of Psychotherapy as a maintenance treatment for chronic depression. *Journal of Consulting and Clinical Psychology, 72,* 681–688.

Koenig, H., Larson, D., & Larson, S. (2001). Religion and coping with serious medical illness. *Annals of Pharmacotherapy, 35,* 352–359.

Kohen, D. (1995). Applications of relaxation/mental imagery (self-hypnosis) to the management of childhood asthma: Behavioral outcomes of a controlled study. *Hypnosis, 22,* 132–144.

Koyama, A. (2005). *Epilepsy—A brief overview.* Retrieved February 13, 2008, from http://www.cogneurosci.com/papers/EpilepsyBriefOverview.pdf

Kozora, E., Ellison, M., Waxmonsky, J., Wamboldt, F., & Patterson, T. (2005). Major life stress, coping styles, and social support in relation to psychological distress in patients with systemic lupus erythematosus. *Lupus, 14,* 363–372.

Krause, N. (1998). Stressors in highly valued roles, religious coping, and mortality. *Psychology and Aging, 13,* 242–255.

Krol, B., Sanderman, R., & Suurmeijer, T. P. (1993). Social support, rheumatoid arthritis and quality of life: Concepts, measurement and research. *Patient Education and Counseling, 20,* 101–120.

Kubzansky, L. D., Cole, S. R., Kawachi, I., Vokonas, P., & Sparrow, D. (2006). Shared and unique contributions of anger, anxiety, and depression to coronary heart disease: A prospective study in the Normative Aging Study. *Annals of Behavioral Medicine, 31,* 21–29.

Lackner, J. M. (2003). Irritable bowel syndrome. In F. Collins & L. Cohen (Eds.), *Handbook of health psychology* (pp. 397–424). Thousand Oaks, CA: Sage.

Lackner, J. M., Coad, M. L., Mertz, H. R., Wack, D. S., Katz, L. A., Krasner, S. S., et al. (2006). Cognitive therapy for irritable bowel syndrome is associated with reduced limbic activity, GI symptoms, and anxiety. *Behaviour Research and Therapy, 44,* 621–638.

Lackner, J. M., Morley, S., Dowzer, C., Mesmer, C., & Hamilton, S. (2004). Psychological treatments for irritable bowel syndrome: A systematic review and meta-analysis, *Journal of Counseling and Clinical Psychology, 72,* 1100–1113.

LaFrance, C., & Devinsky, O. (2004) The treatment of nonepileptic seizures: Historical perspectives and future directions. *Epilepsia, 45,* 15–21.

Lakoff, R. (1983). Interpretive psychotherapy with chronic pain patients. *Canadian Journal of Psychiatry, 28,* 650–653.

Lambert, M. J. (1992). Implications of outcome research for psychotherapy integration. In J. Norcross & M. R. Goldstein (Eds.), *Handbook of psychotherapy integration* (pp. 92–129). New York: Basic Books.

Lambert, M. J., & Barley, D. E. (2002). Research summary on the therapeutic relationship and psychotherapy outcome. In J. C. Norcross (Ed.), *Psychotherapy relationships that work: Therapist contributions and responsiveness to patients* (pp. 17–32). New York: Oxford University Press.

Lask, B., & Matthew, D. (1979). Childhood asthma: A controlled trial of family psychotherapy. *Archives of Diseases of Childhood, 54,* 116–119.

Lau-Walker, M. (2006). Predicting self-efficacy using illness perception components: A patient survey. *British Journal of Health Psychology, 11,* 643–661.

Lee, V., Cohen, S. R., Edgar, L., Laizner, A. M., & Gagnon, A. J. (2006). Meaning-making intervention during breast or colorectal cancer treatment improves self-esteem, optimism, and self-efficacy. *Social Science & Medicine, 62,* 3133–3145.

Lehrer, P., Feldman, J., Giardino, N., Song, H.-S., & Schmaling, K. (2002). Psychological aspects of asthma. *Journal of Counseling and Clinical Psychology, 70,* 691–711.

Lemos, K., Suls, J., Jenson, M., Lounsbury, P., & Gordon, E. E. (2003). How do female and male cardiac patients and their spouses share responsibilities after discharge from the hospital? *Annals of Behavioral Medicine, 25,* 8–15.

Leventhal, H., Diefenbach, M., & Leventhal, E. (1992). Illness cognition: Using common sense to understand treatment adherence and affect in cognitive interactions. *Cognitive Therapy and Research, 16,* 143–163.

Leventhal, H., Leventhal, E., & Cameron, L. (2000). Representation, procedures and affect in illness self-regulation: A perceptual–cognitive model. In A. Baum, T. Revenson, & J. Singer (Eds.), *Handbook of health psychology* (pp. 19–47). Mahwah, NJ: Erlbaum.

Lewin, B. (1997). The psychological and behavioral management of angina. *Journal of Psychosomatic Research, 43,* 452–462.

Lindberg, N., Lindberg, E., Theorell, T., & Larsson, G. (1996). Psychotherapy in rheumatoid arthritis—A parallel-process study of psychic state and course of rheumatic disease. *Zeitschrift für Rheumatologie, 55,* 28–39.

Linden, W., & Moseley, J. V. (2006). The efficacy of behavioral treatments for hypertension. *Applied Psychophysiology and Biofeedback, 31,* 51–63.

Lomax, J., Karff, S., & McKenny, G. (2002). Ethical considerations in the integration of religion and psychotherapy: Three perspectives. *Psychiatric Clinics of North America, 25,* 547–559.

Loney, P., & Stratford, P. (1999). The prevalence of low back pain in adults: A methodological review of the literature. *Physical Therapy, 79,* 384–396.

Lorig, K. (2003). Self-management education: More than a nice extra. *Medical Care, 41*, 699–701.

Lorig, K., Ritter, P., Steward, A., Sobel, D., Brown, B., & Bandura, A. (2001). Chronic disease self-management program: 2-year health status and health care utilization outcomes. *Medical Care, 39*, 1217–1223.

Lucak, S. (2005). Irritable bowel syndrome: Psychiatric factors and therapies. *Psychiatric Times, 22*, 43–61.

Luebbert, K., Dahme, B., & Hasenbring, M. (2001). The effectiveness of relaxation training in reducing treatment-related symptoms and improving emotional adjustment in acute non-surgical cancer treatment: A meta-analytical review. *Psycho-Oncology, 10*, 490–502.

Lustman, P., Griffith, L., Freedland, K., Kissel, S., & Clouse, R. (1998). Cognitive behavior therapy for depression in Type 2 diabetes mellitus: A randomized, controlled trial. *Annals of Internal Medicine, 129*, 613–621.

Lydiard, R. B., & Falsetti, S. A. (1999). Experience with anxiety and depression treatment studies: Implications for designing irritable bowel syndrome clinical trials. *American Journal of Medicine, 107*, 65S–73S.

Maguire, J. L., Stell, B. M., Rafizadeh, M., & Mody, I. (2005). Ovarian cycle-linked changes in $GABA_A$ receptors mediating tonic inhibition alter seizure susceptibility and anxiety. *Nature Neuroscience, 8*, 797–804.

Maharaj, S. J., Rodin, G. M., & Olmstead, M. P. (1998). Eating disturbances, diabetes and the family: An empirical study. *Journal of Psychosomatic Research, 44*, 479–490.

Mann, S. J. (2000). The mind/body link in essential hypertension: Time for a new paradigm. *Alternative Therapies in Health and Medicine, 6*(2), 39–45.

Mann, S. J. (2003). Neurogenic essential hypertension revisited: The case for increased clinical and research attention. *American Journal of Hypertension, 16*, 881–888.

Mann, S. J. (2006). Hypertension and the mindbody connection: A new paradigm. In J. Sarno (Ed.), *The divided mind: The epidemic of mindbody disorders* (pp. 185–226). New York: Regan Books/HarperCollins.

Mann, S. J., & Gerber, L. M. (2001a). Low dose alpha/beta blockade in the treatment of essential hypertension. *American Journal of Hypertension, 14*, 553–558.

Mann, S. J., & Gerber, L. M. (2001b). Psychological characteristics and responses to anti-hypertensive drug therapy. *Journal of Clinical Hypertension, 4*, 25–33.

Mann, S. J., & James, G. D. (1998). Defensiveness and hypertension. *Journal of Psychosomatic Research, 45*, 139–148.

Manzi, S., Meilahn, E., Rairie, J., Conte, C., Medsger, T., Jansen-McWilliams, L., et al. (1997). Age specific incidence rates of myocardial infarction and angina in women with systemic lupus erythematosus: Comparison with the Framingham Study. *American Journal of Epidemiology, 145*, 408–415.

Marrugat, J., Antó, J. M., Sala, J., & Masiá, R. (1994). Influence of gender in acute and long-term cardiac mortality after a first myocardial infarction. *Journal of Clinical Epidemiology, 47*, 111–118.

Martin, D., Garske, J., & Davis, K. (2000). Relation of the therapeutic alliance with outcome and other variables: A meta-analytic review. *Journal of Consulting and Clinical Psychology, 68*, 438–450.

Mayou, R., Bryant, B., Sanders, D., Bass, C., Klimes, I., & Fortar, C. (1997). A controlled trial of cognitive behavioral therapy for non-cardiac chest pain. *Psychological Medicine, 1*, 277–299.

McAdams, D. (1993). *The stories we live by.* New York: William Morrow.

McCracken, L. M., & Yang, S.-Y. (2006). The role of values in a contextual cognitive–behavioral approach to chronic pain. *Pain, 123*, 137–145.

McCullough, J. (2000). *Treatment for chronic depression: Cognitive behavioral analysis system of psychotherapy.* New York: Guilford Press.

McCullough, J. (2005). Cognitive behavioral analysis system of psychotherapy: Treatment for chronic depression. In J. Norcross & M. Goldfried (Eds.), *Handbook of psychotherapy integration* (2nd ed., pp. 281–298). London: Oxford University Press.

McHugh, M. D. (2007). Readiness for change and short-term outcomes of female adolescents in residential treatment for anorexia nervosa. *International Journal of Eating Disorders, 40*, 602–612.

Mensah, S. A., Beavis, J. M., Thapar, A. K., & Kerr, M. (2006). The presence and clinical implications of depression in a community population of adults with epilepsy. *Epilepsy & Behavior, 8*, 213–219.

Meyer, T., & Mark, M. (1995). Effects of psychosocial interventions with adult cancer patients: A meta-analysis of randomized experiments. *Health Psychology, 14*, 101–108.

Michael, E. S., & Burns, J. W. (2004). Catastrophizing and pain sensitivity among chronic pain patients: Moderating effects of sensory and affect focus. *Annals of Behavioral Medicine, 27*, 185–194.

Millar, K., Purushotham, A., McLatchie, E., George, W., & Murray, G. (2005). A 1-year prospective study of individual variation in distress and illnesses perceptions after treatment for breast cancer. *Psychosomatic Research, 58*, 335–342.

Miller, L. (1994). The epilepsy patient: Personality, psychodynamics, and psychotherapy. *Psychotherapy: Theory, Research, Practice, Training, 31*, 735–743.

Milling, L. S., Kirsch, I., Allen, G. J., & Reutenauer, E. L. (2005). The effects of hypnotic and nonhypnotic imaginative suggestion on pain. *Annals of Behavioral Medicine, 29*, 116–127.

Minuchin, S., Rosman, B., & Baker, L. (1978). *Psychosomatic families: Anorexia nervosa in context.* Cambridge, MA: Harvard University Press.

Mitsikostas, D. D., Sfikakis, P., & Goadsby, P. (2004). A meta-analysis for headache in systemic lupus erythematosus: The evidence and the myth. *Brain, 127*, 1200–1209.

Monti, D. A., Peterson, C., Kunkel, E. J. S., Hauck, W. W., Pequignot, E., Rhodes, L., & Brainard, G. C. (2006). A randomized, controlled trial of mindfulness-based art therapy (MBAT) for women with cancer. *Psycho-Oncology, 15*, 363–373.

Moore, D., Petri, M., Manzi, S., Isenberg, D., Gordon, C., Senécal, C., et al. (2000). The use of alternative medical therapies in patients with systemic lupus erythematosus. *Arthritis & Rheumatism, 43*, 1410–1418.

Morgan, M., & Watkins, C. (1988). Managing hypertension: Beliefs and responses to medication among cultural groups. *Sociology of Health and Illness, 10*, 561–578.

Morley, S., & Williams, A. C. (2006). RCTs of psychological treatments for chronic pain: Progress and challenges. *Pain, 121*, 171–172.

Moser, M. (2005). Are lifestyle interventions in the management of hypertension effective? How long should you wait before starting specific medical therapy? An ongoing debate. *Journal of Clinical Hypertension (Greenwich, CT), 7*, 324–326.

Moses, N., Wiggers, J., Nicholas, C., & Cockburn, J. (2005). Prevalence and correlates of perceived unmet needs of people with systemic lupus erythematosus. *Patient Education and Counseling, 57*, 30–38.

Moss-Morris, R., Weinman, J., Petrie, K., Horne, R., Cameron, L., & Buick, D. (2002). The Revised Illness Perception Questionnaire (IPQ-R). *Psychology and Health, 17*, 1–16.

Nakao, M., Myers, P., Fricchione, G., Zuttermeister, P. C., Barsky, A. J., & Benson, H. (2001). Somatization and symptom reduction through a behavioral medicine intervention in a mind/body medical clinic. *Behavioral Medicine (Washington, DC), 26*, 169–176.

National Centers for Chronic Illness Prevention and Health Promotion. (2007). *Chronic diseases and their risk factors.* Retrieved December 18, 2007, from http://www.cdc.gov/nccdphp/n

Neilson-Clayton, H., & Brownlee, K. (2002). Solution-focused brief therapy with cancer patients and their families. *Journal of Psychosocial Oncology, 20*, 1–13.

Nicassio, P. M., Radojevic, V., Weisman, M. H., Culbertson, A. L., Lewis, C., & Clemmey, P. (1993). The role of helplessness in the response to disease modifying drugs in rheumatoid arthritis. *Journal of Rheumatology, 20*, 1114–1120.

Nilsson, L., Ahlbom, A., Farahmand, B. Y., Asberg, M., & Tomson, T. (2002). Risk factors for suicide in epilepsy: A case control study. *Epilepsia, 43*, 644–651.

Norris, S. L., Zhang, X., Avenell, A., Gregg, E., Schmid, C., & Lau, J. (2005). Long-term effectiveness of weight loss interventions in adults with pre-diabetes: A review. *American Journal of Preventive Medicine, 28*, 126–139.

O'Connor, P. (2006). Improving medication adherence. *Archives of Internal Medicine, 166*, 1802–1804.

Opolski, M., & Wilson, I. (2005). Asthma and depression: A pragmatic review of the literature and recommendations for future research. *Clinical Practice and Epidemiology in Mental Health, 1*, 1–18.

Orlinsky, D., Grawe, K., & Parks, B. (1994). Process and outcome in psychotherapy. In A. Bergin & S. Garfield (Eds.), *Handbook of psychotherapy and behavior change* (4th ed., pp. 270–376). New York: Wiley.

Owens, D. M., Nelson, D. K., & Talley, N. J. (1995). The irritable bowel syndrome: Long-term prognosis and the physician-patient interaction. *Annals of Internal Medicine, 122*, 107–112.

Pargament, K. I. (1999). The psychology of religion and spirituality? Yes and no. *International Journal for the Psychology of Religion, 9*, 3–16.

Pargament, K. I., & Brant, C. (1998). Religion and coping. In H. Koenig (Ed.), *Handbook of religion and mental health* (pp. 111–128). San Diego, CA: Academic Press.

Pargament, K., Koenig, H., & Perez, L. (2000). The many methods of religious coping: Development and initial validation of the RCOPE. *Journal of Clinical Psychology, 56*, 519–543.

Pargament, K., Koenig, H., Tarakeswar, N., & Hahn, I. (2001). Religious struggle as a predictor of mortality among medically ill elderly patients: A two-year longitudinal study. *Archives of Internal Medicine, 161*, 1881–1885.

Pargament, K., Koenig, H., Tarakeswar, N., & Hahn, I. (2004). Religious coping methods as predictors of psychological, physical, and spiritual outcomes among medically ill elderly patients: A two-year longitudinal study. *Journal of Health Psychology, 9*, 713–730.

Pedroso de Souza, E. A., & Barioni Salgado, P. C. (2006). A psychosocial view of anxiety and depression in epilepsy. *Epilepsy & Behavior, 8*, 232–238.

Penedo, F. J., Molton, I., Dahn, J. R., Shen, B.-J., Kinsinger, D., Traeger, L., et al. (2006). A randomized clinical trial of group-based cognitive–behavioral stress management in localized prostate cancer: Development of stress management skills improves quality of life and benefit finding. *Annals of Behavioral Medicine, 31*, 261–270.

Perera, F. P. (1997, November 7). Environment and cancer: Who are susceptible? *Science, 278*, 1068-1073.

Petersen, S., Bull, C., Propst, O., Dettinger, S., & Detwiler, L. (2005). Narrative therapy to prevent illness-related stress disorder. *Journal of Counseling and Development, 83*, 41–47.

Petrie, K., Cameron, L., Ellis, C., Buick, D., & Weinman, J. (2002). Changing illness perceptions after myocardial infarction: An early intervention randomized controlled trial. *Psychosomatic Medicine, 64*, 580–586.

Petrie, K., Weinman, J., Sharpe, N., & Buckley, J. (1996). Role of patients' view of their illness in predicting return to work and functioning after myocardial infarction: Longitudinal study. *British Medical Journal, 312*, 1191–1194.

Pincus, T., & Callahan, L. F. (1985). Formal education as a marker for increased mortality and morbidity in rheumatoid arthritis. *Journal of Chronic Diseases, 38*, 973–984.

Pleis, J., & Lethbridge-Cejku, M.(2006). Summary health statistics for U.S. adults: National Health Fitness Survey, 2005. National Center for Health Statistics. *Vital Health Statistics, 10*, 232.

Potter, H. (2007). Battered Black women's use of religious services and spirituality for assistance in leaving abusive relationships. *Violence Against Women, 13*, 262–284.

Poynard, T., Regimbeau, C., & Benhamou, Y. (2001). Meta-analysis of smooth muscle relaxants in the treatment of irritable bowel syndrome. *Alimentary Pharmacology and Therapeutics 15*, 355–361.

Prochaska, J. O., DiClemente, C. C., & Norcross, J. C. (1992). In search of how people change: Applications to addictive behaviors. *American Psychologist, 47*, 1102–1114.

Prochaska, J., Norcross, J., & DiClemente, C. (1994). *Changing for good*. New York: William Morrow.

Redd, W. H., Montgomery, G. H., & DuHamel, K. N. (2001). Behavioral intervention for cancer treatment side effects. *Journal of the National Cancer Institute, 93*, 810–823.

Redman, B. (2004). *Patient self-management of chronic disease: The health care provider's challenge*. Sudbury, MA: Jones & Bartlett.

Rees, G., Fry, A., Cull, A. M., & Sutton, S. (2004). Illness perceptions and distress in women at increased risk of breast cancer. *Psychology and Health, 19*, 749–765.

Rehse, B., & Pukrop, R. (2003). Effects of psychosocial interventions on quality of life in adult cancer patients: Meta-analysis of 37 published controlled outcome studies. *Patient Education and Counseling, 50*, 179–186.

Richards, P. S., & Bergin, A. E. (Eds.). (1999). *The handbook of psychotherapy and religious diversity*. Washington, DC: American Psychological Association.

Rimm, E., Chan, J., Stampfer, M., Colditz, G., & Willett, W. (1995). Prospective study of cigarette smoking, alcohol use, and the risk of diabetes in men. *British Medical Journal, 310*, 555–559.

Rinaldi, S., Ghisi, M., Iaccarino, L., Zampieri, S., Girardello, A., Piercarlo, S., et al. (2006). Influence of coping skills on health-related quality of life in patients with systemic lupus erythematosus. *Arthritis & Rheumatism, 55*, 427–433.

Robertson, J. (1995). The rape of the spine. *Surgical Neurology, 39*, 5–12.

Rodrigue, J. R., Behen, J. M., & Tumlin, T. (1994). Multidimensional determinants of psychological adjustment to cancer. *Psycho-Oncology, 3*, 205–214.

Rogers, C. (1951). *Client-centered therapy*. Boston: Houghton Mifflin.

Rolheiser, R. (1999). *The holy longing: The search for a Christian spirituality*. New York: Doubleday.

Ross, C. J., Davis, T. M., & MacDonald, G. F. (2005). Cognitive–behavioral treatment combined with asthma education for adults with asthma and coexisting panic disorder. *Clinical Nursing Research, 14*, 131–157.

Ross, S., Walker, A., & MacLeod, M. J. (2004). Patient compliance in hypertension: Role of illness perceptions and treatment beliefs. *Journal of Human Hypertension, 18*, 607–613.

Rozanski, A., Blumenthal, J. A., Davidson, K. W., Saab, P. G., & Kubzansky, L. (2005). The epidemiology, pathophysiology, and management of psychosocial risk factors in cardiac practice: The emerging field of behavioral cardiology. *Journal of the American College of Cardiology, 45*, 637–651.

Rubin, R., & Peyrot, M. (1998). Men and diabetes: Psychosocial and behavioral issues. *Diabetes Spectrum, 11*, 81–87.

Rutter, C., & Rutter, D. (2002). Illness representation, coping and outcome in irritable bowel syndrome (IBS). *British Journal of Health Psychology, 7*, 377–391.

Rydall, A. C., Rodin, G. M., Olmstead, M. P., Devenyi, R. G., & Daneman, D. (1997). Disordered eating behavior and microvascular complications in young women with insulin-dependent diabetes mellitus. *New England Journal of Medicine, 336*, 1849–1854.

Schiaffino, K., Shawaryn, J., & Blum, D. (1998). Examining the impact of illness representations on psychological adjustment to chronic illnesses. *Health Psychology, 17*, 262–268.

Schilling, L. S., Grey, M., & Knafl, K. A. (2002). A review of measures of self-management of Type 1 diabetes by youth and their parents. *The Diabetes Educator, 28*, 796–808.

Scicutella, A., & Ettinger, A. B. (2002). Treatment of anxiety in epilepsy. *Epilepsy & Behavior, 3*, S10–S12.

Scottish Intercollegiate Guidelines Network. (2003). *Diagnosis and management of epilepsy in adults.* Edinburgh, Scotland: Royal College of Physicians.

Sears, S. F., Jr., Kovacs, A. H., Azzarello, L., Larsen, K., & Conti, J. B. (2004). Innovations in health psychology: The psychosocial care of adults with implantable cardioverter defibrillators. *Professional Psychology: Research and Practice, 35*, 520–526.

Segui, J., Ramos-Casals, M., Garcia-Carrasco, M., de Flores, T., Cerver, R., Valdes, M., et al. (2000). Psychiatric and psychological disorders in patients with systemic lupus erythematosus: A longitudinal study of active and inactive stages of the disease. *Lupus, 9*, 584–588.

Sheard, T., & Maguire, P. (1999). The effect of psychological interventions on anxiety and depression in cancer patients: Results of two meta-analyses. *British Journal of Cancer, 80*, 1770–1780.

Shick-Tyron, G., & Kane, A. (1993). Relationship of working in alliance to mutual and unilateral termination. *Journal of Counseling Psychology, 40*, 33–36.

Shick-Tyron, G., & Kane, A. (1995). Client involvement, working alliance, and type of termination. *Psychotherapy Research, 5*, 189–198.

Simon, L., Lipman, A. G., Allaire, S. G., Caudill-Slosberg, M., Gill, L. H., & Keefe, F. J. (2002) *Guideline for the management of acute and chronic pain in osteo and rheumatoid arthritis.* Glenview, IL: American Pain Society.

Sin, M.-K., Sanderson, B., Weaver, M., Giger, J., Pemberton, J., & Klapow, J. (2004). Personal characteristics, health status, physical activity, and quality of life in cardiac rehabilitation participants. *International Journal of Nursing Studies, 41*, 173–181.

Sinclair, V. G., & Wallston, K. A. (2001). Predictors of improvement in a cognitive–behavioral intervention for women with rheumatoid arthritis. *Annals of Behavioral Medicine, 23*, 291–297.

Smith, J., Richardson, J., Hoffman, C., & Pilkington, K. (2005). Mindfulness-based stress reduction as supportive therapy in cancer care: Systematic review. *Journal of Advanced Nursing, 52,* 315–327.

Smith, T. W., Peck, J. R., & Ward, J. R. (1990). Helplessness and depression in rheumatoid arthritis. *Health Psychology, 9,* 377–389.

Smyth, J. (1998). Written emotional expression: Effect sizes, outcome types, and moderating variables. *Journal of Consulting and Clinical Psychology, 66,* 174–184.

Snoek, F. J., & Skinner, T. C. (2002). Psychological counseling in problematic diabetes: Does it help? *Diabetic Medicine, 19,* 265–273.

Snoek, F. J., van der Ven, C., & Lubach, C. (1999). Cognitive behavioral group training for poorly controlled Type 1 diabetes patients: A psychoeducational approach. *Diabetes Spectrum, 12,* 147–151.

Snoek, F. J., van der Ven, N., Lubach, C., Chatrou, M., Ader, H., Heine, R., & Jacobson, A. (2001). Effects of cognitive behavioral group training (CBGT) in adult patients with poorly controlled insulin-dependent (Type 1) diabetes: A pilot study. *Patient Education and Counseling, 45,* 143–148.

Sohng, K.-Y. (2003). Effects of a self-management course for patients with systemic lupus erythematosus. *Journal of Advanced Nursing, 42,* 479–486.

Sotile, W. M. (2005). Biopsychosocial care of heart patients: Are we practicing what we preach? *Families, Systems & Health, 23,* 400–403.

Sotsky, S. M., Glass, D. R., Shea, M. T., Pilkonis, P. A., Collins, J. F., Elkin, I., et al. (1991). Patient predictors of response to psychotherapy and pharmacotherapy: Findings in the NIMH treatment of depression collaborative research program. *American Journal of Psychiatry, 148,* 997–1008.

Sperry, L. (2001). *Spirituality in clinical practice: Incorporating the spiritual dimension in psychotherapy and counseling.* New York: Brunner/Routledge.

Sperry, L. (2003). *Handbook of the diagnosis and treatment of the DSM–IV–TR personality disorders* (2nd ed.). New York: Routledge.

Sperry, L. (2005). A therapeutic interviewing strategy for effective counseling practice: Applications to health and medical issues in individual and couples therapy. *The Family Journal, 13,* 477–481.

Sperry, L. (2006a). *Cognitive behavior therapy of the DSM–IV–TR personality disorders: Highly effective interventions for the most common personality disorders* (2nd ed.). Philadelphia: Brunner/Mazel.

Sperry, L. (2006b). *Psychological treatment of chronic illness: The biopsychosocial therapy approach.* Washington, DC: American Psychological Association.

Sperry, L. (2007). Illness perceptions and receptivity to counseling: Implications for individual and couples therapy. *The Family Journal, 15,* 298–302.

Sperry, L., Carlson, J., & Kjos, D. (2003). *Becoming an effective therapist.* Boston: Allyn & Bacon.

Sperry, L., & Shafranske, E. (Eds.). (2006). *Spirituality-oriented psychotherapy.* Washington, DC: American Psychological Association.

Spurgeon, P., Hicks, C., Barwell, F., Walton, I., & Spurgeon, T. (2005). Counselling in primary care: A study of the psychological impact and cost benefits for four chronic conditions. *European Journal of Psychotherapy, Counselling and Health, 7*, 269–290.

Stanos, S., & Houle, T. (2006). Multidisciplinary and interdisciplinary management of chronic pain. *Physical Medicine and Rehabilitation Clinics of North America, 17*, 435–450.

Stiegelis, H., Hagedoorn, M., Sanderman, R., van der Zee, K., Buunk, B., & Alfons, C. (2003). Cognitive adaptation: A comparison of cancer patients and healthy references. *British Journal of Health Psychology, 8*, 303–318.

Stockford, K., Turner, H., & Cooper, M. (2007). Illness perception and its relationship to readiness to change in the eating disorders: A preliminary investigation. *British Journal of Clinical Psychology, 46*, 139–154.

Stoloff, S. W. (2005). Revised asthma guidelines: Summarizing key points. *Journal of Respiratory Diseases, 25*, 210–219.

Strachan, D. P., Butland, B. K., & Anderson, H. R. (1996). Incidence and prognosis of asthma and wheezing illness from early childhood to age 33 in a national British cohort. *British Medical Journal, 312*, 1195–1199.

Strupp, H. (1995). The psychotherapist's skills revisited. *Clinical Psychology, 2*, 70–74.

Sudre, P., Jacquemet, S., Uldry, C., & Perneger, T. V. (1999). Objectives, methods and content of patient education programmes for adults with asthma: Systematic review of studies published between 1979 and 1998. *Thorax, 54*, 681–687.

Suls, J., & Bunde, J. (2005). Anger, anxiety, and depression as risk factors for cardiovascular disease: The problems and implications of overlapping affective dispositions. *Psychological Bulletin, 131*, 260–300.

Suls, J., Wan, C. K., & Costa, P. T. (1995). Relationship of trait anger to blood pressure: A meta-analysis. *Health Psychology, 14*, 444–456.

Szaflarski, M., Szaflarski, J. P., Privitera, M. D., Ficker, D. M., & Horner, R. D. (2006). Racial/ethnic disparities in the treatment of epilepsy: What do we know? What do we need to know? *Epilepsy & Behavior, 9*, 243–264.

Taube, S., & Calman, N. (1992). The psychotherapy of patients with complex partial seizures. *American Journal of Orthopsychiatry, 62*, 35–43.

Taylor, E. E., & Ingleton, C. (2003). Hypnotherapy and cognitive–behaviour therapy in cancer care: The patients' view. *European Journal of Cancer Care, 12*, 137–142.

Taylor, R. R. (2006). *Cognitive behavioral therapy for chronic illness and disability*. New York: Springer Science + Business Media.

Tench, C. M., McCarthy, J., McCurdie, I., White, P., & D'Cruz, D. (2003). Fatigue in systemic lupus erythematosus: A randomized controlled trial of exercise. *Rheumatology, 42*, 1050–1054.

Tennen, H., Affleck, G., & Zautra, A. (2006). Depression history and coping with chronic pain: A daily process analysis. *Health Psychology, 25*, 370–379.

Tucker, M. E. (2008). Psychosocial care set as standard in cancer treatment. *Clinical Psychiatry News. 36*(3), 1, 10.

Tumlin, T. (2001). Treating chronic-pain patients in psychotherapy. *Journal of Clinical Psychology, 57,* 1277–1288.

Turk, D., & Okifuji, A. (2002). Psychological factors in chronic pain: Evolution and revolution. *Journal of Consulting and Clinical Psychology, 70,* 678–690.

Unruh, A. (1996). Gender variations in clinical pain experience. *Pain, 65,* 123–167.

Vadivelu, N., & Sinatra, R. (2005). Recent advances in elucidating pain mechanisms. *Current Opinion in Anaesthesiology, 18,* 540–547.

van der Ven, N., Weinger, K., & Snoek, F. (2002). Cognitive behaviour therapy: How to improve diabetes self-management. *Diabetes Voice, 47*(3), 1–3.

van Middendorp, H., Geenen, R., Sorbi, M. J., Hox, J. J., Vingerhoets, J. J., van Doornen, J. P., & Bijlsma, J. W. (2005). Gender differences in emotion regulation and relationships with perceived health in patients with rheumatoid arthritis. *Women and Health, 42,* 75–97.

Van't Spijker, A., Trijsburg, R. W., & Duivenvoorden, H. J. (1997). Psychological sequaelae of cancer diagnosis: A meta-analytical review of 58 studies after 1980. *Psychosomatic Medicine, 59,* 280–293.

Vazquez, M. I., & Buceta, J. M. (1993). Psychological treatment of asthma: Effectiveness of a self-management program with and without relaxation training. *Journal of Asthma, 30,* 171–183.

Verbrugge, I., & Ascione, F. (1987). Exploring the iceberg: Common symptoms and how people care for them. *Medical Care, 25,* 539–569.

Verhaak, P. F., Kerssen, J. J., Dekker, J., Sorbi, M. J., & Bensing, J. M. (1998). Prevalence of chronic benign pain disorder among adults: A review of the literature. *Pain, 77,* 231–239.

Walker, S., Smarr, K., Parker, J., Weidensaul, D., Nelson, W., & McMurray, R. (2000). Mood states and disease activity in patients with systemic lupus erythematosus treated with bromocriptine. *Lupus, 9,* 527–533.

Wampold, B. (2001). *The great psychotherapy debate.* Mahwah, NJ: Erlbaum.

Watson, W. (2007). Bridging the mind–body split: Towards an integrative framework for thinking about somatoform disorders. *The Family Psychologist, 23,* 30–33.

Weinger, K., Schwartz, E., Davis, A., Rodríguez, M., Simonson, D., & Jacobson, A. (2002). Cognitive behavioral treatment in Type 1 diabetes: A randomized control trial. *Diabetes, 1*(Suppl. 2), A439.

Weinman, J., Petrie, K., Moss-Morris, R., & Horne, R. (1996). The Illness Perception Questionnaire: A new method for assessing illness perceptions. *Psychology and Health, 11,* 431–446.

White, C. (2001). *Cognitive behavior therapy for chronic medical problems.* Chichester, England: Wiley.

Whitehead, W. E. (2006). Hypnosis for irritable bowel syndrome: The empirical evidence of therapeutic effects. *International Journal of Clinical and Experimental Hypnosis, 54,* 7–20.

Whooley, M. A. (2006). Depression and cardiovascular disease: Healing the broken-hearted. *JAMA, 295*, 2874–2881.

Whorwell, P. J. (2006). Effective management of irritable bowel syndrome—The Manchester model. *International Journal of Clinical and Experimental Hypnosis, 54*, 21–26.

Wigington, W., Johnson, W., & Cosman, C. (2003). Comprehensive description of irritable bowel syndrome by subtypes in African-Americans versus Caucasians. *American Journal of Gastroenterology, 98*, S267–S271.

Williams, M. M., Clouse, R. E., & Lustman, P. (2006). Treating depression to prevent diabetes and its complications: Understanding depression as a medical risk factor. *Clinical Diabetes, 24*, 79–86.

Wilson, D. K., & Ampey-Thornhill, G. (2001). The role of gender and family support on dietary compliance in an African-American adolescent hypertension prevention study. *Annals of Behavioral Medicine, 23*, 59–67.

Wilson, S. J., Bladin, P. F., Saling, M. M., & Pattison, P. E. (2005). Characterizing psychosocial outcome trajectories following seizure surgery. *Epilepsy & Behavior, 6*, 570–580.

Winterowd, C., Beck, A. T., & Gruener, D. (2003). *Cognitive therapy with chronic pain patients.* New York: Springer Publishing Company.

Wyllie, E., Luders, H., & Macmillan, J. (1984). Serum prolactin levels after epileptic seizures. *Neurology, 34*, 1601–1604.

Yeh, G., Eisenberg, D., Davis, R., & Phillips, R. (2002). Use of complementary and alternative medicine among persons with diabetes mellitus: Results of a national survey. *American Journal of Public Health, 92*, 1648–1652.

York, J., Fleming, S., & Shuldham, C. (2006). Psychological interventions for children with asthma. *Cochrane Review, 23*, 67–81.

INDEX

Biofeedback
    for arthritis, 96
    for IBS, 225
Biological therapy, 129
Biomarkers, 35, 40
Biopsychosocial assessment, 25–35
    for arthritis, 101
    for asthma, 115
    for cancer, 131
    of capacity/readiness/previous change efforts, 31–32
    for cardiac disease, 149–150
    for chronic pain, 168–169
    of comorbidities/risks, 34
    for diabetes, 185–186
    of diabetes patients, 26–29
    for epilepsy, 202
    for hypertension, 217–218
    for IBS, 231
    of illness phase/course, 34–35
    of illness representation/treatment expectations, 30–31
    for lupus, 246–247
    of personality/roles/relationships/culture, 28–29
    of specific biomarkers/behavioral markers, 35
    of type/severity, 34
Biopsychosocial model, 4, 161
Biopsychosocial pain mechanisms, 96
Blindness, 174–176
Blood clots, 136
Blood-forming tissue, 120
Blood glucose, 175
Blood glucose awareness training, 181
Blood pressure readings, 35, 207, 213
Body language, 67
Bond, 11
Bone mineralization, 140
Borderline personality, 26–27
Brain damage, 192
Brain function
    and cardiac disease, 137
    and IBS, 223
Brain scans, 196
Brain wiring, 193
Breast cancer
    and ethnicity, 122
    and exercise, 125
    and existential therapy, 128
    and group-based cognitive–behavioral stress management, 127
    screening procedures for, 125
Breast examination, 125
Brief Illness Perception Questionnaire, 18
Brief RCOPE, 81
Bromocriptine, 244, 245
Bronchodilators, 113–114
Bumex, 148
Bupropion, 148, 184
Butterfly rash, 236
Bypass surgery, 139, 147

CAD. See Coronary artery disease
Calcium channel blockers, 147, 148, 208
CAM. See Complementary and alternative medical treatments
Cancer, 119–133
    case study, 132–133
    causal factors of, 122
    combined treatment for, 129–132
    diagnosis/screening for, 124–125
    epidemiology of, 120
    and gender/ethnicity, 121–122
    illness representations in, 124
    and lifestyle modification, 125–126
    medical treatment for, 129
    prognosis for, 123
    psychiatric comorbidities with, 122–123
    psychoeducational interventions for, 126–129
    severity of, 120–121
    treatment interventions for, 123–124
    types of, 120
"Cancer Care for the Whole Patient" (Institute of Medicine), 124
Capacity for change, 27
Captopril, 148
Carbamazepine, 200
Carcinomas, 120
Cardiac disease, 135–152
    case study, 151–152
    combined treatment for, 149–151
    epidemiology of, 135–136
    and exercise/physical therapy, 147
    and gender/age/ethnicity, 137–138
    and implanted cardioverter defibrillators, 140
    medical comorbidities with, 138
    medical treatment for, 147
    medication for, 147–148
    prognosis for, 141
    psychiatric comorbidities with, 139–140

for symptom reduction, 68–69
Cognitive coping skills, 96
Cognitive map, 39
Cognitive restructuring, 97
Cognitive therapy (CT)
    for hypertension, 214
    for IBS, 225
Collaboration, 23
Colon, 221–223
Colorectal cancer, 125, 128
Combined treatment
    for arthritis, 100–102
    for asthma, 114–116
    for cancer, 129–132
    for cardiac disease, 149–151
    for chronic pain, 167–170
    for diabetes, 184–187
    for epilepsy, 201–203
    for hypertension, 216–219
    for IBS, 230–233
    implementation of, 40
    for lupus, 246–248
Communication, of symptoms, 67–68
Comorbidities, 34
Complementary and alternative medical
    treatments (CAM), 244–245
Compliance (treatment compliance), 55–64
    for asthma, 110
    for cardiac disease, 143
    CBT strategy for, 57–58
    defined, 55
    diabetes case illustration, 58–64
    and family dynamics, 56–57
    for hypertension, 213
    strategies for, 57
Congestive heart failure. See Heart failure
Connective tissue, 120
Consequences (illness representation), 17,
    70–73
Constipation-dominant IBS, 222, 230
Contemplation stage, 27–28
Context, as noncompliance factor, 57
Control coping style, 95
Coping questions, 128
Coping styles, 95
Core conditions, 11
Corgard, 148
Coronary artery bypass, 139
Coronary artery disease (CAD), 135–139,
    148, 149
    age differences with, 138
    description of, 136

and diabetes, 175
    ethnic differences with, 138
    quality of life with, 141
    SSRIs for, 148
    and stress, 139
Coronary heart disease (CHD)
    description of, 137
    illness representations of, 142
Corticosteroids
    for arthritis, 99
    for asthma, 113, 114
    for lupus, 245
Couples group therapy, 244
Course of disease, 35
C-reactive protein, 140
Crepitus, 90
Crestor, 148
Crisis phase, 34, 44
Crohn's disease, 226
CT. See Cognitive therapy
Cultural factors, 11, 29, 122
Cure/control (illness representation), 17
CVD. See Cardiovascular disease
Cyclophosphamide, 245
Cytokines, 107
Cytoxan, 245

Decadron, 245
Decision stage, 28
Defensiveness, 210
Defibrillator-generated shock, 145
Deltasone, 245
Dental pain, 160
Depakene, 200
Dependent personality, 31–32
Depression
    and arthritis, 92, 93, 103
    and asthma, 108, 115
    and cancer, 121
    and cardiac disease, 139–140
    CBASP for treatment of, 38
    and chronic pain, 158
    and diabetes, 177
    and epilepsy, 194
    and lupus, 238
    and religious coping, 80–81
Desipramine, 229, 230
Dexamethasone, 245
Diabetes mellitus, 173–188
    CAM for, 245
    case study, 187–188
    causal factors of, 175

ABOUT THE AUTHOR

Len Sperry, MD, PhD, is professor and coordinator of the doctoral program in counseling at Florida Atlantic University, Boca Raton, and is clinical professor of psychiatry at the Medical College of Wisconsin, Milwaukee. A fellow of the American Psychological Association, he is also a distinguished fellow of the American Psychiatric Association and a fellow of the American College of Preventive Medicine. In addition to being a diplomate in clinical psychology of the American Board of Professional Psychology, he is certified by the American Board of Psychiatry and Neurology and the American Board of Preventive Medicine. Among his more than 300 publications are 47 professional books, including *Spirituality in Clinical Practice: Incorporating the Spiritual Dimension in Psychotherapy and Counseling; Sex, Priestly Ministry and the Church; Transforming Self and Community: Revisioning Pastoral Counseling and Spiritual Direction; Ministry and Community: Recognizing, Healing and Predicting Ministry Impairment;* and *Psychological Treatment of Chronic Illness: The Biopsychosocial Therapy Approach.* He is listed in *Who's Who in America, Best Doctors in America,* and *Guide to America's Top Physicians* and is a recipient of two lifetime achievement awards, including the Harry Levinson Award from the American Psychological Association. He has served on editorial boards for several journals, including *Counseling and Values,* the *Journal of Family Psychology, The Family Journal,* the *American Journal of Family Therapy,* the *Journal of Individual Psychology, Depression and Stress,* the *Journal of Child Psychiatry and Human Development,* and the *Journal of Pastoral Counseling.*